Business Ratios Guidebook

Fourth Edition

Steven M. Bragg

For more information about AccountingTools® products, visit our Web site at www.accountingtools.com.

ISBN-13: 978-1-64221-055-2

Printed in the United States of America

Table of Contents

Preface

A typical business churns out an enormous amount of financial and operational information. It can be quite difficult to sort through this information to understand how a company is performing. Ratios and other types of measurements can play a valuable role in analyzing this information. In addition, a system of measurements can be used to monitor and control the operations of an organization. The *Business Ratios Guidebook* is full of ratios and other measurements that can assist in these interpretation and control tasks. The topics covered include both general and more specific functional areas of analysis. General analysis topics include measurements for such areas as performance, liquidity, cash flow, return on investment, and share performance. More specific functional analysis topics include measurements for such areas as cash management, credit and collections, fixed assets, inventory, and product design. As examples of the measurements covered, *Business Ratios* provides answers to the following questions:

- How can I test the quality of earnings reported by a business?
- What are the components of the cash conversion cycle?
- How can I tell if the amount of cash flow being generated is adequate?
- What variations on the return on investment concept are available?
- Can I incorporate inflation into the analysis of corporate growth?
- How can I measure the effectiveness of usage of a bottleneck operation?
- How can I measure the effectiveness of the collections operation?
- What measures can be used to track different aspects of customer orders?
- Are there ways to test the ability of the human resources department to fill open jobs?
- How can I tell if any inventory items are obsolete?
- How can I measure the efficiency of the payroll operation?
- Is there a way to measure the rate of flow through the production process?

The *Business Ratios Guidebook* is intended for managers, analysts, accountants, consultants, and students, who can benefit from its broad range of measurement topics. The book also provides references to the author's popular Accounting Best Practices podcast, which provides additional coverage of many measurement topics. As such, it may earn a place on your book shelf as a reference tool for years to come.

Centennial, Colorado
October 2020

About the Author

Steven Bragg, CPA, has been the chief financial officer or controller of four companies, as well as a consulting manager at Ernst & Young. He received a master's degree in finance from Bentley College, an MBA from Babson College, and a Bachelor's degree in Economics from the University of Maine. He has been a two-time president of the Colorado Mountain Club, and is an avid alpine skier, mountain biker, and certified master diver. Mr. Bragg resides in Centennial, Colorado. He has written more than 250 books and courses, including *New Controller Guidebook*, *GAAP Guidebook*, and *Payroll Management*.

Steven maintains the accountingtools.com web site, which contains continuing professional education courses, the Accounting Best Practices podcast, and thousands of articles on accounting subjects.

Buy Additional AccountingTools Courses

AccountingTools offers more than 1,200 hours of CPE courses, with concentrations in accounting, auditing, finance, taxation, and ethics. Related courses that you might like include:

- Constraint Management
- Financial Analysis
- Financial Forecasting and Modeling
- The Interpretation of Financial Statements

Go to accountingtools.com/cpe to view these additional courses.

Chapter 1
Overview of Measurements

Introduction

When someone receives the financial statements of a business, they may not know how to interpret the presented information. These statements contain a great deal of information, and yet they do not present it in a manner that allows a reader to evaluate how certain line items compare to other information, or whether results or liquidity levels are unusually good or bad. To circumvent this problem, we use various measurements to interpret financial statements. In addition, managers may aggregate operational information and use it as the basis for additional measurements that either deal solely with operations, or which are meshed with financial information to reveal additional insights into a business. Thus, measurements are used to interpret both financial and operational information.

Measurements also play a key role in controlling operations. Once a system of measurements has been created, employees will expect that measurements calculated in one period will be roughly similar to historical results. If not, then an unusual measurement outcome should trigger an investigation to determine the reason for the change.

In general, we use ratios as the basis for a system of measurements. Ratios are used to compare different types of information, so that users can more easily interpret how one type of information is changing in relation to another. While other types of measurements are noted in this book, such as trend analysis and various formulas, the bulk of the measurements described are ratios.

In this chapter, we focus on the interpretation and control aspects of measurements by discussing which measurements to use, how they should be used, and the frequency of measurement reporting, as well as several related matters.

> **Related Podcast Episodes:** Episodes 222 and 234 of the Accounting Best Practices Podcast discuss the reporting of performance measurements and how to find the right metrics, respectively. The episodes are available at: **accountingtools.com/podcasts** or **iTunes**

What to Measure

When setting up a measurement system, a key concern is what to measure. Employees have a strong tendency to improve whatever is being measured, so focusing their attention on the wrong measurement can lead to results that are injurious to a business. Here are several examples of the issue:

- *Sales growth.* A common focus of attention is period-over-period increases in sales. Typically, a business starts with a small number of products and customer accounts that are sufficiently profitable to pay for additional rounds of sales growth. However, these additional rounds of growth may come at the expense of profitability, which gradually declines. In particular, there is a danger of specifically targeting customers only to obtain more sales volume, with no regard to how they will contribute to profits.
- *Expense growth.* Management may closely monitor expenses in order to keep expense growth in check. However, doing so may lead to the reduction of several key discretionary expenses, such as research and development, that are needed to fund future growth.
- *Days sales outstanding.* A commonly-followed metric is days sales outstanding, which compares the amount of receivables to sales. The number of days sales outstanding should generally be kept as low as possible, thereby reducing the investment in accounts receivable. However, an undue focus on this measurement could lead to the restriction of credit to customers, which will in turn result in reduced sales.
- *Square feet per person.* One of the larger expenses in most organizations is the cost of facilities, which means that the number of square feet per person may be closely monitored. A typical outcome of this focus is the installation of large numbers of cubicles. However, some employees, such as engineers, require minimal noise in order to concentrate on their work, and so must have a certain amount of square feet of office space in order to function effectively.

Consequently, the selection of the most appropriate measurements is crucial. Management should consider the negative impact of using a particular measurement before rolling it out, and should also monitor the results of its use. In some cases, it may be necessary to terminate a measurement at once, to keep contrary behavior from occurring.

There is no ideal set of measurements to follow. Instead, measurements must be tailored to the circumstances in which a business finds itself. For example, a company whose investors are willing to plow money into the business in order to obtain significant market share may be willing to focus solely on sales growth, even at the expense of profits. Conversely, a company in a monopoly position in a low-growth industry may have a greater interest in maximizing cash flow. Or, if a market demands a constant flow of new products, the emphasis may instead be on the time required to generate new products.

The focus of a business may change over time, necessitating a change in measurements. Most commonly, a business will shift from an initial growth phase to a low-growth situation, and so alters its measurements to focus less on sales and more on profitability. The same issue arises when a business enters a new market. It is entirely possible that different rules apply to each market, which requires the use of different measurements. For example, a business may sell its goods through a chain of retail stores, as well as through an Internet-based direct sales channel. The measurements for the retail stores may include a same-store sales growth trend line, while the Internet store may require a measurement for the number of page views converted into sales. In short, a completely different set of measurements may be required for each market in which a company competes; there may be no common measurements that are applicable to *all* of the markets.

Mandatory Measurements

The person most likely to create a formal measurements report is the company controller, who releases the report as an attachment to the financial statements following the end of each reporting period. The controller should be mindful of requirements that certain measurements *will* be reported, even if they are not critical to the goals of the company. The need for these measurements is generally triggered by specific legal or regulatory requirements, or by their traditional use with outside parties. Consider the following situations:

- *Loan covenants*. A lender may require that the borrower report on specific ratios, such as the current ratio, and has the right to call the related loan if the specified ratio falls below a threshold level. In this case, management should be made aware of both the current status of the measurement and the threshold level below which the measurement cannot be allowed to go.
- *Public reporting*. When a publicly-held company issues financial statements to the public by way of the Securities and Exchange Commission, it may choose to include certain ratios or other measurements that provide information considered useful for investors. If so, the company should be consistent in providing the same information for all reporting periods presented.
- *Regulatory requirements*. In some regulated industries, it is required that certain information be accumulated and reported to the governing regulatory authority.

Managers should be made aware of the measurements associated with all three of the preceding areas. However, since these measurements are not necessarily critical to the long-term value-creating ability of a business, consider shifting them into a separate part of the measurement report, away from the most critical measurements.

Breaking with Tradition

Many of the measurements described in this book are standard ones that have been used in business for ages, such as the gross profit ratio, breakeven point, and current ratio. However, these measurements routinely focus the attention of users on short-term effects that call for the highest possible levels of liquidity and profitability – right now. Instead, we advocate the use of a different set of measurements that focus attention further out in the future. By doing so, it becomes more acceptable to trade off lower levels of liquidity and profitability now, in exchange for the creation of value over the long term. This approach should yield a greater return to investors over a number of years, rather than a short-sighted focus that may quickly drive a company into bankruptcy.

When developing an ideal set of measurements that can be used to drive long-term value creation, be aware that the measurements initially selected may not have a direct cause-and-effect relationship with the desired outcomes. For example, higher levels of employee training may *not* result in the generation of more ideas to drive down costs, and reduced employee turnover may *not* lead to increased customer service levels. Managers may simply have assumed that there was a cause-and-effect relationship, and chose to use certain measurements based on their long-held beliefs about which measurements should work. To avoid this problem, continually test whether the use of a certain measurement actually leads to a specific outcome; if not, eliminate the measurement in favor of a more relevant one.

While we have advocated breaking with tradition and using more long-term measurements, this also creates a conundrum in the evaluation of managers. On the one hand, we are reducing the emphasis on short-term performance measurements, which are commonly used to evaluate the tactical abilities of a manager. On the other hand, the realization of value over the long-term may not be determinable for quite some time. This means that a long-range measurement system may result in the performance of an inadequate manager not being noticed for several years. To avoid this concern, it is useful to continue monitoring short-term performance to ensure that management is still paying attention to operations, while employing a series of milestone performance reviews to ensure that managers are also attending to long-term goals.

Measurement Usage Levels

One danger of using measurements is that they will be presented to an excessive extent, with every possible ratio and formula crammed into a report. The recipients of these reports do not know which outcomes are important, and so tend to ignore the entire report. A better approach is to select only those measurements that represent a critical issue for the company, and to present them with clear explanations of why the information is important. Another possibility is to use a green/yellow/red color code to highlight the status of measurements, in order to more easily identify outlier results.

When measurement results are curated and then presented with accompanying information, the presentation can be in several formats. Consider the following approaches:

- *Variances from baseline.* A company may have a historical record of various measurements that reveals little variation over time. Managers want to see only those measurements that depart from the historical baseline. In this case, the measurements reported will vary in each period, depending upon the size of the variance. If there are no variances, no measurements are reported. This approach works well in a relatively static environment.

- *Goal monitoring.* The management team may have decided that certain goals are to be attained, such as increasing the number of customers, expanding the number of products offered, or reducing the amount of accounts receivable. To monitor the company's progress toward these goals, a specific set of related measurements are reported. Since the goals may change over time, so too may the measurements. However, management may still want to see a few measurements related to prior goals, to ensure that the company is still complying with previous management mandates.
- *Strategic and tactical insights.* The person assembling measurements may note that a few measurements are leading indicators of issues or opportunities for the company, and decides to present them to management along with a detailed commentary regarding their importance. For example, a sudden sharp decline in the ratio of sales backlog to sales is a leading indicator of a future decline in sales. Or, a spike in bad debts may indicate a decline in the credit-worthiness of customers that may call for a change in the company's credit policy.

Ideally, measurement systems should be incorporated into the planning and feedback loops of a company. For example, a rapidly-growing company will likely experience a cash shortfall as it funds the assets needed to expand operations. Accordingly, there is a tight focus on accelerating the receipt of accounts receivable. In this case, the measurement system can be inserted into the following parts of business operations:

- The budgeting model, so that days of receivables are estimated as part of budgeted cash flows.
- The bonus compensation plan, to reward the credit and collection staff if days of receivables are kept below a certain level.
- The daily collection plan, to direct resources toward those receivables in danger of passing the days of receivables target.

This detailed analysis can only be accomplished with a few measurements, given the high level of participation and monitoring that is required. All other measurements that are considered of less importance can be reviewed by a financial analyst and brought to the attention of management only if there is a notable variance from expected results.

Measurement Timing

The timing of measurements can have an impact on the extent to which the information is acted upon. Of particular concern is avoiding situations where measurements are being spewed out so frequently that recipients feel inundated with information, and so take no action. Conversely, a measurement that is only issued at long intervals can result in the passage of too much time before corrective action is taken.

To avoid either situation, discuss the appropriate timing of measurement reports with recipients. In rare cases where constant monitoring is required, a few measurements may be issued on a daily or continual basis. In most other cases, the default reporting interval is likely to be monthly or quarterly. If daily or continual measurements are needed, a different reporting system will probably be needed, such as an automated system that transmits information to desktop dashboards, or which is manually posted on whiteboards.

Measurement Consistency

When a measurement is being presented for multiple periods, the calculation should be identical for all periods presented. For example, the inclusion of sales in a return on sales figure should always be net sales, not gross sales in one period and net sales in others. Otherwise, results will be so unreliable that managers will learn not to rely upon the presented information. There are several steps that can be taken to ensure a high degree of measurement consistency. Consider the following:

- *Audits*. Have the company's internal auditors occasionally review the measurements to ensure that they are being consistently calculated, and report to a senior manager if this is not the case.
- *Standards sheet*. Create a report on which are listed the calculations for all measurements. This standards sheet can be distributed to all recipients of measurement reports, as well as anyone whose performance is being monitored through the measurements. By doing so, everyone is aware of exactly how measurements are being developed.
- *Measurement locks*. Ideally, measurements should be included in the financial statements report writer, and then locked down with password access. By doing so, it is very difficult for anyone to adjust the calculations without proper authorization.

An issue with the use of a standards sheet is that the person responsible for reporting measurements will be pressured by those employees whose performance is being monitored through the measurements. This pressure will take the form of requests to use alternative calculations that cast the employees' performance in a better light. To counteract this pressure, require the measurements person to seek the approval of a senior manager (such as the president) before any measurement calculation changes are allowed.

Measurements and the Soft Close

A soft close refers to closing the books at the end of a reporting period without the use of many normal closing steps, such as the use of adjusting entries. A soft close is used to reduce the amount of effort required to close the books, and is considered acceptable when the resulting financial statements are not being issued outside of the company. The soft close is not used for more formal financial statement issuances, such as the year-end financials, because the results may not be entirely accurate.

When the accounting department employs a soft close, any measurements derived from the financial statements may be somewhat suspect. The results are more likely to be inaccurate if either the numerator or denominator of a ratio includes information that would normally have been adjusted with a journal entry as part of the closing process. For example, the absence of a wage accrual in the income statement would artificially increase the amount of net profit reported, and therefore alter the results of any ratio involving the net profit figure.

There are several approaches to consider when deriving measurements from soft close information:

- *Skip selected measurements.* If the results are sufficiently inaccurate, skip certain measurements entirely, and only calculate them in periods when a full set of closing activities have been completed.
- *Skip all measurements.* The main point behind a soft close is to avoid the effort required for a full close – which includes the preparation of a set of performance metrics. Management might agree to avoid all measurements as part of a soft close.
- *Determine variability of results.* It is entirely possible that the adjusting entries not being made in a soft close will result in only minor changes to measurements. This can be tested by comparing the results of measurements from soft close periods and normal close periods. If so, the results can still be released, perhaps along with a cautionary message to recipients.
- *Lengthen measurement period.* The size of adjusting entries tends to decline over lengthy measurement periods in relation to the reported results. This means that a measurement covering a quarterly soft close period is more likely to be accurate than a measurement spanning just one month for which a soft close was employed. If testing proves that this is correct, consider using measurements that cover a trailing three-month period.

Measurement Clutter

The concept of measurement clutter is rarely considered. Clutter arises in the report format when a large number of measurements are jammed into a report, which recipients must then sort through for useful information. The following exhibit illustrates the problem.

A Cluttered Measurement Report

	April	May	June	July
Current ratio	2.0:1	1.9:1	2.1:1	2.2:1
Days sales outstanding	48	49	50	57
Debt to equity ratio	0.48:1	0.53:1	0.55:1	0.93:1
Earnings on invested funds	1.32%	1.35%	1.09%	1.13%
Net profit ratio	11.3%	10.9%	12.2%	10.7%
Order fill rate	88.1%	90.9%	91.0%	67.6%
Price/earnings ratio	11.0x	13.7x	12.1x	10.8x

The exhibit suffers from several problems. First, it covers multiple periods, when managers are probably most interested in only the most recent measurements. Second, an excess degree of precision is being used, which is irrelevant in determining whether a problem exists. Finally, most of the measurements do not change over time to a significant extent, and so are irrelevant from the perspective of triggering any remedial action. All of these issues can be resolved by focusing solely on those measurements requiring immediate attention. The result is a more narrative report format, such as the following exhibit that is based on the prior example.

Narrative Analysis of Measurements

Measurement	July Result	Comments
Days sales outstanding	57 days	Jump of seven days caused by the Dorado Ltd. receivable
Debt to equity ratio	0.9:1	Ratio doubled due to borrowings for Atlas acquisition
Order fill rate	68%	Caused by raw materials shortage for red widgets

Note how the revised report does not even mention a number of measurements. This is because those metrics did not change sufficiently during the reporting period to be worthy of management attention. Instead, the report focuses solely upon actionable items. This approach completely eliminates management clutter.

Limitations of Ratio Analysis

Ratio analysis is a useful tool, especially for an outsider such as a credit analyst, lender, or stock analyst. These people need to create a picture of the financial results and position of a business just from its financial statements. Ratio analysis can be used to compare information taken from different parts of the financial statements to gain a general understanding of the results, financial position, and cash flows of a business. However, there are a number of limitations of ratio analysis to be aware of. They are:

- *Historical.* All of the information used in ratio analysis is derived from actual historical results. This does not mean that the same results will carry forward into the future. However, you can use ratio analysis on pro forma information and compare it to historical results for consistency.

- *Historical versus current cost.* The information on the income statement is stated in current costs (or close to it), whereas some elements of the balance sheet may be stated at historical cost (which could vary substantially from current costs). This disparity can result in unusual ratio results.
- *Inflation.* If the rate of inflation has changed in any of the periods under review, this can mean that the numbers are not comparable across periods. For example, if the inflation rate was 100% in one year, sales would appear to have doubled over the preceding year, when in fact sales did not change at all.
- *Aggregation.* The information in a financial statement line item that is being used for a ratio analysis may have been aggregated differently in the past, so that running the ratio analysis on a trend line does not compare the same information through the entire trend period.
- *Operational changes.* A company may change its underlying operational structure to such an extent that a ratio calculated several years ago and compared to the same ratio today would yield a misleading conclusion. For example, if a constraint analysis system has been implemented, this might lead to a reduced investment in fixed assets, whereas a ratio analysis might conclude that the company is letting its fixed asset base become too old.
- *Accounting policies.* Different companies may have different policies for recording the same accounting transaction. This means that comparing the ratio results of different companies may be like comparing apples and oranges. For example, one company might use accelerated depreciation while another company uses straight-line depreciation, or one company records a sale at gross while the other company does so at net.
- *Business conditions.* Ratio analysis needs to be placed in the context of the general business environment. For example, 60 days of sales outstanding might be considered poor in a period of rapidly growing sales, but might be excellent during an economic contraction when customers are in severe financial condition and unable to pay their bills.
- *Interpretation.* It can be quite difficult to ascertain the reason for the results of a ratio. For example, a current ratio of 2:1 might appear to be excellent, until you realize that the company just sold a large amount of its stock to bolster its cash position. A more detailed analysis might reveal that the current ratio will only temporarily be at that level, and will probably decline in the near future.
- *Company strategy.* It can be dangerous to conduct a ratio analysis comparison between two firms that are pursuing different strategies. For example, one company may be following a low-cost strategy, and so is willing to accept a lower gross margin in exchange for more market share. Conversely, a company in the same industry is focusing on a high customer service strategy where its prices are higher and gross margins are higher, but it will never attain the revenue levels of the first company.
- *Point in time.* Some ratios extract information from the balance sheet. Be aware that the information on the balance sheet is only as of the last day of

the reporting period. If there was an unusual spike or decline in the account balance on the last day of the reporting period, this can impact the outcome of the ratio analysis.

In short, ratio analysis has a variety of limitations that can limit its usefulness. However, as long as you are aware of these problems and use alternative and supplemental methods to collect and interpret information, this approach is still useful.

The Measurement Surrogate Problem

When a company develops a strategy, it typically links a set of measurements to the strategy. This linkage is based on the assumption that strategic goals will be met by improving upon the measurements. This is not necessarily the case, for several reasons. First, the linkage between a measurement and a strategy may be relatively weak. For example, if the strategy is to provide the best customer service in the industry, does it really make sense to measure the proportion of the day that the customer service function is open? It is entirely possible that customers only contact the company during its normal business hours, so measuring the hours of availability outside of this time period may not translate into better customer service.

The second concern, and a much more important one, is that the measurements can be viewed as a surrogate for the corporate strategy. This means that employees are continually trying to improve the measurements, on the assumption that doing so will automatically enhance the associated strategy. For example, when a car company creates a strategy of cross-selling warranties and insurance products to the buyers of its vehicles, the sales staff might be overly pushy in selling the warranties and insurance, thereby driving away customers and reducing overall sales. In short, assuming that measurement improvement can fulfill a firm's strategy can damage a company.

These concerns can be mitigated by taking a hard look at the operational behavior being driven by measurements. If they appear to be causing actions that run against the firm's strategic goals, then the measurements should either be de-emphasized or eliminated. De-emphasizing a measurement means making sure that employees are not rewarded for improving it. Another remediation option is to compensate employees based on their ability to achieve a *set* of measurements that more closely match the firm's strategic objectives, rather than linking pay to a single measurement. The use of multiple measurements makes it more difficult to evaluate employee performance, but is needed to focus employees more tightly on the company strategy.

EXAMPLE

A customer-focused company decides that "delighting the customer" is a core target of its strategy, and decides to measure it with a customer survey, where happiness with the company is rated by customers on a scale of one to 10. Employees begin to think that improving these scores is one of their main goals, rather than improving the customer experience. Consequently, they pester customers to give them higher scores, rather than working to improve the customer experience.

10

EXAMPLE

One of a company's strategic targets is to reduce the number of flawed products it manufactures, so it decides to start tracking the percentage of goods that are returned under warranty. Since employee pay is partially based on this measurement, they start to contact any customers who are claiming a warranty return, offering them a cash payment to keep the products. The result is a rapid decline in the percentage of warranty returns, even though there has been no real change in product quality.

Summary

A system of measurements can be a powerful tool for interpreting information and controlling the results of a business. However, measurements are only indicators of underlying issues. When a measurement yields an unusual result, it is always necessary to dig deep into the underlying information to fully understand the reasons for the result. This means that the highest-quality measurement report reads more like an essay than a spreadsheet – the measurement result is presented, along with an interpretation of the underlying information, and a recommendation regarding the actions to be taken. Given the volume of research required for an unusual measurement result, it is necessary to focus on only a small number of measurements. Otherwise, the analyst will be so buried in work that few meaningful and in-depth analyses will ever reach management.

Chapter 2
Performance Measurements

Introduction

Performance measures are designed to evaluate the information on a company's income statement at a relatively high level. They make note of the quality of revenues, and then quantify the proportions of income being generated by different aspects of the entity. These measures can also be used to evaluate the quality of earnings, and how closely a business is operating to its breakeven level. In this chapter, we address an array of performance measurements that can lead to an understanding of the profit-making capabilities of a business.

> **Related Podcast Episodes:** Episodes 70 and 282 of the Accounting Best Practices Podcast discuss breakeven and the margin of safety, as well as key performance indicators. The episodes are available at: **accountingtools.com/podcasts** or **iTunes**

Overview of Performance Measurements

Performance measurements are based on information in the income statement. As such, we can begin at the top of the income statement to extract information about revenues, and then work our way down the statement to derive additional types of information. For example, we can compare sales returns and allowances to gross sales, which can reveal the extent to which customers are returning goods or demanding billing reductions.

There are also several sub-headings of information that can reveal the ability of a company to earn different types of profits. For example, we describe ratios for the contribution margin (which uses variable costing concepts), gross profit (which incorporates factory overhead), operating income (which excludes non-operating transactions), and net profit (which encompasses all of the earning activities of a business).

We then work through a number of additional measurements that provide insights into the performance capabilities of an organization. For example, we can adjust profits for the effects of inflation, strip away non-operating transactions to focus on the core earnings capability of a business, and look at the relative proportions of different types of expenses. It is also possible to evaluate the risk of earnings declines by examining the breakeven point of a business, as well as by measuring the extent to which sales can decline before losses will be incurred.

A thorough examination of the performance measurements of a business can yield an excellent overview of its earning capabilities, which can lead to more detailed investigations that go beyond ratio analysis.

Sales Returns and Allowances to Sales

Sales returns are credits paid to customers when they return goods to the seller, while sales allowances are reductions in the purchase price of goods granted to customers to keep them from returning goods. In both cases, a high proportion of credits allowed to customers is a strong indicator of problems with the underlying product. Consequently, it is useful to track the proportion of sales returns and allowances to sales on a trend line, to see if there are any spikes in the percentage.

To calculate the ratio, aggregate all sales returns and allowances for the reporting period and divide them by gross sales for the same period. The formula is:

$$\frac{\text{Sales returns} + \text{Sales allowances}}{\text{Gross sales}}$$

There are two issues with this ratio. First, sales returns and allowances may be recorded in the same account as gross sales, making it difficult to locate individual transactions. To remedy the situation, create separate accounts for sales returns and sales allowances, and store the transactions there. Second, sales returns and allowances are usually recorded when customers return merchandise or complain about goods, which may not be the same reporting period in which the related gross sales were recorded. This can create a mismatch in the ratio, where the returns and allowances are paired with gross sales for a different period. The issue can be mitigated by using a broader reporting period, such as quarterly, for calculating the ratio.

EXAMPLE

Green Lawn Care launched a new battery-powered leaf blower three months ago, and the customer service department is hearing complaints from customers that the batteries in some of the units are catching on fire. To track the issue, management asks that the sales returns and allowances to sales ratio be tracked on a monthly basis, just for sales of the leaf blower. The result is the following table:

	May	June	July
Sales returns and allowances	$13,500	$72,000	$143,000
Gross leaf blower sales	$330,000	$365,000	$402,000
Sales returns and allowances to sales	4%	20%	36%

The ratio analysis shows minimal activity for the first month of sales, followed by a hard spike in returns. This is likely to be a delayed issue with the battery that is not evident during initial use. Management decides to enact a general recall of the product.

Contribution Margin Ratio

The contribution margin ratio is the percentage of a firm's contribution margin to its sales. Contribution margin is a product's price minus its variable costs, resulting in

13

the incremental profit earned for each unit sold. The total contribution margin generated by an entity represents the total earnings available to pay for fixed expenses and generate a profit.

The contribution margin formula is useful for determining the proportion of profit earned from a sale. The contribution margin should be relatively high, since it must be sufficient to also cover fixed costs and administrative overhead. Also, the measure is useful for determining whether to allow a lower price in special pricing situations. If the contribution margin ratio is excessively low or negative, it would be unwise to continue selling a product at that price point, since the company would have some difficulty earning a profit over the long term. The contribution margin ratio is also useful for determining the profits that will arise from various sales levels (see the example).

The contribution margin is also useful for determining the impact on profits of changes in sales. In particular, it can be used to estimate the decline in profits if sales drop, and so is a standard tool in the formulation of budgets.

To calculate the contribution margin ratio, divide the contribution margin by sales. The formula is:

$$\frac{\text{Sales} - \text{Variable expenses}}{\text{Sales}}$$

The contribution margin ratio does not account for the impact of a product on the bottleneck operation of a company. A low contribution margin may be entirely acceptable, as long as it requires little or no processing time by the bottleneck operation. See the Constraint and Throughput Measurements chapter for more information.

EXAMPLE

The Iverson Drum Company sells drum sets to high schools. In the most recent period, it sold $1,000,000 of drum sets that had related variable costs of $400,000. Iverson had $660,000 of fixed costs during the period, resulting in a loss of $60,000. The key information is:

Revenue	$1,000,000
Variable expenses	400,000
Contribution margin	600,000
Fixed expenses	660,000
Net loss	-$60,000

Iverson's contribution margin ratio is 60%, so if it wants to break even, the company must either reduce its fixed expenses by $60,000 or increase its sales by $100,000 (calculated as the $60,000 loss divided by the 60% contribution margin ratio).

Gross Profit Ratio

The gross profit ratio shows the proportion of profits generated by the sale of goods or services, before selling and administrative expenses. In essence, it reveals the ability of a business to create sellable products in a cost-effective manner. The ratio is of some importance from an analysis perspective, especially when tracked on a trend line, to see if a business is continuing to provide products to the marketplace for which customers are willing to pay.

The gross margin ratio is calculated as sales minus the cost of goods sold, divided by sales. The formula is:

$$\frac{Sales - Cost\ of\ goods\ sold}{Sales}$$

The ratio can vary over time as sales volumes change, since the cost of goods sold contains some fixed cost elements that will not vary with sales volume.

EXAMPLE

An analyst is reviewing a credit application from Quest Adventure Gear, which includes financial statements for the past three years. The analyst extracts the following information from the financial statements of Quest:

	20X1	20X2	20X3
Sales	$12,000,000	$13,500,000	$14,800,000
Cost of goods sold	$5,000,000	$5,100,000	$4,700,000
Gross profit ratio	58%	62%	68%

The analysis reveals that Quest is suffering from an ongoing decline in its gross profits, which should certainly be a concern from the perspective of allowing credit.

Operating Income Ratio

The standard performance measurement for a business is the net profit ratio, but that ratio suffers from the inclusion of one-time and non-operating gains and losses. For example, there may be an insurance loss or investment income – neither of which reveals the true state of the underlying business operations. A way to discern the underlying level of profitability is to use the operating income ratio, which compares operating income to only those sales related to operations. To calculate the operating income ratio, follow these steps:

1. Clean up the sales figure by eliminating any "sales" transactions that are really interest income or one-time gains.

2. Clean up the net profit ratio by eliminating all financing-related interest and income, as well as gains and losses on one-time transactions. The result is operating income.
3. Divide the operating income figure by the adjusted sales figure.

The formulation of the operating income ratio is:

$$\frac{\text{Net profit} - \text{Non-operating gain and loss transactions}}{\text{Net sales} - \text{Non-operating transactions recorded as sales}}$$

When the operating income ratio is calculated in aggregate for an entire entity, it can mask operating losses at the business unit level, since these losses may be offset by gains elsewhere in the company. Consequently, it is best to generate the measurement at a level as far down within the company as possible.

EXAMPLE

Quest Clothiers, maker of rugged outdoor gear, raised $100 million in a private stock placement two years ago. The company has reported net profits of $4,500,000 and $5,200,000 in the following two years, but this may be masking losses that are being netted against interest income on the $100 million of cash. An investor quizzes the company controller about this issue, and learns that $4,200,000 and $3,100,000 of interest income have been recorded as revenue in the past two years. Total revenues reported were $62,000,000 and $67,000,000, respectively, in years 1 and 2. The following table eliminates the interest income to arrive at the company's operating income ratio:

	Year 1	Year 2
Reported revenue	$62,000,000	$67,000,000
Less: Interest income	-4,200,000	-3,900,000
Adjusted revenue	$57,800,000	$63,100,000
Reported net profits	$4,500,000	$5,200,000
Less: Interest income	-4,200,000	-3,900,000
Operating income	$300,000	$1,300,000
Operating income ratio	0.5%	2.1%

The ratio reveals that most of the income reported by the company has really been derived from its investment of the $100 million of cash, rather than from operations. However, the situation appears to be improving, since the operating profit quadrupled in Year 2.

Net Profit Ratio

The net profit ratio is a comparison of after-tax profits to net sales. It reveals the remaining profit after all costs of production and administration have been deducted from sales, and income taxes recognized. As such, it is one of the best measures of the overall results of a firm, especially when combined with an evaluation of how well it is using its working capital. The measure is commonly reported on a trend line, to judge performance over time. It is also used to compare the results of a business with its competitors.

The net profit ratio is really a short-term measurement, because it does not reveal a company's actions to maintain profitability over the long term, as may be indicated by the level of capital investment or research and development expenditures. Also, a company may delay a variety of discretionary expenses, such as maintenance or training, to make its net profit ratio look better than it normally is. Consequently, evaluate this ratio alongside an array of other metrics to gain a full picture of a company's ability to continue as a going concern.

Another issue with the net profit ratio is that a company may intentionally keep it low through a variety of expense recognition strategies in order to avoid paying taxes. If so, review the statement of cash flows to determine the real cash-generating ability of the business.

To calculate the net profit ratio, divide net profits by net sales and then multiply by 100. The formula is:

$$(\text{Net profit} \div \text{Net sales}) \times 100$$

EXAMPLE

Kelvin Corporation has $1,000,000 of sales in its most recent month, as well as sales returns of $40,000, a cost of goods sold of $550,000, and administrative expenses of $360,000. The income tax rate is 35%. The calculation of its net profit percentage is:

$1,000,000 Sales - $40,000 Sales returns = $960,000 Net sales

$960,000 Net sales - $550,000 Cost of goods - $360,000 Administrative expenses
= $50,000 Income before tax

$50,000 Income before tax $\times (1 - 0.35) = $32,500 Profit after tax

($32,500 Profit after tax $\div$ $960,000 Net Sales) $\times$ 100

= 3.4% Net profit ratio

Deflated Profit Growth

When a business operates in a highly inflationary environment, a decline in the value of its home currency can cause the business to report unusually high profits in comparison to prior periods. To gain a better understanding of the underlying profit growth of the business, it is necessary to deflate the profits for the current period and then compare them to the profits reported for the prior period. To calculate deflated profit growth, follow these steps:

1. Divide the price index for the prior reporting period by the price index for the current reporting period.
2. Multiply the result by the net profit figure reported for the current reporting period.
3. Subtract the net profits for the prior reporting period from the result.
4. Divide the result by the net profit figure for the prior reporting period.

The formula is:

$$\frac{\text{Current period net profit} \times \dfrac{\text{Price index for prior period}}{\text{Price index for current period}} - \text{Prior period net profit}}{\text{Prior period net profit}}$$

The use of price indexes only approximates the true impact of inflation on a business. A price index is based on the changes in prices for a mix of common goods and services, which a company may not use in the same proportions built into the index. For example, a price index may have increased primarily because of a jump in the price of oil, but a company may have minimum expenditures for oil. Consequently, there can be differences between the deflated profit growth calculation and the actual impact of inflation on a business.

EXAMPLE

Aphelion Corporation operates telescopes in the Atacama Desert in northern Chile, and uses the Chilean peso as its home currency. The company reported profits of 5,000,000 pesos in the most recent year, and 4,500,000 pesos in the immediately preceding year. The price index for the current year was 127, as opposed to 106 for the preceding year. Based on this information, the deflated profit growth of the company is:

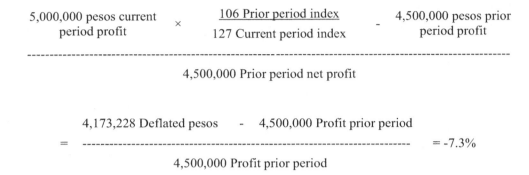

$$\frac{5{,}000{,}000 \text{ pesos current period profit} \times \frac{106 \text{ Prior period index}}{127 \text{ Current period index}} - 4{,}500{,}000 \text{ pesos prior period profit}}{4{,}500{,}000 \text{ Prior period net profit}}$$

$$= \frac{4{,}173{,}228 \text{ Deflated pesos} - 4{,}500{,}000 \text{ Profit prior period}}{4{,}500{,}000 \text{ Profit prior period}} = -7.3\%$$

Thus, when adjusted for inflation, the profits of Aphelion declined by 7.3% in the current reporting period.

Effective Tax Rate

A major determinant of the net profit ratio just described is the ability of a business to avoid or defer the payment of income taxes. There are a number of strategies available for lowering the statutory tax rate to a level far below what would normally be expected. If a company can successfully engage in a tax reduction or deferral strategy over a long period of time, the result can be a massive increase in net profits, with an attendant increase in cash flows.

To calculate the effective tax rate, divide the aggregate amount of income tax expense stated on the income statement by the amount of before-tax profit reported on the same document.

$$\frac{\text{Recognized tax expense}}{\text{Before-tax profit}}$$

It can be useful to track the effective tax rate over multiple years, to see if a business is capable of maintaining a low tax rate over the long term, usually by shifting reportable income to low-tax locations. A one-year decline in the tax rate is much less indicative of a corporate tax-reduction strategy, since a company may simply have blundered into a tax-reduction scenario without intending to do so.

EXAMPLE

Clyde Shotguns manufactures extremely high-end shotguns for wealthy collectors around the world. The company has a long-term strategy of building production facilities in multiple countries, each one owned by a separate legal entity. This means that Clyde can utilize favorable transfer pricing to recognize the bulk of the company's income in its Ireland facility, where the tax rate is substantially lower than in other parts of the world where its other subsidiaries operate. The result in the past year was the recognition of $800,000 of tax expense on $5,333,000 of before-tax profit, which is an effective tax rate of 15%.

Core Earnings Ratio

There are many ways in which the net profit ratio of a business can be skewed by events that have little to do with the core operating capabilities of a business. To get to the root of the issue and concentrate on only the essential operations of a business, Standard & Poor's has promulgated the concept of core earnings, which strips away all non-operational transactions from a company's reported results.

There are a multitude of unrelated transactions that can be eliminated from net profits, some of which are so specific to certain industries that Standard & Poor's probably never thought of them. The most common of these unrelated transactions are:

- Asset impairment charges
- Costs related to merger activities
- Costs related to the issuance of bonds and other forms of financing
- Gains or losses on hedging activities that have not yet been realized
- Gains or losses on the sale of assets
- Gains or losses related to the outcome of litigation
- Profits or losses from pension income
- Recognized cost of stock options issued to employees
- Recognized cost of warrants issued to third parties
- The accrued cost of restructuring operations that have not yet occurred

Many of these special adjustments only occur at long intervals, so a company may find that its core earnings ratio is quite close to its net profit ratio in one year, and substantially different in the next year. The difference tends to be much larger when a company adds complexity to the nature of its operations, so that more factors can impact net profits.

The calculation of the core earnings ratio is to adjust reported net income for as many of the preceding items as are present, and divide by net sales. The formula is:

$$\frac{\text{Net profits} - \text{Core earnings adjustments}}{\text{Net sales}}$$

EXAMPLE

Subterranean Access, maker of drilling equipment, has reported a fabulous year, with profits of $10,000,000 on sales of $50,000,000. A credit analyst that rates the company's bonds is suspicious of this good fortune, and digs through the company's annual report to derive the core earnings ratio of the business. She uncovers the following items:

Profit from favorable settlement of a lawsuit	$8,000,000
Profit on earnings from pension fund	500,000
Gain on sale of a subsidiary	3,500,000
Impairment charge on acquired intangible assets	-1,000,000
Total	$11,000,000

When these adjustments are factored out of the company's net profits, it turns out that the core earnings figure is actually a $1,000,000 loss, which results in a core earnings ratio of -2%. Based on this information, the analyst issues a downgrade on the company's debt, on the assumption that the multitude of favorable adjustments will not continue.

Quality of Earnings Ratio

The "real" performance of a business equates to the cash flows that it generates, irrespective of the results that appear in its income statement. Any number of accruals and aggressive or conservative interpretations of the accounting standards can lead to a wide divergence between the reported amounts of cash flows and net income. The greater the divergence, the more an observer must wonder about the reliability of the information being presented. This issue is addressed by the quality of earnings ratio, which compares the reported level of earnings to the reported cash flows. Earnings are considered to be of high quality if the two figures are relatively close to each other. To calculate the quality of earnings, follow these steps:

1. Obtain the "Cash from operations" line item in the statement of cash flows.
2. Subtract the cash from operations figure from the net profit figure in the income statement.
3. Divide the result by the average asset figure for the business during the measurement period.

The formula is:

$$\frac{\text{Net profits} - \text{Cash from operations}}{\text{Average assets}}$$

An occasional spike in this ratio can be explained by a company's compliance with the accounting standards in regard to a specific issue, and can be entirely legitimate. However, if the amount of net profits is persistently higher than cash from operations for a number of reporting periods, it is likely that management is actively engaged in the inflation of the net profits figure.

EXAMPLE

The Red Herring Fish Company has been having difficulty meeting its loan covenants over the past few months, and the loan officer is beginning to suspect that something fishy is going on. She reviews the company's latest set of financial statements, and extracts the following information:

Cash from operations	$2,300,000
Net profits	4,700,000
Beginning assets	11,000,000
Ending assets	11,400,000

Based on this information, she compiles the following quality of earnings ratio:

$$\frac{\$4,700,000 \text{ Net profits} - \$2,300,000 \text{ Cash from operations}}{(\$11,000,000 \text{ Beginning assets} - \$11,400,000 \text{ Ending assets}) \div 2}$$

$$= 21\%$$

The ratio reveals quite a substantial difference between the cash flows and reported (and possibly inflated) earnings of Red Herring. The loan officer decides that it is time to send in an audit team to review the company's books.

Operating Ratio

The operating ratio is the ratio of production and administrative expenses to net sales. It excludes financing costs, non-operating expenses, and taxes. Essentially, it is the cost per sales dollar of operating a business. A lower operating ratio is a good indicator of operational efficiency.

The operating ratio is only useful for seeing if the core business is able to generate a profit. Since several potentially significant expenses are not included, it is not a good indicator of the overall performance of a business, and so can be misleading when used without any other performance metrics.

To calculate the operating ratio, add together all production costs (i.e., the cost of goods sold) and administrative expenses (which include general, administrative, and selling expenses) and divide by net sales (which is gross sales minus sales discounts, returns, and allowances). The calculation is:

$$\frac{\text{Production expenses} + \text{Administrative expenses}}{\text{Net sales}}$$

A variation on the formula is to exclude production expenses, so that only administrative expenses are matched against net sales. This version yields a much lower ratio, and is useful for determining the amount of fixed administrative costs that must be covered by sales. As such, it is a variation on the breakeven calculation (which is described later in this chapter). The ratio is:

$$\frac{\text{Administrative expenses}}{\text{Net sales}}$$

The operating ratio indicates little when taken as a single measure for one time period. Since operating expenses can vary considerably across multiple months, it is better to track the ratio on a trend line.

EXAMPLE

Horton Corporation has production expenses of $600,000, administrative expenses of $200,000, and net sales of $1,000,000. Its operating ratio is:

$$\frac{\$600,000 \text{ Production expenses} + \$200,000 \text{ Administrative expenses}}{\$1,000,000 \text{ Net sales}}$$

$$= 80\% \text{ Operating ratio}$$

Thus, operating expenses are 80% of net sales.

Operating Leverage

Operating leverage measures a company's fixed costs as a percentage of all of its costs. The following two scenarios describe an organization having high operating leverage and low operating leverage.

1. *High operating leverage.* A large proportion of the company's costs are fixed costs. In this case, the firm earns a large profit on each incremental sale, but must attain sufficient sales volume to cover its substantial fixed costs. If it can do so, then the entity will earn a substantial profit on all sales *after* it has paid for its fixed costs.
2. *Lower operating leverage.* A large proportion of the company's costs are variable costs, so it only incurs these costs if there is a sale. In this case, the firm earns a smaller profit on each incremental sale, but does not have to generate much sales volume in order to cover its lower fixed costs. It is easier for this type of company to earn a profit at low sales levels, but it does not earn outsized profits if it can generate additional sales.

For example, a software company has substantial fixed costs in the form of developer salaries, but has almost no variable costs associated with each incremental software sale; this firm has high operating leverage. Conversely, a consulting firm bills its

23

clients by the hour, and incurs variable costs in the form of consultant wages. This firm has low operating leverage.

To calculate operating leverage, divide an entity's contribution margin (sales minus variable costs) by its net operating income. The ratio is:

$$\frac{\text{Sales} - \text{Variable expenses}}{\text{Net operating income}}$$

Constant monitoring of operating leverage is more important for a firm having high operating leverage, since a small percentage change in sales can result in a dramatic increase (or decrease) in profits. A firm must be especially careful when forecasting its revenues in such situations, since a small forecasting error translates into large errors in both net income and cash flows.

EXAMPLE

Nascent Corporation has the following financial results:

Revenues	$100,000
Variable expenses	30,000
Fixed expenses	60,000
Net operating income	$10,000

Nascent has a contribution margin of 70% and net operating income of $10,000, which gives it a degree of operating leverage of 7. Nascent's sales then increase by 20%, resulting in the following financial results:

Revenues	$120,000
Variable expenses	36,000
Fixed expenses	60,000
Net operating income	$24,000

The contribution margin of 70% has stayed the same, and fixed costs have not changed. Because of Nascent's high degree of operating leverage, the 20% increase in sales translates into a greater than doubling of its net operating income.

Breakeven Point

The breakeven point is the sales volume at which a business earns exactly no money. It is mostly used for internal analysis purposes, but it is also useful for a credit analyst, who can use it to determine the amount of losses that could be sustained if a credit applicant were to suffer a sales downturn.

To calculate the breakeven point, divide total fixed expenses by the contribution margin. Contribution margin is sales minus all variable expenses, divided by sales. The formula is:

$$\frac{\text{Total fixed expenses}}{\text{Contribution margin percentage}}$$

A more refined approach is to eliminate all non-cash expenses (such as depreciation) from the numerator, so that the calculation focuses on the breakeven cash flow level.

EXAMPLE

A credit analyst is reviewing the financial statements of a customer that has a large amount of fixed costs. The industry is highly cyclical, so the analyst wants to know what a large downturn in sales will do to the customer. The customer has total fixed expenses of $3,000,000, sales of $8,000,000, and variable expenses of $4,000,000. Based on this information, the customer's contribution margin is 50%. The breakeven calculation is:

$$\frac{\$3,000,000 \text{ Total fixed costs}}{50\% \text{ Contribution margin}}$$

$$= \$6,000,000 \text{ Breakeven sales level}$$

Thus, the customer's sales can decline by $2,000,000 from their current level before the customer will begin to lose money.

Margin of Safety

The margin of safety is the reduction in sales that can occur before the breakeven point of a business is reached. The amount of this buffer is expressed as a percentage. The concept is especially useful when a significant proportion of sales are at risk of decline or elimination, as may be the case when a sales contract is coming to an end. By knowing the amount of the margin of safety, management can gain a better understanding of the risk of loss to which a business is subjected by changes in sales. The opposite situation may also arise, where the margin is so large that a business is well-protected from sales variations.

The margin of safety concept does not work well when sales are strongly seasonal, since some months will yield catastrophically low results. In such cases, annualize the information in order to integrate all seasonal fluctuations into the outcome.

To calculate the margin of safety, subtract the current breakeven point from sales, and divide by sales. The formula is:

$$\frac{\text{Current sales level} - \text{Breakeven point}}{\text{Current sales level}}$$

Here are two alternative versions of the margin of safety:

1. *Budget based.* A company may want to project its margin of safety under a budget for a future period. If so, replace the current sales level in the formula with the budgeted sales level.
2. *Unit based.* To translate the margin of safety into the number of units sold, use the following formula instead (though note that this version works best if a company only sells one product):

$$\frac{\text{Current sales level} - \text{Breakeven point}}{\text{Selling price per unit}}$$

The margin of safety concept is also applied to investing, where it refers to the difference between the intrinsic value of a company's share price and its current market value. An investor wants to see a large variance between the two figures (which is the margin of safety) before buying stock. This implies that there is substantial upside potential for the stock price – or at least, it means any error in deriving the intrinsic value must be a big one in order to erase the margin of safety.

EXAMPLE

Lowry Locomotion is considering the purchase of new equipment to expand the production capacity of its toy tractor product line. The addition will increase Lowry's operating costs by $100,000 per year, though sales will also be increased. Relevant information is noted in the following table:

	Before Machinery Purchase	After Machinery Purchase
Sales	$4,000,000	$4,200,000
Gross margin percentage	48%	48%
Fixed expenses	$1,800,000	$1,900,000
Breakeven point	$3,750,000	$3,958,000
Profits	$120,000	$116,000
Margin of safety	6.3%	5.8%

The table reveals that both the margin of safety and profits worsen slightly as a result of the equipment purchase, so expanding production capacity is probably not a good idea.

Discretionary Cost Ratio

Discretionary costs are costs that management can choose to avoid during the short term without interfering with the basic operation of a business. Examples of discretionary expenses are advertising, research and development, maintenance on facilities and equipment, and employee training. These costs are typically reduced when management is attempting to avoid a cash squeeze or wants to bolster short-term earnings.

However, these expenditures must be made over the long term, or else a company will lose its best employees and experience declining market share and reduced profits. The discretionary cost ratio is designed to highlight these expenditures in comparison to sales, preferably on a trend line. If an outside observer sees a declining ratio over time, this is a clear indicator that management is deliberately scaling back on these expenses.

To calculate the discretionary cost ratio, aggregate all types of discretionary costs for the reporting period and divide by net sales. The formula is:

$$\frac{\sum \text{All types of discretionary costs}}{\text{Net sales}}$$

This ratio can be difficult for an outsider to discern, for not all of the discretionary costs may be separately stated in a company's income statement. Instead, they may be aggregated into more general line items, such as "general and administrative." This level of aggregation can be a particular concern when these costs used to be separately stated, and are now aggregated, indicating that management wishes to hide the information.

A decline in the ratio does not always mean that management is deliberately attempting to bolster short-term results at the expense of long-term results. Instead, it is possible that changes in the structure of the business have resulted in different levels of discretionary expenditure. For example, if management decides to outsource its manufacturing to a third party, then all of the repairs and maintenance expense associated with the in-house facility will be eliminated. Similarly, all of the training costs for the production staff will no longer be needed. Thus, the outcome of this ratio should be examined in light of changes in a company's underlying operations.

EXAMPLE

Pulsed Laser Drilling manufactures a laser that drills through solid rock, and which is used for oil and gas drilling. The product requires a large research and development expenditure, especially since drillers are demanding a wider bore hole, which requires a much more high-powered laser. Pulsed Laser's management decides in 20X3 that it can no longer afford the amount of research required to support the product, and so sells it to a larger multi-national company that has greater financial resources. This triggers a massive decline in the company's discretionary cost ratio, as noted in the following table:

	20X2	20X3
Training costs	$320,000	$290,000
Repairs and maintenance	820,000	805,000
Advertising	230,000	190,000
Research and development	4,290,000	1,050,000
Total discretionary costs	$5,660,000	$2,335,000
Net sales	$22,600,000	$19,450,000
Discretionary cost ratio	25%	12%

In short, the ratio declines, but for a justifiable reason – the company is unable to support a product, and so accepts fewer discretionary expenses in exchange for a reduced level of sales.

Summary

When conducting an analysis of a business, many people restrict themselves to the performance measurements described in this chapter. While performance measures do form the core of an analysis effort, we must caution that the other ratios presented in this book must be addressed, particularly those that focus on the liquidity of an organization. For example, an analyst will conclude that a company is growing at a fast and profitable clip, and does not extend the analysis to see that the business does not have sufficient cash to support its growth – resulting in severe financial difficulties. Consequently, use a broad range of measurements to gain a complete understanding of a business, rather than using just performance measures to view one aspect of operations.

Chapter 3
Liquidity Measurements

Introduction

The liquidity of a business is a primary concern of outside parties. Lenders want to understand the ability of a borrower to pay back a loan, while suppliers want to feel secure in extending credit to a customer. Similarly, a prospective investor will not buy a company's stock if there is a reasonable risk that the business does not have sufficient cash to meet its obligations. Given the concerns of these parties, we present a broad range of measurements that can be used to discern the liquidity of an organization, using the balance sheet as the primary source of information.

> **Related Podcast Episode:** Episode 28 of the Accounting Best Practices Podcast discusses liquidity measurements. The episode is available at: **accountingtools.com/podcasts** or **iTunes**

Overview of Liquidity Measurements

Liquidity measurements are used to estimate the ability of an organization to pay its bills. These measurements are rarely used within a company, which has access to much more detailed cash forecast information. However, they are critical to suppliers, lenders, and investors, who must infer the state of a company's liquidity from information in its financial statements, especially its balance sheet.

The foundation of liquidity is a company's cash conversion cycle, which is the time it takes to pay for inbound raw materials, sell them as finished goods, and collect cash from customers. A business must have sufficient cash reserves to survive through this process. Accordingly, we examine the components of the cash conversion cycle, and how to derive each component.

A third party can more easily derive several simpler measures of liquidity than the cash conversion cycle, simply by comparing different elements of the balance sheet. The classic liquidity measure is the current ratio, though several issues can yield misleading results. Consequently, we also note the more conservative quick ratio and cash ratio, which focus on the most liquid assets and exclude items that may not be so readily convertible into cash.

We then relate the liquidity of a business to its ongoing expenditures, to see how long it can survive on anticipated cash flows. This approach is useful when a target date must be reached with little additional incoming cash expected in the interim. Another variation is to relate liquidity to sales, which reveals the amount of assets required to support a certain level of sales. This approach can also be used to compare current asset levels to expected future sales, to examine asset utilization levels.

We also make note of those assets that can twist the result of a liquidity ratio by including items that are not readily convertible into cash. This is a particular problem when a business has recognized large amounts of inventory, customized equipment, and intangible assets.

Finally, there is a discussion of the ability of a business to support its long-term obligations. However, long-term liquidity is not the point of the bulk of the ratios in this chapter, for long-term issues can be resolved in many ways, such as through the sale of assets, sale of stock, or roll forward of debt agreements. Instead, we primarily focus on short-term measures, where these alternative forms of funding may not be available, and a business must instead rely upon its ability to convert current assets into cash.

When reviewing the following ratios, keep in mind that there is no perfect target for a liquidity measurement. While a high level of liquidity is considered to be best, this may mean that a business is not putting its cash and investments to the best possible use. Instead, a better alternative could be investing in less-liquid assets, such as fixed assets, that can generate more cash flow. Also, a company should be able to meet its payment obligations even with a lower liquidity level by closely tracking projected cash inflows and outflows. Thus, a lower level of liquidity, if properly managed, can be indicative of better management than a higher level of liquidity.

Cash Conversion Cycle

The cash conversion cycle is the time period extending from the payment of cash for the production of goods, until cash is received from the sale of those goods to customers. The activities involved in the cash conversion cycle include the purchasing of raw materials or items to be resold, their storage, the production process, payments to employees related to the production process, and the sale of goods to customers. If a company only provides services, then the cash conversion cycle extends from the date of payments to employees to the receipt of cash from the sale of services to customers. The cash conversion cycle tends to be much shorter for the provision of services.

It is important to know the duration of the cash conversion cycle, for this is the time period over which cash is invested in a business. If the conversion cycle can be shortened, then cash can be permanently extracted from a business and made available for other purposes. The steps in the cash conversion cycle that can potentially be compressed include:

- Placement of orders for goods with suppliers
- Time required for goods to be delivered to the company
- Time required to inspect and log in received goods
- Inventory holding period
- Duration of production process
- Time required to prepare goods for shipment
- The delay incorporated into payment terms with customers
- The time required to collect overdue accounts receivable

The cash conversion cycle can be severely compressed through the use of a just-in-time "pull" system that only produces goods just as they are needed for immediate sale to customers.

To calculate the amount of the cash conversion cycle, add together the days of sales in accounts receivable and the days of sales in inventory, and subtract the days of payables outstanding. For example, a company has 60 days of sales in accounts receivable, 80 days of sales in inventory, and 30 days of payables outstanding. Its cash conversion cycle is therefore:

$$60 \text{ Days receivables} + 80 \text{ Days inventory} - 30 \text{ Days payables}$$

$$= 110 \text{ Days cash conversion cycle}$$

The calculations for days of sales in accounts receivable, days of sales in inventory, and days payables outstanding are explained next.

Days Sales in Accounts Receivable

Days sales in accounts receivable is the number of days that a customer invoice is outstanding before it is collected. The measurement is usually applied to the entire set of invoices that a company has outstanding at any point in time, rather than to a single invoice. The point of the measurement is to determine the effectiveness of a company's credit and collection efforts in allowing credit to reputable customers, as well as its ability to collect from them. When measured at the individual customer level, it can indicate when a customer is having cash flow troubles, since the customer will attempt to stretch out the amount of time before it pays invoices.

There is not an absolute number of accounts receivable days that represents excellent or poor accounts receivable management, since the figure varies considerably by industry and the underlying payment terms. Generally, a figure of 25% more than the standard terms allowed may represent an opportunity for improvement. Conversely, an accounts receivable days figure that is very close to the payment terms granted to a customer probably indicates that a company's credit policy is too tight.

The formula for accounts receivable days is:

$$(\text{Accounts receivable} \div \text{Annual revenue}) \times \text{Number of days in the year}$$

For example, if a company has an average accounts receivable balance of $200,000 and annual sales of $1,200,000, then its accounts receivable days figure is:

$$(\$200,000 \text{ Accounts receivable} \div \$1,200,000 \text{ Annual revenue}) \times 365 \text{ Days}$$

$$= 60.8 \text{ Accounts receivable days}$$

The calculation indicates that the company requires 60.8 days to collect a typical invoice.

An effective way to use the accounts receivable days measurement is to track it on a trend line, month by month. Doing so shows any changes in the ability of the company to collect from its customers. If a business is highly seasonal, a variation is to compare the measurement to the same metric for the same month in the preceding year; this provides a more reasonable basis for comparison.

No matter how this measurement is used, remember that it is usually compiled from a large number of outstanding invoices, and so provides no insights into the collectability of a specific invoice. Thus, it should be supplemented with an ongoing examination of the aged accounts receivable report and the collection notes of the collection staff.

Days Sales in Inventory

Days sales in inventory (DSI) is a way to measure the average amount of time that it takes for a company to convert its inventory into sales. A relatively small number of days sales in inventory indicates that a company is more efficient in selling off its inventory, while a large number indicates that a company may have invested too much in inventory, and may even have obsolete inventory on hand.

To calculate days sales in inventory, divide the average inventory for the year by the cost of goods sold for the same period, and then multiply by 365. For example, if a company has average inventory of $1.5 million and an annual cost of goods sold of $6 million, then its days sales in inventory is calculated as:

($1.5 million inventory ÷ $6 million cost of goods sold) × 365 days

= 91.3 days sales in inventory

The days sales in inventory figure can be misleading, for the following reasons:

- A company could post financial results that indicate a low DSI, but only because it has sold off a large amount of inventory at a discount, or has written off some inventory as obsolete. An indicator of these actions is when profits decline at the same time that the number of days sales in inventory declines.
- A company could change its method for calculating the cost of goods sold, such as by capitalizing more or fewer expenses into overhead. If this calculation method varies significantly from the method the company used in the past, it can lead to a sudden alteration in the results of the measurement.
- The person creating the metrics might use the amount of ending inventory in the numerator, rather than the average inventory figure for the entire measurement period. If the ending inventory figure varies significantly from the average inventory figure, this can result in a sharp change in the measurement.
- A company may switch to contract manufacturing, where a supplier produces and holds goods on behalf of the company. Depending upon the arrangement, the company may have no inventory to report at all, which renders the DSI measurement useless.

Days Payables Outstanding

The accounts payable days formula measures the number of days that a company takes to pay its suppliers. If the number of days increases from one period to the next, this indicates that the company is paying its suppliers more slowly. A change in the number of payable days can also indicate altered payment terms with suppliers, though this rarely has more than a slight impact on the total number of days. If a company is paying its suppliers very quickly, it may mean that the suppliers are demanding short payment terms because they are suspicious of the company's ability to pay.

To calculate days payables outstanding, summarize all purchases from suppliers during the measurement period, and divide by the average amount of accounts payable during that period. The formula is:

$$\frac{\text{Total supplier purchases}}{(\text{Beginning accounts payable} + \text{Ending accounts payable}) \div 2}$$

This formula reveals the total accounts payable turnover. Then divide the resulting turnover figure into 365 days to arrive at the number of accounts payable days.

The formula can be modified to exclude cash payments to suppliers, since the numerator should include only purchases on credit from suppliers. However, the amount of up-front cash payments to suppliers is normally so small that this modification is not necessary.

As an example, a treasurer wants to determine his company's accounts payable days for the past year. In the beginning of this period, the beginning accounts payable balance was $800,000, and the ending balance was $884,000. Purchases for the last 12 months were $7,500,000. Based on this information, the treasurer calculates the accounts payable turnover as:

$$\frac{\$7,500,000 \text{ Purchases}}{(\$800,000 \text{ Beginning payables} + \$884,000 \text{ Ending payables}) \div 2}$$

$$=$$

$$\frac{\$7,500,000 \text{ Purchases}}{\$842,000 \text{ Average accounts payable}}$$

$$= 8.9 \text{ Accounts payable turnover}$$

Thus, the company's accounts payable is turning over at a rate of 8.9 times per year. To calculate the turnover in days, the treasurer divides the 8.9 turns into 365 days, which yields:

$$365 \text{ Days} \div 8.9 \text{ Turns} = 41 \text{ Days}$$

Companies sometimes measure accounts payable days by only using the cost of goods sold in the numerator. This is incorrect, since there may be a large amount of administrative expenses that should also be included. If a company only uses the cost of goods sold in the numerator, this creates an excessively small number of payable days.

A significant failing of the days payables outstanding measurement is that it does not factor in all of the short-term liabilities of a business. There may be substantial liabilities related to payroll, interest, and taxes that exceed the size of payables outstanding. This issue can be eliminated by incorporating all short-term liabilities into the days payables outstanding measurement.

Liquidity Index

The liquidity index calculates the days required to convert a company's trade receivables and inventory into cash. The index is used to estimate the ability of a business to generate the cash needed to meet current liabilities. Use the following steps to calculate the liquidity index:

1. Multiply the ending trade receivables balance by the average collection period.
2. Multiply the ending inventory balance by the average inventory liquidation period. This includes the average days to sell inventory and to collect the resulting receivables.
3. Summarize the first two items and divide by the total of all trade receivables and inventory.

The liquidity index formula is:

$$\frac{(\text{Trade receivables} \times \text{Days to liquidate}) + (\text{Inventory} \times \text{Days to liquidate})}{\text{Trade receivables} + \text{Inventory}}$$

The liquidation days information in the formula is based on historical averages, which may not translate well to the receivables and inventory currently on hand. Actual cash flows may vary substantially around the averages indicated by the formula.

EXAMPLE

A financial analyst wants to understand the ability of a customer, Hassle Corporation, to convert its receivables and inventory into cash. Hassle has $400,000 of trade receivables on hand, which can normally be converted to cash within 50 days. Hassle also has $650,000 of inventory, which can be liquidated in an average of 90 days. When combined with the receivable collection period, this means it takes 140 days to fully liquidate inventory *and* collect the proceeds. Based on this information, the liquidity index is:

$$\frac{(\$400,000 \text{ Receivables} \times 50 \text{ Days to liquidate}) + (\$650,000 \text{ Inventory} \times 90 \text{ Days to liquidate})}{\$400,000 \text{ Receivables} + \$650,000 \text{ Inventory}}$$

$$= 106 \text{ Days to convert assets to cash}$$

The larger proportion of inventory in this calculation tends to skew the number of days well past the liquidation days for trade receivables. In short, Hassle will require a lengthy period to convert several current assets to cash, which may impact its ability to pay bills in the short term.

It may appear difficult to obtain the liquidation days information required for this formula. However, using industry averages can yield a reasonable estimate of the liquidity index for a business.

Current Ratio

One of the first ratios that a lender or supplier reviews when examining a company is its current ratio. The current ratio measures the short-term liquidity of a business; that is, it gives an indication of the ability of a business to pay its bills. A ratio of 2:1 is preferred, with a lower proportion indicating a reduced ability to pay in a timely manner. Since the ratio is current assets divided by current liabilities, the ratio essentially implies that current assets can be liquidated to pay for current liabilities.

To calculate the current ratio, divide the total of all current assets by the total of all current liabilities. The formula is:

$$\frac{\text{Current assets}}{\text{Current liabilities}}$$

The current ratio can yield misleading results under the following circumstances:

- *Inventory component.* When the current assets figure includes a large proportion of inventory assets, since these assets can be difficult to liquidate. This can be a particular problem if management is using aggressive accounting techniques to apply an unusually large amount of overhead costs to inventory, which further inflates the recorded amount of inventory.
- *Paying from debt.* When a company is drawing upon its line of credit to pay bills as they come due, which means that the cash balance is near zero. In this case, the current ratio could be fairly low, and yet the presence of a line of credit still allows a business to pay in a timely manner.

EXAMPLE

A supplier wants to learn about the financial condition of Lowry Locomotion. The supplier calculates the current ratio of Lowry for the past three years:

	Year 1	Year 2	Year 3
Current assets	$8,000,000	$16,400,000	$23,400,000
Current liabilities	$4,000,000	$9,650,000	$18,000,000
Current ratio	2:1	1.7:1	1.3:1

The sudden rise in current assets over the past two years indicates that Lowry has undergone a rapid expansion of its operations. Of particular concern is the increase in accounts payable in Year 3, which indicates a rapidly deteriorating ability to pay suppliers. Based on this information, the supplier elects to restrict the extension of credit to Lowry.

Inventory to Current Assets Ratio

We just noted a key problem with the current ratio, which is that the inventory component of the measurement is far less convertible into cash than receivables. We can measure the extent of this problem by tracking the inventory to current assets ratio, preferably on a trend line. This ratio can also be used on a prospective basis, to estimate the amount of investment in inventory as a proportion of current assets. For example, if management wants to increase the speed of customer order fulfillment, this translates into keeping more inventory on hand, which increases the inventory proportion within the ratio.

To calculate the inventory to current assets ratio, divide the total of all inventory in the balance sheet by current assets. This means that any reserves for obsolete inventory are also netted against the inventory figure in the denominator. The calculation is:

$$\frac{\text{Inventory} - \text{Related inventory reserves}}{\text{Current assets}}$$

The measure can be affected by changes in how the cost of inventory is compiled, such as a change from the first in, first out method to the last in, first out method. A change in the method of overhead allocation can also affect the numerator.

This ratio should not be treated as a stand-alone measurement. Management will want to know the reason for a sudden change in the metric, which will call for a detailed report showing exactly which inventory items changed.

EXAMPLE

The owner of Dude Skis is contemplating a change from the company's historical reliance on custom ski manufacturing to bulk manufacturing for the middle of the ski market. Doing so will require stocking substantially more inventory than was the case in the past for prepaid customer orders. The before and after forecasted changes resulting from this decision are as follows:

	Custom Skis Only	Mass Market Skis
Inventory	$200,000	$800,000
Current assets	$1,000,000	$2,670,000
Inventory to current assets ratio	20%	30%

The ratio indicates that the company will have to maintain a higher proportion of inventory within its current assets. What the analysis does not reveal is the profits resulting from this strategic move, which could justify the increase in inventory.

Quick Ratio

The quick ratio formula matches the most easily liquidated portions of current assets with current liabilities. The intent of this ratio is to see if a business has sufficient assets that are immediately convertible to cash to pay its bills. The key elements of current assets that are included in the quick ratio are cash, marketable securities, and accounts receivable. Inventory is not included in the quick ratio, since it can be quite difficult to sell off in the short term. Because of the exclusion of inventory from the formula, the quick ratio is a better indicator than the current ratio of the ability of a company to pay its obligations.

To calculate the quick ratio, summarize cash, marketable securities and trade receivables, and divide by current liabilities. Do not include in the numerator any excessively old receivables that are unlikely to be paid. The formula is:

$$\frac{\text{Cash} + \text{Marketable securities} + \text{Accounts receivable}}{\text{Current liabilities}}$$

Despite the absence of inventory from the calculation, the quick ratio may still not yield a good view of immediate liquidity, if current liabilities are payable right now, while receipts from receivables are not expected for several more weeks.

EXAMPLE

Rapunzel Hair Products appears to have a respectable current ratio of 4:1. The breakdown of the ratio components is:

Item	Amount
Cash	$100,000
Marketable securities	50,000
Accounts receivable	420,000
Inventory	3,430,000
Current liabilities	1,000,000
Current ratio	4:1
Quick ratio	0.57:1

The component breakdown reveals that nearly all of Rapunzel's current assets are in the inventory area, where short-term liquidity is questionable. This issue is only visible when the quick ratio is substituted for the current ratio.

> **Tip:** It may be necessary to determine the ability of a business to pay off its most essential liabilities in the short term. If so, strip away from the quick ratio all liabilities that can be safely delayed, and use the remaining liabilities in the denominator.

Cash Ratio

The cash ratio compares the most liquid assets to current liabilities, to determine if a company can meet its short-term obligations. It is the most conservative of all the liquidity measurements, since it excludes inventory (which is used in the current ratio) and accounts receivable (which is included in the quick ratio).

To calculate the cash ratio, add together cash and cash equivalents, and divide by current liabilities. A variation that may be slightly more accurate is to exclude accrued expenses from the current liabilities in the denominator, since it may not be necessary to pay for these items in the near term. The calculation is:

$$\frac{\text{Cash} + \text{Cash equivalents}}{\text{Current liabilities}}$$

If a company wants to show a high cash ratio to the outside world, it must keep a large amount of cash on hand as of the measurement date, probably more than is prudent. Another issue is that the ratio only measures cash balances as of a specific point in time, which may vary considerably on a daily basis, as receivables are collected and suppliers are paid. Further, the ratio essentially assumes that the cash on hand now will be used to pay for all accounts payable, when in reality the cash from an ongoing series of receivable payments will also be used. Consequently, a better measure of liquidity is the quick ratio, which includes accounts receivable in the numerator.

EXAMPLE

Quest Adventure Gear has $100,000 of cash and $400,000 of cash equivalents on its balance sheet at the end of May. On that date, its current liabilities are $1,000,000. Its cash ratio is:

$$\frac{\$100,000 \text{ Cash} + \$400,000 \text{ Cash equivalents}}{\$1,000,000 \text{ Current liabilities}}$$

$$= 0.5{:}1 \text{ Cash ratio}$$

Defensive Interval Ratio

A variation on the preceding quick ratio is to use the same set of liquid assets to determine how long a business can continue to pay its bills. There is no correct answer to the number of days over which existing assets will provide sufficient funds to support company operations. Instead, review the measurement over time to see if the defensive interval is declining; this is an indicator that the company's buffer of liquid assets is gradually declining in proportion to its immediate payment liabilities.

To calculate the defensive interval ratio, aggregate the amounts of cash, marketable securities, and trade accounts receivable on hand, and then divide by the average amount of daily expenditures. Note that the denominator is not the average amount of *expenses*, since this can exclude any ongoing expenditures made for assets. Also, only put trade accounts receivable in the numerator, since other receivables (such as from officers of the company) may not be collectible in the short term. The formula is:

$$\frac{\text{Cash} + \text{Marketable Securities} + \text{Trade accounts receivable}}{\text{Average daily expenditures}}$$

There are several issues with this calculation that should be considered when evaluating its results, which are:

- *Expenditure inconsistency.* The central flaw is that the average amount of expenses that a business incurs on a daily basis is not consistent. On the contrary, it is extremely lumpy. For example, there may be no significant expenditure required for several days, followed by a large payroll payment, and then a large payment to a specific supplier. Because of the uneven timing of expenditures, the ratio does not yield an overly accurate view of exactly how long a company's assets will support operations.
- *Receivable replenishment.* The cash and accounts receivable figures used in the numerator are constantly being replenished by new sales, so there should be more cash available from this source than is indicated by the ratio.
- *Receipt inconsistency.* Cash receipts tend to be just as uneven as expenditures, so the amount of cash available to actually pay for expenditures may not be adequate.

EXAMPLE

Hammer Industries is suffering through a cyclical decline in the heavy equipment industry, but the cycle appears to be turning up. The company expects a cash-in-advance payment from a major customer in 60 days. In the meantime, the CEO wants to understand the ability of the company to stay in business at its current rate of expenditure. The following information applies to the analysis:

Cash	$1,200,000
Marketable securities	3,700,000
Trade receivables	4,100,000
Average daily expenditures	$138,500

The calculation of the defensive interval ratio is:

$$\frac{\$1,200,000 \text{ Cash} + \$3,700,000 \text{ Marketable securities} + \$4,100,000 \text{ Receivables}}{\$138,500 \text{ Average daily expenditures}}$$

$$= 65 \text{ days}$$

The ratio reveals that the company has sufficient cash to remain in operation for 65 days. However, this figure is so close to the projected receipt of cash from the customer that it may make sense to eliminate all discretionary expenses for the next few months, to extend the period over which remaining cash can be stretched.

Net Working Capital Ratio

The net working capital ratio is not actually a ratio at all, but rather the net of all elements of working capital. It is intended to reveal whether a business has a sufficient amount of net funds available in the short term to stay in operation. Use the following formula to calculate the net working capital ratio:

Current assets – Current liabilities = Net working capital

This measurement only provides a general idea of the liquidity of a business, for the following reasons:

- It does not relate the total amount of negative or positive outcome to the amount of current liabilities to be paid off, as would be the case with a real ratio.
- It does not compare the timing of when current assets are to be liquidated to the timing of when current liabilities must be paid off. Thus, a positive net working capital ratio could be generated in a situation where there is not sufficient immediate liquidity in current assets to pay off the immediate requirements of current liabilities.

An alternative version of the ratio compares net working capital to the total amount of assets on the balance sheet. The formula is:

$$\frac{\text{Current assets} - \text{Current liabilities}}{\text{Total assets}}$$

Under this second version, the intent is to track the proportion of short-term net funds to assets, usually on a trend line. By doing so, you can tell if a business is gradually shifting more of its assets into or out of long-term assets, such as fixed assets. An increasing ratio is considered good, since it implies that a business is minimizing its investment in fixed assets and keeping its asset reserves as liquid as possible.

EXAMPLE

Spud Potato Farms has $100,000 of cash, $250,000 of accounts receivable, and $400,000 of inventory, against which are offset $325,000 of accounts payable and $125,000 of the current portion of a long-term loan. The calculation of the net working capital ratio would indicate a positive balance of $300,000. However, it can take a long time to liquidate inventory, so the business might actually find itself in need of additional cash to meet its obligations in the short term, despite the positive outcome of the calculation.

Working Capital Productivity

The working capital productivity measurement compares sales to working capital. The intent is to measure whether a business has invested in a sufficient amount of working capital to support its sales. From a financing perspective, management wants to maintain low working capital levels in order to keep from having to raise more cash to operate the business. This can be achieved by such techniques as issuing less credit to customers, implementing just-in-time systems to avoid investing in inventory, and lengthening payment terms to suppliers.

Conversely, if the ratio indicates that a business has a large amount of receivables and inventory, this means that the organization is investing too much capital in return for the amount of sales that it is generating.

To decide whether the working capital productivity ratio is reasonable, compare a company's results to those of competitors or benchmark businesses.

To derive working capital productivity, divide annual revenues by the total amount of working capital. The formula is:

$$\frac{\text{Annual revenues}}{\text{Total working capital}}$$

When using this measurement, consider including the annualized quarterly sales in order to gain a better short-term understanding of the relationship between working capital and sales. Also, the measurement can be misleading if calculated during a seasonal spike in sales, since the formula will match high sales with a depleted inventory level to produce an unusually high ratio.

EXAMPLE

A lender is concerned that Pianoforte International does not have sufficient financing to support its sales. The lender obtains Pianoforte's financial statements, which contain the following information:

Annual revenues	$7,800,000
Cash	200,000
Accounts receivable	800,000
Inventory	2,000,000
Accounts payable	400,000

With this information, the lender derives the working capital productivity measurement as follows:

$$\frac{\$7,800,000 \text{ Annual revenues}}{\$200,000 \text{ Cash} + \$800,000 \text{ Receivables} + \$2,000,000 \text{ Inventory} - \$400,000 \text{ Payables}}$$

$$= 3:1 \text{ Working capital productivity}$$

This ratio is lower than the industry average of 4:1, which indicates poor management of the company's receivables and inventory. The lender should investigate further to see if the receivable and inventory figures may contain large amounts of overdue or obsolete items, respectively.

Working Capital Roll Forward

As a business expands over time, it is possible to use a ratio to estimate whether the amount of working capital now being used is appropriate. We do this by assuming that the historical ratio of working capital to sales represents a reasonable proportion, and then roll this ratio forward to the current period to see how it compares to the current proportion. If the current proportion has declined, this represents a reduction in the amount of working capital needed to support sales, and vice versa. To derive the working capital roll forward measurement, follow these steps:

1. Calculate the percentage change in revenue from the baseline period to the current period.
2. Multiply this percentage change by the working capital figure for the baseline period.
3. Subtract the result from the working capital figure for the current period.

The working capital roll forward formula is:

Current period working capital – (Baseline period ending working capital × (1 + percent change in revenue from baseline period)) = Working capital roll forward

This measurement is most useful when a company is comparing results between periods that have not been modified by alterations to the business plan, such as changes in price points, expansions into new geographic regions, and so forth. Such changes may alter the amount of working capital that must be maintained, rendering a comparison to working capital in a prior period less applicable to the current circumstances.

EXAMPLE

Quest Adventure Gear has been expanding rapidly in its core market of rugged travel equipment. In the immediately preceding year, the company required $1,200,000 of working capital to support sales of $5,000,000. In the current year, sales increased by 20%, to $6,000,000, while working capital increased to $1,680,000. The working capital roll forward for the current year is calculated as follows:

$1,680,000 Current period working capital – ($1,200,000 Baseline working capital × 1.2)

= $240,000

The ratio reveals that Quest's working capital increased by $240,000 more than expected, based on a proportional comparison to the baseline period. Further investigation reveals that the sales manager granted longer payment terms to a large retailer in exchange for its agreement to sell the Quest line of products.

Illiquid Asset Conversion Ratio

One of the main issues with the validity of liquidity ratios is that some assets on a company's balance sheet are unlikely to be convertible into much cash, if any. For example, intangible assets, goodwill, and heavily customized assets may yield little or no cash. This is a major concern for lenders and potential acquirers, who want to know how much cash they can extract from a business.

To calculate the ratio, aggregate the net book value of all assets for which conversion to cash may be difficult, and divide by the carrying amount of total assets. The formula is:

$$\frac{\sum \text{Net book value of illiquid assets}}{\text{Total recorded cost of all assets}}$$

Note that the numerator merely identifies those assets for which conversion to cash may be difficult. There is no attempt to derive the amount of cash (if any) that can be extracted from these assets. Thus, the ratio is half an answer − a high ratio indicates the presence of a potential problem, but it does not reveal the extent of the problem.

A further issue is that a company may need to hire an outside appraiser to identify the extent of its illiquid assets. Corporate insiders usually have a good idea of the cash flows that can be derived from the ongoing operation of assets, but not of the amount of cash for which an asset can be sold.

EXAMPLE

Muscular Corporation is contemplating the purchase of Active Exercise Machines (AEM), which manufactures and sells treadmills into the home market. AEM acquired several key patents related to advanced features of treadmills from a third party for $1,000,000. AEM also bought a competitor in order to grow into the Seattle market, resulting in the recognition of a $100,000 customer list asset, plus $250,000 of goodwill. The total amount of assets recognized by AEM is $1,800,000. Based on this information, Muscular calculates the following illiquid asset conversion ratio:

$$\frac{\$1,000,000 \text{ Patents} + \$100,000 \text{ Customer list} + \$250,000 \text{ Goodwill}}{\$1,800,000 \text{ Total assets}}$$

$$= 75\% \text{ Illiquid asset conversion ratio}$$

The ratio is quite high, and initially indicates that AEM's assets may not be readily convertible into cash. However, Muscular's management realizes that the $1,000,000 cost of patents purchased may result in a notable competitive advantage for AEM, especially if Muscular can use

43

the patents to block the product development activities of competitors. Consequently, Muscular extends an offer to the shareholders of AEM to acquire the business.

Solvency Ratio

The solvency ratio is specifically targeted at the ability of a business to meet its long-term obligations. The ratio is derived from the information stated in a company's income statement and balance sheet, and so will not be accurate to the extent that an organization does not recognize contingent liabilities. The solvency ratio calculation involves the following steps:

1. Add all non-cash expenses back to after-tax net income. This should approximate the amount of cash flow generated by the business.
2. Aggregate all short-term and long-term obligations of the business.
3. Divide the adjusted net income figure by the liabilities total.

The formula is:

$$\frac{\text{Net after-tax income} + \text{Non-cash expenses}}{\text{Short-term liabilities} + \text{Long-term liabilities}}$$

A higher percentage indicates an increased ability to support the liabilities of a business over the long term.

Though this measurement appears simple, its derivation hides a number of problems. Consider the following issues:

*   A company may have reported an unusually high proportion of earnings not related to its core operations, and which may therefore not be repeatable during the time period required to pay off the company's liabilities. Consequently, net after-tax operating income is a better figure to use in the numerator.
*   The short-term liabilities used in the denominator are more likely to fluctuate considerably in the short-term, so the measurement results could vary widely if calculated just a few months apart. This issue can be mitigated by using an average short-term liabilities figure.
*   The ratio assumes that a company will pay off all of its long-term liabilities, when it may be quite likely that the business can instead roll forward the debt or convert it to equity. If so, even a low solvency ratio may not indicate eventual bankruptcy.

In short, there are so many variables that can impact the ability to pay over the long term that using any ratio to estimate solvency can be misleading.

EXAMPLE

A lender is reviewing an application submitted by Pensive Corporation to roll over its outstanding debt of $5,000,000 for an additional three-year period. Pensive reports net after-tax income of $600,000 and non-cash expenses of $150,000. In addition to the outstanding debt, Pensive also reports short-term liabilities of $800,000. This information yields the following solvency ratio:

$$\frac{\$600,000 \text{ Net after-tax income} + \$150,000 \text{ Non-cash expenses}}{\$800,000 \text{ Short-term liabilities} + \$5,000,000 \text{ Long-term liabilities}}$$

$$= 12.9\%$$

The ratio indicates that Pensive could potentially pay off its obligations with earnings over a period of approximately 7¾ years. The lender must decide whether it wishes to undertake the risk of being repaid over a longer period of time, or whether it should demand repayment now.

Altman Z Score

The Altman Z Score was developed by Edward Altman, and is used to predict the likelihood that a business will go bankrupt within the next two years. The formula is based on information found in the income statement and balance sheet of an organization; as such, it can be readily derived from commonly-available information. In its original form, the Z score formula is as follows:

$$Z = 1.2A \times 1.4B \times 3.3C \times 0.6D \times 0.99E$$

The letters in the formula designate the following measures:

A = Working capital ÷ Total assets [measures the relative amount of liquid assets]

B = Retained earnings ÷ Total assets [determines cumulative profitability]

C = Earnings before interest and taxes ÷ Total assets [measures earnings away from the effects of taxes and leverage]

D = Market value of equity ÷ Book value of total liabilities [incorporates the effects of a decline in market value of a company's shares]

E = Sales ÷ Total assets [measures asset turnover]

A Z score of greater than 2.99 means that the entity being measured is safe from bankruptcy. A score of less than 1.81 means that a business is at considerable risk of going into bankruptcy, while scores in between should be considered a red flag for possible problems. The model has proven to be reasonably accurate in predicting the future bankruptcy of entities under analysis.

This scoring system was originally designed for manufacturing firms having assets of $1 million or more. Given the targeted nature of the model, it has since been modified to be applicable to other types of organizations.

This approach to evaluating businesses is better than using just a single ratio, since it brings together the effects of multiple items - assets, profits, and market value. As such, it is most commonly used by creditors and lenders to determine the risk associated with extending funds to customers and borrowers.

Summary

This chapter has addressed the various proportions of assets and liabilities on a company's balance sheet, and how you can infer the liquidity of a business from these ratios. However, the key missing element is no real knowledge of the timing of or extent to which cash can be extracted from assets, or when liabilities must be paid. The result is potentially incorrect approximations and inferences from a balance sheet.

For an alternative viewpoint on liquidity, see the following Cash Flow Measurements chapter; this provides an historical view of the cash flows that a company has been able to generate. This chapter and the Cash Flow Measurements chapter, when combined, give a more complete view of the ability of a company to generate sufficient cash to pay for its current and future liabilities.

Chapter 4
Cash Flow Measurements

Introduction

The profitability of a business is usually the main focus of a measurement system. However, because of the vagaries of the accrual basis of accounting, profitability does not necessarily equate to the underlying financial health of a business. In this chapter, we look at measurements related to cash flow, which is a more reliable indicator. Measurements covered include free cash flow, several variations on cash flow returns, the sources of cash, and how cash is being used within a business.

Related Podcast Episodes: Episodes 29 and 250 of the Accounting Best Practices Podcast discuss cash flow measurements and the burn rate, respectively. The episodes are available at: **accountingtools.com/podcasts** or **iTunes**

Overview of Cash Flow Measurements

An outsider reviewing the results of a business would be wise to rely heavily upon cash flow measurements to form an opinion of the entity. Cash flow analysis strips away the use of accruals that are mandated under the accrual basis of accounting, making it much easier to discern the underlying capabilities of an organization.

The most comprehensive measure of cash flow is the concept of free cash flow, which we introduce as the first (and most important) measurement. It is not a ratio, but rather an aggregate total of the amount of cash generated by a business, less a variety of uses. We also note a number of ways in which management can boost free cash flow. Peruse these items carefully, to be aware of how cash flows can be bolstered, and not always to the benefit of an organization.

We then turn to several ways in which cash flows can be compared or presented – on a per-share basis, as a percentage of sales, and as a percentage of assets. These are all variations on how profits are presented, but with cash flows inserted into the numerator of the ratios.

There is also a discussion of the source of cash flows. Ideally, nearly all cash flows should come from operations. If so, this is a strong indicator of the long-term viability of a business. If cash is instead scraped up from other sources, such as the proceeds of lawsuits or from minor side businesses, then a company may lack strategic focus.

We finish the discussion of cash flows with a review of cash usage measurements. These ratios are used to determine the extent to which internally-generated cash flows are sufficient to fulfill such ongoing requirements as investments in fixed assets and working capital. A variation on this concept is used to examine budgeted cash flows.

Not many cash flow ratios are needed, but having a few of them in the mix of corporate reports should be considered essential. They can provide a useful early warning if they reveal results not in line with the net profit ratio and other profit-based measurements.

Free Cash Flow

Free cash flow is the net change in cash generated by the operations of a business during a reporting period, minus cash outlays for working capital, capital expenditures, and dividends during the same period. Thus, the calculation of free cash flow is:

Operating cash flow ± Working capital changes − Capital Expenditures − Dividends

The "operating cash flow" component of that equation is calculated as:

Net income + Depreciation + Amortization

Free cash flow is important because it is an indicator of the financial health of a business, and particularly of its ability to invest in new business opportunities. The measure is also used by investors to estimate the amount of cash flow that may be available for distribution to them in the form of dividends. However, there can be a variety of situations in which a company can report positive free cash flow, and which are due to circumstances not necessarily related to a healthy long-term situation. For example, positive free cash flow can be caused by:

- Selling off major corporate assets
- Cutting back on or delaying capital expenditures
- Delaying the payment of accounts payable
- Accelerating receivable receipts with high-cost early payment discounts
- Foregoing a dividend
- Cutting back on key maintenance expenditures
- Reducing marketing expenditures
- Curtailing scheduled pay increases
- Entering into sale and lease back arrangements for key assets

In these examples, management has taken steps to reduce the long-term viability of a business in order to improve its short-term free cash flows. Other actions, such as accelerating the collection of accounts receivable through changes in payment terms or switching to just-in-time materials management systems, can be beneficial to a business while still reducing its outgoing cash flows.

Free cash flow can also be impacted by the growth rate of a business. If a company is growing rapidly, it requires a significant investment in accounts receivable and inventory, which increases its working capital investment and therefore decreases the amount of free cash flow. Conversely, if a business is shrinking, it is converting some of its working capital back into cash as receivables are paid off and inventory liquidated, resulting in an increasing amount of free cash flow.

An additional consideration is the ability of a business to repatriate cash from a subsidiary. If a subsidiary is spinning off enormous amounts of cash, the ability to do so makes little difference to the corporate parent if it cannot access the cash, due to stringent controls over cash repatriation by the government.

In short, be aware of the general condition and strategic direction of a business when evaluating whether the state of its free cash flows is beneficial or not.

Cash Flow Returns

In this chapter, we are essentially substituting cash for profitability when developing measurements. Since the cornerstone of profitability measurement is the return generated, we will do the same for cash. In this section, we present cash flow per share, which is a variation on earnings per share. We also present the cash flow return on sales and cash flow return on assets, which are equivalent to the net profit ratio and the return on assets, respectively.

Cash Flow per Share

In the Share Performance Measurement chapter, we noted that earnings per share can be artificially altered via a number of accounting tricks, such as the use of accelerated revenue recognition and the capitalization of expenditures that would normally be charged to expense as incurred. It is much more difficult to alter the reported amount of cash flows that a company generates, so the cash flow per share figure is a superior way to discern its ability to generate a return for investors. The measure also indicates the ability of a business to pay a dividend, though any positive cash flows could be directed to other uses than the payment of investors.

To calculate cash flow per share, add non-cash expenses back to net income, and divide by fully diluted earnings per share. The calculation is:

$$\frac{\text{Net profit} + \text{Non-cash expenses}}{\text{Average number of common shares outstanding}}$$

The numerator in this measurement is not a totally accurate depiction of cash flows, for it does not incorporate any changes in working capital or new investments in assets. If these additional changes are significant, factor them into the numerator.

EXAMPLE

The board of directors of Dillinger Designs replaces the retiring CEO with an outsider known for his aggressively optimistic dealings with investors. The new CEO promptly orders the company controller to switch from accelerated depreciation to straight-line depreciation, as well as to pare back the size of the allowance for doubtful accounts. The result is an immediate boost in earnings per share.

A discerning analyst is suspicious of the rapid increase in earnings per share, and revises the calculation by stripping out non-cash expenses. Her findings are noted in the following table, which reveals that the cash flow results of the company have worsened under the new CEO:

Cash Flow Measurements

	Last Annual Results Reported by Old CEO	First Annual Results Reported by New CEO
Net profit	$18,600,000	$20,900,000
Non-cash expenses	$4,800,000	$1,300,000
Average common shares	24,000,000	24,000,000
Earnings per share	$0.78	$0.87
Cash flow per share	$0.98	$0.93

Upon learning of the financial trickery imposed by the CEO, the board promptly fires him and persuades the former CEO to return to the position.

Cash Flow Return on Sales

When a business uses the accrual basis of accounting to record its performance, it is entirely possible that various accruals will twist the reported results to such an extent that the net profit ratio (net profit divided by sales) will not accurately reflect the amount of profit from each dollar of sales. If there is a disparity between cash flows and net profit reported, consider using the cash flow return on sales instead. This approach focuses on the amount of cash generated from each dollar of sales, and so provides a more accurate representation of the results of a business.

To calculate the cash flow return on sales, we must first convert the net income figure into an approximation of cash flows by adding back non-cash expenses (though this does not factor in changes in working capital or fixed assets), and divide by net sales for the measurement period. The formula is:

$$\frac{\text{Net profit} + \text{Non-cash expenses}}{\text{Total net sales}}$$

This measurement should be tracked on a trend line to spot long-term tendencies for cash flows to decline. If this is the case, management should engage in a thorough review that may culminate in corrective action to reverse the decline. Also, compare this result to the same measurement for competitors, to see how the company performs in relation to a common benchmark.

EXAMPLE

Grissom Granaries operates grain barges and a tugboat on the Mississippi River, transporting grain on behalf of clients. The new president of Grissom is concerned about the company's low ongoing cash balance, and asks the CFO to calculate the cash flow return on sales for the business. The result shows minimal cash flow. The hefty depreciation charge provides a clue as to where the problem lies. Further investigation reveals that the barges and tugboat are continually running aground, resulting in much faster hull replacement cycles than had been originally anticipated, and therefore excessive investments in fixed assets. The president responds by firing the tugboat captain and installing sonar on the tugboat.

Net profit	-$1,800,000
Depreciation	$2,000,000
Net sales	$25,000,000
Cash flow return on sales	0.8%

Cash Flow Return on Assets

In an asset-intensive industry, it makes sense to measure the productivity of the large investment in assets by calculating the amount of cash flow generated by those assets. When linked to a performance measurement system, the likely result is a continual reduction in the amount of fixed assets and inventory in proportion to sales.

To calculate the cash flow return on sales, we must first convert the net income figure into an approximation of cash flows by adding back non-cash expenses (though this does not factor in changes in working capital or fixed assets), and divide by total assets as of the end of the measurement period. The formula is:

$$\frac{\text{Net profit} + \text{Non-cash expenses}}{\text{Total assets}}$$

Though a generally useful measure, there are two concerns to be aware of:

- *Depreciation.* If a company uses an accelerated depreciation method and there is a large investment in fixed assets, the total assets figure in the denominator will decline with great rapidity, resulting in improved ratio performance without management actually doing anything. This problem can be rectified by using straight-line depreciation instead.
- *Replenishment.* Fixed assets should be replaced when their useful lives have ended, to keep from incurring too much maintenance expense. If management wants to manipulate the asset base to improve the ratio, it could elect to retain assets well past the point at which they should have been retired.

This measurement is not overly useful in those industries where there is a minimal fixed asset investment, such as service industries or those relying on intangible assets.

Cash Flow from Operations Ratio

Ideally, the bulk of the cash flow generated by a business should come from its core operations. The cash flows from ancillary activities should be quite minor. Otherwise, the entity is relying on non-core activities to support its core activities.

The calculation of this ratio first requires the derivation of cash flow from operations, which requires the calculation noted in the following exhibit.

Cash Flow from Operations

	Income from operations
+	Non-cash expenses
-	Non-cash revenue
=	Cash flow from operations

An example of non-cash revenue is deferred revenue that is being recognized over time, such as an advance payment on services that will be provided over several months.

Once cash flow from operations has been derived, we then divide it by the total net income for the entity. The calculation is:

$$\frac{\text{Cash flow from operations}}{\text{Net income}}$$

Ideally, the ratio should be fairly close to 1:1. A much smaller ratio indicates that a business is deriving much of its cash flow from sources other than its core operating capabilities.

EXAMPLE

Blitz Communications recently raised $50 million through an initial public offering, and promptly parked all of the cash in investments. In the following quarter, the company's net income rose from $400,000 to $900,000. Further investigation reveals the following cash flow from operations ratio:

	Preceding Quarter	Current Quarter
Cash flow from operations	$390,000	$375,000
Net income	$400,000	$900,000
Cash flow from operations ratio	98%	42%

The ratio reveals that the core operations of the business have generated less cash than had been the case before the company went public. The entire source of the increased net income has been the investment income generated by the cash the company obtained from investors when it went public.

Cash Reinvestment Measurements

It may be useful to track the uses to which a company puts its cash flows. In this section, we review one ratio designed to examine *actual* cash usage, as well as another ratio that is intended to examine the usage of *expected* cash flows.

Cash Reinvestment Ratio

One of the more interesting cash flow ratios does not examine the sources of cash flow, but rather how cash flow is used. The cash reinvestment ratio focuses on the proportion of cash flow that is invested back into the business – specifically, in fixed assets and working capital. The inverse of this ratio would reveal the amount of cash flowing out of a business, such as through dividends paid to investors. If the ratio is very high, it can be indicative of a business that is rapidly growing, and which therefore needs all of its excess cash to fund further expansion. However, a high ratio can also indicate that a business is barely profitable, so all of its cash is needed to maintain operations.

To calculate the cash reinvestment ratio, aggregate the amount of any increases in the gross amount of fixed assets, as well as any changes in working capital, and then divide by net income plus non-cash expenses. The gross amount of fixed assets is used instead of the net amount, so that the effects of depreciation are excluded. The calculation is:

$$\frac{\text{Increase in gross amount of fixed assets} \pm \text{Changes in working capital}}{\text{Net income} + \text{non-cash expenses}}$$

When interpreting this ratio, it is of some importance to recognize when a business is using more assets than would be required by a lean operation. This calls for the development of turnover ratios for receivables, inventory, and fixed assets, which can then be compared to other companies in the industry. If these ratios indicate low asset turnover levels, there could be a problem with the manner in which a business is being managed.

EXAMPLE

A prospective buyer is reviewing the financial statements of Giro Cabinetry, which reveals a very high cash reinvestment ratio of 95%. However, the company is generating net profits of 20%, which indicates a high level of available cash, while sales are only increasing at a rate of 10% per year. The buyer digs further and examines the company's asset turnover ratios. Accounts receivable average 45 days old, which is normal for the industry. The proportion of fixed assets to sales is also normal. However, average inventory is 200 days old, which is far beyond the industry average. After more investigation, the buyer learns that Giro has an antiquated materials management system that results in very large amounts of excess inventory. The inventory is still usable, so the investor decides to buy the company, install a new job control system, and sell off the excess inventory.

Funds-Flow Adequacy Ratio

A key component of a corporate budgeting process is the examination of forecasted cash flows, to see if the cash flows will be sufficient for all projected company requirements, such as additions to working capital and fixed assets, as well as planned dividends to shareholders. This examination can be conducted with the funds-flow adequacy ratio. To calculate the ratio, aggregate all of the cash requirements just noted and divide this total into the projected net cash outflows from the operations of the business. The formula is:

$$\frac{\text{Net budgeted cash available from operations}}{\text{Budgeted increase in fixed assets} + \text{Budgeted increase in working capital} + \text{Expected dividends}}$$

If the outcome of this ratio is more than 1:1, then the business can internally generate sufficient funds for all of its needs. If the ratio is less than 1:1, then the budget can be recast to require fewer expenditures, or additional financing can be included in the budget to cover the shortfall.

The ratio can also be used to judge the historical ability of a company to fund its own cash requirements. If the company has continually suffered cash shortfalls in prior years, it is entirely likely that a more optimistic target in the budget will not be achieved.

EXAMPLE

The budget analyst for Camelot Construction (maker of wedding props) is reviewing the first draft of management's budget for the next year. She is suspicious of the amount of cash flow projected to be produced by the company, and decides to compare it to actual results for previous years. She does so using the funds-flow adequacy ratio, as shown in the following table:

	20X1 Actual Results	20X2 Actual Results	20X3 Budgeted Results
Cash available from operations	$250,000	$235,000	$680,000
Cash usage	$280,000	$305,000	$400,000
Funds-flow adequacy ratio	89%	77%	170%

The table reveals that the proposed budget is a fantasy. Based on its historical results, Camelot is quite unlikely to generate anywhere near the cash flow noted in the first iteration. The analyst appears before a round table of company managers to state her findings.

Summary

One note of caution in regard to cash flow measurements is that the numerator of many ratios calls for an *approximation* of cash flows. This approximation is derived by adding non-cash expenses back to net income and subtracting out the effects of any accrued revenue that is being recognized in the period. However, the result may not match actual cash flows, for it does not incorporate any changes related to working capital or fixed assets. For an increased level of accuracy, consider including these additional items in your cash flow measurements.

This chapter is primarily designed to highlight the cash-generating ability of a business. For additional information about cash-related topics, read the Liquidity Measurements chapter; this chapter addresses whether a business has sufficient cash flows to meet its obligations.

Chapter 5
Return on Investment

Introduction

From the perspective of the investor, the most vital information is the return on invested funds. This information can be derived in a variety of ways, such as by examining the return on equity, or comparing the cost of capital to the return generated on invested funds, or perhaps by examining the book value of a company's assets. Other investors are more focused on an examination of dividends, and especially in proportion to reported profits. In short, there are many ways to view the concept of return on investment.

In this chapter, we examine the ways in which return on investment can be measured, and also point out how each approach can yield inaccurate or misleading results, or force managers to adopt incorrect strategies. As we note in the Summary section, all of these measurements are flawed to some extent, and so should be supplemented by an examination of the competitive fundamentals of a business.

Return on Equity

The return on equity (ROE) ratio reveals the amount of return earned by investors on their investments in a business. It is one of the metrics most closely watched by investors. Given the intense focus on ROE, it is frequently used as the basis for bonus compensation for senior managers.

ROE is essentially net income divided by shareholders' equity. ROE performance can be enhanced by focusing on improvements to three underlying measurements, all of which roll up into ROE. These sub-level measurements are:

- *Profit margin*. Calculated as net income divided by sales. Can be improved by trimming expenses, increasing prices, or altering the mix of products or services sold.
- *Asset turnover*. Calculated as sales divided by assets. Can be improved by reducing receivable balances, inventory levels, and/or the investment in fixed assets, as well as by lengthening payables payment terms.
- *Financial leverage*. Calculated as assets divided by shareholders' equity. Can be improved by buying back shares, paying dividends, or using more debt to fund operations.

Or, stated as a formula, the return on equity is noted in the following exhibit.

Return on Equity Formula

Return on Equity	=	Net income / Sales	×	Sales / Assets	×	Assets / Shareholders' equity

---

EXAMPLE

Hammer Industries manufactures construction equipment. The company's return on equity has declined from a high of 25% five years ago to a current level of 10%. The CFO wants to know what is causing the problem, and assigns the task to a financial analyst, Wendy. She reviews the components of ROE for both periods, and derives the following information:

	ROE		Profit Margin		Asset Turnover		Financial Leverage
Five Years Ago	25%	=	12%	×	1.2x	×	1.75x
Today	10%	=	10%	×	0.6x	×	1.70x

The information in the table reveals that the primary culprit causing the decline is a sharp reduction in the company's asset turnover. This has been caused by a large buildup in the company's inventory levels, which have been caused by management's insistence on stocking larger amounts of finished goods in order to increase the speed of order fulfillment.

The multiple components of the ROE calculation present an opportunity for a business to generate a high ROE in several ways. For example, a grocery store has low profits on a per-unit basis, but turns over its assets at a rapid rate, so that it earns a profit on many sale transactions over the course of a year. Conversely, a manufacturer of custom goods realizes large profits on each sale, but also maintains a significant amount of component parts that reduce asset turnover. The following illustration shows how both entities can earn an identical ROE, despite having such a different emphasis on profits and asset turnover. In the illustration, we ignore the effects of financial leverage.

Comparison of Returns on Equity

	ROE		Profit Margin		Asset Turnover
Grocery Store	20%	=	2%	×	10x
Custom manufacturer	20%	=	40%	×	0.5x

Usually, a successful business is able to focus on either a robust profit margin *or* a high rate of asset turnover. If it were able to generate both, its return on equity would be so high that the company would likely attract competitors who want to emulate the underlying business model. If so, the increased level of competition usually drives down the overall return on equity in the market to a more reasonable level.

A high level of financial leverage can increase the return on equity, because it means a business is using the minimum possible amount of equity, instead relying on debt to fund its operations. By doing so, the amount of equity in the denominator of the return on equity equation is minimized. If any profits are generated by funding activities with debt, these changes are added to the numerator in the equation, thereby increasing the return on equity.

The trouble with employing financial leverage is that it imposes a new fixed expense in the form of interest payments. If sales decline, this added cost of debt could trigger a steep decline in profits that could end in bankruptcy. Thus, a business that relies too much on debt to enhance its shareholder returns may find itself in significant financial trouble. A more prudent path is to employ a modest amount of additional debt that a company can comfortably handle even through a business downturn.

EXAMPLE

The president of Finchley Fireworks has been granted a bonus plan that is triggered by an increase in the return on equity. Finchley has $2,000,000 of equity, of which the president plans to buy back $600,000 with the proceeds of a loan that has a 6% after-tax interest rate. The following table models this plan:

	Before Buyback	After Buyback
Sales	$10,000,000	$10,000,000
Expenses	9,700,000	9,700,000
Debt interest expense	---	36,000
Profits	300,000	264,000
Equity	2,000,000	1,400,000
Return on equity	15%	19%

The model indicates that this strategy will work. Expenses will be increased by the new amount of interest expense, but the offset is a steep decline in equity, which increases the return on equity. An additional issue to be investigated is whether the company's cash flows are stable enough to support this extra level of debt.

A business that has a significant asset base (and therefore a low asset turnover rate) is more likely to engage in a larger amount of financial leverage. This situation arises because the large asset base can be used as collateral for loans. Conversely, if a company has high asset turnover, the amount of assets on hand at any point in time is relatively low, giving a lender few assets to designate as collateral for a loan.

> **Tip:** A highly successful company that spins off large amounts of cash may generate a low return on equity, because it chooses to retain a large part of the cash. Cash retention increases assets and so results in a low asset turnover rate, which in turn drives down the return on equity. Actual ROE can be derived by stripping the excess amount of cash from the ROE equation.

Return on equity is one of the primary tools used to measure the performance of a business, particularly in regard to how well management is enhancing shareholder value. As noted in this section, there are multiple ways to enhance ROE. However, we must warn against the excessive use of financial leverage to improve ROE, since the use of debt can turn into a burden if cash flows decline.

A case can be made that ROE should be ignored, since an excessive focus on it may drive management to pare back on a number of discretionary expenses that are needed to build the long-term value of a company. For example, the senior management team may cut back on expenditures for research and development, training, and marketing in order to boost profits in the short term and elevate ROE. However, doing so impairs the ability of the business to build its brand and compete effectively over the long term. Some management teams will even buy their companies back from investors, so that they are not faced with the ongoing pressure to enhance ROE. In a buyback situation, managers see that a lower ROE combined with a proper level of reinvestment in the business is a better path to long-term value.

Economic Value Added

The economic value added (EVA) measurement compares the cost of capital of a business to the rate of return it generates, to see if the business is creating any value in excess of its cost of funds. If the economic value added measurement turns out to be negative, this means a business is destroying value on the funds invested in it. It is essential to review all of the components of this measurement to see which areas of a business can be adjusted to create a higher level of EVA. A possible outcome of the measurement is that a business is destroying so much value that it should be sold off or shut down, and any residual funds returned to investors.

To calculate EVA, determine the difference between the actual rate of return on assets and the cost of capital, and multiply this difference by the net investment in the business. Additional details regarding the calculation are:

- Eliminate any unusual income items from net income that do not relate to ongoing operational results.
- The net investment in the business should be the net book value of all fixed assets, assuming that straight-line depreciation is used.
- The expenses for training and research and development should be considered part of the investment in the business.
- The fair value of leased assets should be included in the investment figure.
- If the calculation is being derived for individual business units, the allocation of costs to each business unit is likely to involve extensive negotiation, since

the outcome will affect the calculation for each business unit. This can mean that the best negotiators will avoid expense allocations, making their EVA results look better.

These bullet points should make it clear that EVA is not a simple ratio – it is a carefully calculated formulation that requires a lengthy analysis to derive. Thus, the following formula for EVA masks a great deal of cost accounting:

Net investment × (Actual return on investment – Percentage cost of capital) = EVA

EXAMPLE

The president of the Hegemony Toy Company has just returned from a management seminar in which the benefits of EVA have been trumpeted. He wants to know what the calculation would be for Hegemony, and asks his financial analyst to find out.

The financial analyst knows that the company's cost of capital is 12.5%, having recently calculated it from the company's mix of debt, preferred stock, and common stock. He then reconfigures information from the income statement and balance sheet into the following matrix, where some expense line items are instead treated as investments.

Account Description	Performance	Net Investment
Revenue	$6,050,000	
Cost of goods sold	4,000,000	
General & administrative	660,000	
Sales department	505,000	
Training department		$75,000
Research & development		230,000
Marketing department	240,000	
Net income	**$645,000**	
Fixed assets		3,100,000
Cost of patent protection		82,000
Cost of trademark protection		145,000
Total net investment		**$3,632,000**

The return on investment for Hegemony is 17.8%, using the information from the preceding matrix. The calculation is $645,000 of net income divided by $3,632,000 of net investment. Finally, he includes the return on investment, cost of capital, and net investment into the following calculation to derive the EVA:

($3,632,000 Net investment) × (17.8% Actual return − 12.5% Cost of capital)

= $3,632,000 Net investment × 5.3%

= $192,496 Economic value added

Thus, the company is generating a healthy EVA on the funds invested in it.

The EVA concept can be expanded upon to include an examination of changes in EVA over time. While a simple trend line can be used, an alternative measure is to compare changes in EVA to sales over time. To do so, divide the change in EVA by annualized sales. The formula is:

$$\frac{\text{Ending EVA} - \text{Beginning EVA}}{\text{Annualized sales}}$$

This approach reveals the ability of a company to maintain positive EVA growth as it (presumably) increases sales. If the result is negative, then it is likely that the effort and funding expended to gain additional sales resulted in a net destruction of shareholder value.

EXAMPLE

As of the beginning of the current fiscal year, Hegemony Toy Company had recorded positive EVA of $192,000. During the current year, the president of Hegemony has pursued a strategy of expanding distribution in the Far East market. The result has been a stellar 25% increase in sales, to $8,000,000. However, doing so has required a significant investment in inventory and regional warehouses, as well as up-front fees. The result is a decline in EVA to $150,000. The EVA momentum calculation for this year of activity is:

$$\frac{\$150,000 \text{ Ending EVA} - \$192,000 \text{ Beginning EVA}}{\$8,000,000 \text{ Sales}}$$

= -0.5% EVA momentum

The decision to expand may still be the correct one. Despite the loss in EVA momentum, the geographic expansion might still pay off, if the company can increase income on its new and larger asset base, and by tweaking its distribution system to generate more profits.

The EVA concept will certainly focus the attention of management on the returns generated on invested funds. However, a case can be made that an excessive focus on

EVA will drive management away from riskier or longer-term investments, where the payback may not occur at all, or not for a long time (as noted in the last example). These types of investments are critical to the long-term competitiveness of a business, and yet might be avoided by management in favor of less-risky investments or ones with more assured payoffs.

Book Value Analysis

The book value of a business is the amount of assets stated on its balance sheet, minus the liabilities listed on the balance sheet. Or, stated as a formula, book value is:

$$\text{Assets} - \text{Liabilities} = \text{Book value}$$

Book value is a commonly-used measure of the value of a business, probably because it is so easily derived from the published balance sheet of a company. The information could be used to estimate the most appropriate price of a company's stock, such as by comparing the market price of the stock to its book value. Or, the book value concept could be one possible basis for deriving the value of a company, when a potential acquirer wants to issue a bid to the owners of the target company. Also, lenders commonly use book value to estimate whether a prospective or current borrower is a good credit risk. In short, book value has many possible uses.

Despite the widespread use of book value, it is a seriously flawed measurement. The problem is that the amounts stated in a company's balance sheet do not necessarily match their current market values. Instead, some are recorded at their original purchase prices, while others are adjusted to their market values as of the balance sheet date. The problem is exacerbated by the Generally Accepted Accounting Principles (GAAP) framework, which enforces the recordation of the most conservative values for assets. The issue is less of a problem if the International Financial Reporting Standards (IFRS) framework is used, since IFRS allows for the upward revaluation of some assets. The following bullet points illustrate the problem for a selection of transactions that are recorded and updated using GAAP:

- *Investments*. Depending on the types of securities held as investments, they are marked to market at the end of each reporting period. When this is not possible for longer-term investments for which there are no fair market values available, the recorded cost remains the purchase cost.
- *Inventory*. The lower of cost or market rule states that the recorded value of inventory must be reduced to its market value if market value declines below recorded cost. However, there is no provision for increasing the recorded amount of inventory if the market value of inventory increases. Further, the last in, first out (LIFO) inventory costing method is designed to record the lowest possible inventory cost in environments where prices are increasing over time.
- *Fixed assets*. Fixed assets are only recorded at their initial purchase costs, after which these amounts are reduced over time by depreciation. They may also be reduced more rapidly if it is determined that their values have been

impaired. However, there is no way to increase the recorded amount of a fixed asset if the market value of the asset increases.

A further issue with book value is the incorporation of intangible assets into the balance sheet. An intangible asset is a non-physical asset that has a useful life spanning more than one accounting period. Examples of intangible assets are software developed for internal use, patents, and copyrights. If a company internally generates intangible assets, the business cannot record these assets on its balance sheet. In some cases, the value of these assets represents the primary value of an entire business, so the book value calculation may wildly underestimate the value of the organization.

Conversely, an acquirer is allowed to record that portion of the purchase price of an acquiree that can be allocated to the intangible assets of the acquiree. For example, a portion of the purchase price may be allocated to an intangible asset called "customer relationships," which is then amortized over the presumed remaining life of those relationships. In some cases, these intangible assets can be considered specious at best, and yet are included in the book value calculation because they are listed on the balance sheet.

A further problem with acquisitions is that any portion of the purchase price that cannot be allocated to tangible or intangible assets is recorded as "goodwill," which appears in the balance sheet as an asset. In some cases, goodwill can represent a large part of the assets listed on a company's balance sheet, and so can radically skew the calculation of book value.

For the reasons enumerated here, we do not recommend using the book value concept for the purposes of assigning a value to an entire business. The value derived would be nearly arbitrary, and could bear little relationship to the actual market value of the entity. That being said, it may be possible to apply the book value concept to an individual asset, which is called *net book value*. Another alternative is to strip away intangible assets from the book value calculation, resulting in *tangible book value*. These concepts are discussed next.

Net Book Value

Net book value is the original cost of an asset, less any accumulated depreciation, accumulated depletion, accumulated amortization, and accumulated impairment. These elements are:

- *Original cost.* This is the acquisition cost of an asset, which is the cost required to not only purchase or construct the asset, but also to bring it to the location and condition intended for it by management. Thus, the original cost of an asset may include such items as the purchase price, sales taxes, delivery charges, and setup costs.

- *Depreciation.* The depreciation, depletion, or amortization associated with an asset is the process by which the original cost of an asset is ratably charged to expense over its useful life, less any estimated salvage value. Thus, the net book value of an asset should decline continually over its useful life.
- *Impairment.* This is a situation where the market value of an asset is less than its net book value, in which case the remaining net book value of the asset is written down to its market value. Thus, an impairment charge can have a sudden downward impact on the net book value of an asset.

While net book value also does not necessarily equate to market value, it is devoid of the goodwill issue that plagues use of the book value concept when applied to an entire business. Also, the net book value concept can bear some relationship to the lowest possible market value of an asset, since the use of impairment will keep an asset value from rising too high. As such, this concept tends to establish the lower end of the actual value of an individual asset.

EXAMPLE

Fireball Flight Services operates a small business jet, which it acquired for $5,000,000. Management expects that the jet will have a salvage value of $2,000,000 in ten years. The company uses the straight line method to depreciate the jet over its 10-year expected useful life. This means that the jet is being depreciated at a rate of $300,000 per year, which is calculated as:

($5,000,000 cost - $2,000,000 salvage value) ÷ 10 years = $300,000 per year

After three years, Fireball has recorded depreciation of $900,000 for the jet, which means that it now has a net book value of $4,100,000. At that time, the company conducts an annual impairment test, and concludes that the market value of the jet has declined to $3,500,000. The company records an impairment charge of $600,000, which brings its net book value down to $3,500,000. At the time of the impairment charge, the net book value of the jet approximates its market value.

Tangible Book Value

Another variation on the book value concept is to remove all intangible assets from the book value formula. Doing so eliminates the inflation of asset values caused by the presence of goodwill, as well as other assets created as part of a corporate acquisition. However, some of these intangible assets may have significant value, so anyone using the tangible book value concept should sort through the various intangible assets and determine which are to be eliminated and which ones retained. This can turn into a qualitative exercise, where different analysts arrive at different tangible book values based on their own perceptions of the worth of certain intangible assets. Consequently, if this measurement is to be used, it should be accompanied by a detailed analysis of each intangible asset included in or excluded from the measurement, as well as justifications for the amounts included.

The calculation of tangible net worth is to subtract all liabilities listed on a company's balance sheet from all tangible net assets stated on the balance sheet. By "net assets," we refer to assets from which all contra accounts, such as the allowance for bad debts, depreciation, and amortization, have been subtracted. The formula is:

Tangible net assets – Liabilities = Tangible book value

EXAMPLE

Nefarious Industries has engaged in a number of hostile takeovers in the past decade, resulting in a group of subsidiaries for which Nefarious paid a total of $15,000,000 more than could be assigned to the tangible assets of the subsidiaries. The result is the following intangible assets recorded on the consolidated financial statements of the company:

Intangible Asset Type	Amount
Customer lists	$1,500,000
Internet domain names	500,000
Licensing agreements	4,000,000
Water rights	3,500,000
Goodwill	5,500,000
Total	$15,000,000

The consolidated balance sheet of Nefarious reveals a total of $32,000,000 in assets and $8,000,000 in liabilities. A prospective investor is attempting to determine the tangible book value of the company, and concludes that the licensing agreements and water rights listed as intangible assets have actual value. The other intangible assets are discarded. Based on this review, the investor concludes that the adjusted tangible book value of the company is:

$32,000,000 assets - $7,500,000 intangible assets with no value - $8,000,000 liabilities = $16,500,000 Adjusted tangible book value

---

Book Value per Share

We have provided extensive warnings about why book value should not be used. If you still insist upon using it, the best method is to calculate book value on a per-share basis. The main reason for doing so is that the primary user of book value is an outside investor, who wants to compare the market value of shares owned to their book value, and so needs a measurement that is presented on a per-share basis.

The measurement is typically calculated on the basis of just common stock, with the effects of preferred stock eliminated from the calculation. By doing so, the result shows the amount that a common shareholder might receive upon the liquidation of a business.

To calculate book value per share, subtract preferred stock from stockholders' equity and divide by the number of common shares outstanding. Be sure to use the average number of shares in the denominator, since the period-end amount may incorporate a recent stock buyback or issuance, and so could skew the results. The formula is:

(Stockholders' equity – Preferred stock) ÷ Average common shares = Book value per share

Note that the numerator in this formula appears to differ from the classic definition of book value, which is assets minus liabilities. However, since assets minus liabilities equal shareholders' equity, the resulting numbers are identical.

EXAMPLE

Grissom Granaries has $15,000,000 of stockholders' equity, $3,000,000 of preferred stock, and an average of 2,000,000 shares outstanding during the measurement period. The calculation of its book value per share is:

$$\frac{\$15,000,000 \text{ Stockholders' equity} - \$3,000,000 \text{ Preferred stock}}{2,000,000 \text{ Average common shares outstanding}}$$

$$= \$6.00 \text{ Book value per share}$$

Return on Assets

A central reason why a business asks investors for money is to fund the acquisition of assets, of which there are many types – receivables, inventory, fixed assets, and so forth. Consequently, it behooves an investor to inquire into the return subsequently generated from those assets, which is called the return on assets ratio. Ideally, the assets as a group should generate a significant return, indicating that the company is capable of investing shareholder funds in an effective manner.

The return on assets measurement can be misleading, for a variety of reasons. Consider the following situations:

- *Request for additional funds.* A company has thus far generated a high return on assets, and asks investors for more funds, so that it can acquire additional equipment. In this case, investors are making the assumption that the return generated in the past will continue in the future, which may not be the case. The additional funds may be used for an entirely different purpose than the funds invested previously. Consequently, simply basing an investment on the historical return on assets is dangerous; there should also be an inquiry into how the additional funds will be used, and how this varies from previous investments.
- *Small asset base.* In some cases, a company does not require a large amount of assets in order to conduct operations. For example, it may provide services, in which case its primary asset may only be accounts receivable. In these situations, the return on assets may appear astronomical. However, because

there are so few assets, it is questionable whether the measurement should even be used. Instead, use it only for asset-intensive operations.

- *Asset replenishment.* The fixed assets upon which this measurement is partially based are being continually reduced by depreciation, which makes the return on assets figure appear to increase over time as the carrying amount of the assets declines. This issue is not material if a company is continually replenishing its fixed assets with new purchases, thereby keeping the total amount of fixed assets relatively consistent from period to period. However, if management is not reinvesting in the business, then the impact of depreciation will gradually reduce the total carrying amount of assets, resulting in a higher return on assets, but also an older and less-efficient infrastructure. This issue can be spotted by reviewing the trend line of maintenance expenses; if the expense is rising over time, it could mean that an entity is spending more money to maintain older machines.

Given these issues, any measure of the return on assets should be treated with a certain amount of caution.

Next, we will address the primary return on assets calculation, followed by a variation on the concept that focuses on those assets actually being used to operate a business.

Return on Assets

The generic return on assets measurement is designed to measure the total return from all sources of income from all assets. The formula is:

$$\frac{\text{Net income}}{\text{Total assets}}$$

The measurement is certainly a simple one, but its all-encompassing nature also means that the result may not yield the type of information needed. Consider the following issues:

- *Non-operating income.* The numerator of the ratio is net income, which includes income from all sources, some of which may not be even remotely related to the assets of the business. For example, net income may include one-time gains or losses from lawsuits or hedging activities, as well as interest income or expense. This issue can be avoided by only using operating income in the numerator.
- *Tax rate.* The net income figure is net of the company's income tax liability. This liability is a result of the company's tax strategy, which may yield an inordinately low (or high) tax rate. Also, depending on the tax strategy, the tax rate could change markedly from year to year. Because of the effect of tax planning, a non-operational technical issue could have a major impact on the calculated amount of return on assets. This concern can be sidestepped by only using before-tax information in the measurement.

- *Cash basis*. The net income figure can be significantly skewed if a company operates on the cash basis of accounting, where transactions are recorded when cash is received or paid out. This issue can be avoided by only using the measurement on a business that employs the accrual basis of accounting.
- *Cash holdings*. The total assets figure in the denominator includes *all* assets; this means that a company with a significant amount of undistributed cash reserves will reveal a lower return on assets, simply because it has not chosen to employ the cash. This problem can arise not only for a successful company with a large amount of cash earned, but also for a company that has recently sold a large amount of stock, and has not yet employed the resulting cash hoard. This issue can be avoided by subtracting cash from the total assets figure in the measurement, or by using a cash amount considered sufficient to support the ongoing operation of the business.

These concerns are in addition to the asset replenishment issue already noted earlier in this section. Given these problems, we suggest an alternative measurement, which uses operating income in the numerator and subtracts all cash from the denominator. The formula is:

$$\frac{\text{Operating income}}{\text{Total assets - Cash}}$$

EXAMPLE

Bland Cabinets, a maker of mass-produced cabinets for apartment complexes, has net income of $2,000,000, which includes a one-time lawsuit settlement cost of $500,000. The company has assets of $11,000,000, of which $1,000,000 is excess cash that the board of directors intends to issue to shareholders as a dividend. For the purposes of calculating Bland's return on assets, the lawsuit settlement cost is added back to the net income figure, while the $1,000,000 of excess cash is subtracted from its total assets figure. The resulting calculation is:

$$\frac{\$2,500,000 \text{ Adjusted income}}{\$10,000,000 \text{ Assets net of excess cash}}$$

$$= 25\% \text{ Return on assets}$$

Return on Operating Assets

The general version of the return on assets just noted is based on the assumption that all of the assets recorded in a company's balance sheet are actually being used productively to generate income. This is extremely unlikely, as there are always excess amounts of receivables, inventory, and fixed assets that are not needed or should never have been acquired. For example:

- *Receivables*. A company may be allowing employees to borrow cash from the company, which are recorded as non-trade receivables. There may also be trade receivables on the books that are unlikely to be paid, and for which there is not a sufficient reserve in the allowance for doubtful accounts.

- *Inventory.* There may be a large amount of inventory on hand that is effectively obsolete, in that it will not be used for a long time, if ever. If there is not a reserve that offsets the amount of this obsolete inventory, the reported inventory asset is likely too high in comparison to the profits being generated.
- *Fixed assets.* Some fixed assets may have fallen into disuse, and so are no longer involved in the generation of income. These assets are likely to be tucked away in odd corners of the business, and are still being depreciated down to their salvage values.

An alternative format for the return on assets measurement can be used that sidesteps all of these issues. The return on operating assets measurement focuses attention on only those assets used to generate a profit. This means that all unnecessary receivables, inventory, and fixed assets are removed from the assets listed in the denominator of the return on assets calculation, yielding the theoretical return that could be achieved if a company were making optimal use of its assets. The formula is:

$$\frac{\text{Net income}}{\text{Total assets} - \text{Assets not used to generate income}}$$

The return on operating assets figure can be extremely effective if used properly. Management can use the resulting measurement as a target figure, and then determine how to eliminate the excess assets that were subtracted from the denominator. The result should be a gradual decline in the asset base of the business, which may generate extra cash that can either be returned to investors through a dividend or stock buyback, or used to invest in more productive assets.

EXAMPLE

The Hegemony Toy Company, maker of military games, has acquired a number of assets through acquisitions, and may no longer need some of the assets. The president tells the controller to develop a return on operating assets measurement, with the intent of spotting equipment that can be disposed of. The controller assembles the following information:

Net income	$500,000
Total assets listed on balance sheet	17,000,000
Excess assembly line	500,000
Excess plastic molding facility	1,500,000
Excess warehouse	750,000

Based on this information, the controller suggests that the return on operating assets is:

$$\frac{\$500,000 \text{ Net income}}{\$17,000,000 \text{ Total assets} - \$2,750,000 \text{ Excess assets}}$$

$$= 3.5\%$$

The behavior that can be engendered by use of this measurement can be troubling, so it should be employed with caution. The following scenarios may arise:

- *Gaming*. Managers will realize that any assets not included in the measurement will eventually be considered excess, and therefore likely to be eliminated. Consequently, expect them to game the system by classifying unnecessary assets as necessary assets.
- *Excessive asset reduction*. Some assets may not be used frequently, but can be useful if production levels spike, when they can be used as excess capacity. This is a particular issue when assets are stripped away that were being used to maintain an even flow of goods into a bottleneck operation. The result can be foregone profits that the terminated assets might otherwise have generated.
- *Tighter credit*. Management may conclude that the accounts receivable asset can be reduced by restricting the amount of credit granted to customers. However, doing so may also reduce the amount of net income, since there may be fewer resulting sales. If this situation arises, be sure to adjust the numerator by a reasonable estimate of lost profits.

Earnings per Share

One of the classic measures of the value of a company's shares is earnings per share (EPS). EPS measures the amount of a company's net income that is theoretically available for payment to the holders of its common stock. A company with a high EPS is capable of generating a significant dividend for investors, or it may plow the funds back into its operations to generate more growth; in either case, a high EPS is presumed to indicate a potentially worthwhile investment, if the market price of the stock is acceptable to the investor.

When researching the performance of a company, EPS is likely to be the first metric found. Despite its prevalence, EPS only yields a snippet of information about the underlying valuation of a company. Consider the following issues:

- *Accrual basis*. EPS information is only reported by publicly-held companies, all of which report their financial statements using the accrual basis of accounting. Because of the accounting rules used for the accrual basis, there can be a significant difference between the cash flows generated and the profits or losses reported. It is quite possible that a company might report skyrocketing profits, and yet have no cash on hand that could be used to pay dividends. This issue can be avoided by focusing instead on the cash information reported in the statement of cash flows.

- *EPS orientation.* Company managers can artificially bolster EPS by cutting back on such discretionary expenditures as marketing, training, and research and development. This excessive focus on short-term results will likely lead to a long-term decline in the competitiveness of a business.
- *Quarterly basis.* A publicly-held company reports its financial results once every three months, so the focus of EPS is only on the last three months. Given the vagaries of many markets, it is entirely possible that a company's reported EPS will fluctuate over the course of a year, giving investors the impression that earnings are unreliable. This issue can be avoided by only focusing on annual EPS.
- *Dilution.* EPS information is reported by a company in two formats, one of which is fully diluted earnings per share. Diluted EPS incorporates every possible financial instrument issued by a company that might be convertible into common stock. This is an extremely conservative ratio, since many common stock equivalents are never converted into common stock. Consequently, the measurement can report an unusually low EPS number that is not indicative of the actual performance of an entity. The issue can at least be mitigated by instead using the basic earnings per share figure, which does not presume dilution from common stock equivalents.

Given these issues, EPS should not be the only measurement used when evaluating an investment in a company.

To calculate earnings per share, subtract any dividend payments due to the holders of preferred stock from net income after tax, and divide by the average number of common shares outstanding during the measurement period. The calculation is:

$$\frac{\text{Net income after tax} - \text{Preferred stock dividends}}{\text{Average number of common shares outstanding}}$$

EXAMPLE

Kelvin Corporation has net income after tax of $1,000,000 and also must pay out $200,000 in preferred dividends. The company has both bought back and sold its own stock during the measurement period; the weighted average number of common shares outstanding during the period was 400,000 shares. Kelvin's earnings per share is:

$$\frac{\$1,000,000 \text{ Net income} - \$200,000 \text{ Preferred stock dividends}}{400,000 \text{ Common shares}}$$

$$= \$2.00 \text{ Earnings per share}$$

A variation on the EPS concept is to track it on an annual trend line. If the trend is positive, then an organization is either generating an increasing amount of earnings (thereby improving the numerator in the ratio) or buying back its stock (thereby improving the denominator in the ratio).

An alternative to tracking EPS on a trend line is to measure the percentage change in earnings per share over time. This yields a quantitative examination of EPS, rather than the more visual representation of a trend line. To calculate the percentage change, divide the incremental change in EPS by the EPS for the preceding reporting period. The calculation is:

$$\frac{\text{Incremental change in EPS}}{\text{EPS from preceding reporting period}}$$

EXAMPLE

Kelvin Corporation reported earnings per share of $2.00 in last year's financial results, and has reported $2.10 earnings per share in this year's financial statements. The percentage change in EPS is:

$$\frac{\$2.10 \text{ Latest EPS} - \$2.00 \text{ Preceding EPS}}{\$2.00 \text{ Preceding EPS}}$$

$$= 5\% \text{ Incremental change in EPS}$$

The use of a trend line or the percentage change in EPS calculation focuses attention on the long-term ability of a company to create value by increasing earnings per share. However, it also places pressure on management to do so, sometimes to the extent that they will stretch the accounting rules to continue reporting increasing EPS. This issue can only be spotted with an intensive review of a company's financial statements and accompanying disclosures, to see if management is using more aggressive accounting techniques over time. If so, a likely result is a long series of EPS increases, followed by a sudden and significant decline in EPS, when management can no longer use trickery to maintain its reported results.

Dividend Performance

When an investor is inclined to buy the shares of a company that issues dividends, this person or entity is called an *income investor*. An income investor values the stock based on the ability of the issuer to reliably pay out a predictable dividend on an ongoing basis. This type of investor is likely to use the dividend payout ratio to determine the proportion of company income being paid out in the form of dividends, to see if the dividends are sufficiently large, and if they can be sustained. Investors also use the dividend yield ratio to calculate the return on their investment, based on a comparison of dividends paid and the market price of the stock. Both ratios are described in this section.

Dividend performance ratios are primarily used by investors, not the companies in which they invest. Nonetheless, the board of directors (which authorizes dividends) should be aware of the impact of their decisions on dividends. Also, the investor relations officer, who is the primary point of contact with the company for investors, should also be conversant with these ratios.

Dividend Payout Ratio

Investors who want a dividend will evaluate a company based on its dividend payout ratio. This ratio is the percentage of a company's earnings paid out to its shareholders in the form of dividends. There are two ways to calculate the dividend payout ratio; each one results in the same outcome. One version is to divide total dividends paid by net income. The calculation is:

$$\frac{\text{Total dividends paid}}{\text{Net income}}$$

The alternative version essentially calculates the same information, but at the individual share level. The formula is to divide total dividend payments over the course of a year on a per-share basis by earnings per share for the same period. The calculation is:

$$\frac{\text{Annual dividend paid per share}}{\text{Earnings per share}}$$

EXAMPLE

The Conemaugh Cell Phone Company paid out $1,000,000 in dividends to its common shareholders in the last year. In the same time period, the company earned $2,500,000 in net income. The dividend payout ratio is:

$$\frac{\$1,000,000 \text{ Dividends paid}}{\$2,500,000 \text{ Net income}}$$

$$= 40\% \text{ Dividend payout ratio}$$

Investors interested in the long-term viability of a series of dividend payments will likely track the dividend payout ratio on a trend line, to see if a business is generating enough income to support its dividend payments over a number of years. If not, they may sell off their shares, thereby driving down the stock price. If an investor sees that the payout ratio is nearly 100% or greater than that amount, then the current dividend level is probably not sustainable. Conversely, if the ratio is quite low, investors will consider the risk of a dividend cutback to also be low, and so will be more inclined to buy the stock, thereby driving up its price.

Investors may also look at the reverse of the dividend payout ratio to see how much of earnings are being retained within a business. If the retention amount is declining, this indicates that the company does not see a sufficient return on investment to be worthy of plowing additional cash back into the business. From this perspective, a declining retention rate will drive away those growth-oriented investors who rely on an increasing share price.

In short, investors rely on ratio analysis on a trend line to determine whether a business is issuing an appropriate amount of dividends, and may alter their stock holdings based on the outcome of this analysis.

From the perspective of a company that is issuing dividends, the main concern is whether the business is capable of issuing a certain dividend amount on a sustained basis. If cash flows have a history of being quite variable, then it will make more sense to set a dividend that can be paid even when the company is suffering through a low point in its business cycle. Conversely, if cash flows are quite stable, then a higher dividend can likely be sustained over time. An additional concern is whether there are internal uses for cash that will generate greater returns for investors over the long term than an immediate dividend. If so, the company's board of directors must weigh the two alternatives and decide how the cash should be used.

Dividend Yield Ratio

The dividend yield ratio reveals the amount of dividends that a company pays to its investors in comparison to the market price of its stock. Thus, the ratio is the return on investment if an investor were to have bought shares at the market price on the measurement date.

To calculate the ratio, divide the annual dividends paid per share by the market price of the stock at the end of the measurement period. Since the stock price is measured on a single date, and that measurement may not be representative of the stock price over the measurement period, consider using an average stock price instead. The calculation is:

$$\frac{\text{Annual dividends paid per share}}{\text{Market price of the stock}}$$

EXAMPLE

Horton Corporation pays dividends of $4.50 and $5.50 per share to its investors in the current fiscal year. At the end of the fiscal year, the market price of its stock is $80.00, which is a representative value for its shares over the entire year. Horton's dividend yield ratio is:

$$\frac{\$10 \text{ Dividends paid}}{\$80 \text{ Share price}}$$

$$= 12.5\% \text{ Dividend yield ratio}$$

When deriving and using this measurement, be aware of the following issues:

- *Consistent dividend measurement.* The calculation should be based only on dividends paid, not on dividends declared but not yet paid. Otherwise, there is a risk of double-counting, where dividends declared are included in the measurement for one period, and then included again in the measurement for the next period when the dividends are actually paid.

- *Consistent share price measurement.* If you elect to use an average market price for the stock that spans a number of days or months, use the same averaging technique for all measured periods. Otherwise, a likely result is inconsistent measurements that reveal little about the actual yield being generated. This is a particular problem when a company's share price is highly variable.

Summary

The return on investment concept is based on the ability of a business to generate an adequate return for investors over a long period of time. This return is ultimately based on non-financial measures, such as product design skill, a monopoly situation, excellent store locations, or a productive research and development department. None of these items are readily apparent in any of the measurements described in this chapter. Instead, the measurements discussed here rely upon reported financial information or market prices, which are the best financial evidence of company performance. Nonetheless, these ratios are a weak alternative to a more in-depth analysis of the competitive positioning and future prospects of a business, which requires a great deal of investigative work. Only by engaging in this advanced level of examination is it possible to develop a comprehensive view of the likely return on investment of a business. Company managers should also attend more to the fundamentals of a business, rather than using financial engineering to give the appearance of improved performance to investors.

Chapter 6
Share Performance Measurements

Introduction

A key concern of the investment community is whether to invest in the shares of a company, which involves multiple types of analysis. Investors are also interested in leading indicators of possible changes in the value of their shares, which they can use to decide whether to sell or hold the shares. In this chapter, we address a number of measurements that can assist in the investment decision, as well as other measures that can provide clues regarding future share prices.

Overview of Share Performance Measurements

The decision to invest in a company is based on a wide array of factors, encompassing the measurements in many chapters of this book that can be used to interpret the operating and financial condition of an entity. In addition, an investor must evaluate the price of a company's stock, and whether that price fairly reflects the earnings power of the business.

In this chapter, we address several measurements that can be used to evaluate the price at which a share is currently selling. The price/earnings ratio compares the price of the stock to the most recently reported earnings of a business, while the capitalization rate derives the implied rate of return on share holdings. We also review the concept of total shareholder return, which compiles the total return for shareholders, based on dividends received and changes in the price of the stock.

We also look at the market value added concept, which calculates the difference between the market value of a business (i.e., the extended price at which all of its shares are currently selling) and the book value of invested capital. This measure provides a clue to the ability of management to generate value. A less-relevant (though common) measurement is the market to book ratio, which compares the market value of a business to its book value; the trouble is that book value is an accounting measure that may have little relevance when deriving the underlying value of a business.

We then turn to the prediction of the direction of a company's future stock price. One approach is the insider buy/sell ratio, under which the buying and selling activities of corporate insiders can be used to guesstimate whether insiders believe the current share price is too high or low. Another indicative measure is the options and warrants to common stock ratio; this ratio can be used to predict how many stock options and warrants may be converted to stock, which can in turn lead to a decline in the price of the stock, since more shares now have a claim on the residual value of a business. Yet another indicative measure is the short interest ratio, which quantifies the amount of interest by short sellers in a company's stock. Since short sellers usually conduct a large amount of investigation into the financial statements of a business, it is possible that a spike in short interest indicates problems that will lead to a stock price decline.

We conclude with the institutional holdings ratio, which measures the amount of a company's shares held by institutional investors in relation to the amount of trading volume. The outcome of this measurement is neither good nor bad; it merely reflects how large blocks of stock holdings can impact a variety of issues related to a business.

Price/Earnings Ratio

The price/earnings ratio is the price currently paid on the open market for a share of a company's stock, divided by its earnings per share. The ratio reveals the multiple of earnings that the investment community is willing to pay to own the stock. A very high multiple indicates that investors believe the company's earnings will improve dramatically, while a low multiple indicates the reverse. If the ratio is already high, there is little chance for the stock price to climb even higher, so there is significant risk that the share price will slide lower in the future.

The investment community usually forces a stock price upward based on future expectations for such issues as new patents, new products, favorable changes in the laws impacting a company, and so forth.

To calculate the price/earnings ratio, divide the current market price per share by fully diluted earnings per share. The formula is:

$$\frac{\text{Current market price per share}}{\text{Fully diluted earnings per share}}$$

It is also possible to derive the ratio by dividing the total current company capitalization by net after-tax earnings. In this case, the formula is:

$$\frac{\text{Current company market capitalization}}{\text{Net after-tax earnings}}$$

Yet another variation is to build an expected price earnings ratio by dividing future earnings expectations per share into the current market price. This is not a firm indicator of where the ratio will actually be in the future, but is a good basis for deciding whether the stock is undervalued or overvalued.

There are several issues with the price/earnings ratio to be aware of. Consider the following problems:

- *Manipulation.* Earnings information can be manipulated by accelerating or deferring expense recognition, as well as through a variety of revenue recognition schemes. A more accurate measure of the value that the investment community is placing on a company's stock is the price to cash flow ratio. Cash flow is a good indicator of the results of operations.
- *Industry-wide effects.* Changes in the ratio tend to impact every company in an industry at the same time, because they are all subject to the same market forces, with slight differences between the various companies. Thus, a

favorable change in the ratio may not be cause for excessive jubilation for a job well done, since the change may not be traceable to a company's performance at all, but rather to changes in its business environment.

- *Timing.* The price of a company stock may fluctuate wildly in the short term, as such factors as takeover rumors and large customer orders excite investors and impact the price. Consequently, the ratio can be dramatically different if the timing of the measurement varies by just a few days.

EXAMPLE

The common stock of the Cupertino Beanery is currently selling for $15 per share on the open market. The company reported $3.00 of fully diluted earnings per share in its last annual report. Therefore, its price/earnings ratio is:

$$\frac{\$15 \text{ Market price per share}}{\$3 \text{ Earnings per share}}$$

$$= 5:1 \text{ Price/earnings ratio}$$

Capitalization Rate

It can be useful to derive the rate of return that investors expect on a company's stock, based on its current market price and the associated price/earnings ratio. We do this by simply reversing the price/earnings ratio, so that fully diluted earnings per share are divided by the current market price per share. The formula is:

$$\frac{\text{Fully diluted earnings per share}}{\text{Current market price per share}}$$

Since it contains the same information used for the price/earnings ratio noted in the last section, the capitalization rate should be considered to suffer from the same issues. Therefore, allow for possible manipulation of reported earnings, effects impacting the entire industry, and short-term variations in the price of the stock being examined.

EXAMPLE

A major institutional investor is interested in purchasing the shares of Atlas Machining Company, which has seen a major decline in its share price over the past year, due to concerns about its facilities in a country where there is a major ongoing insurgency. Despite the insurgency, Atlas has continued to report robust earnings of $3.50 per share in each of the last two years. The investor's target rate of return on its investments is 15%. The capitalization rate for Atlas for the past two years is as follows:

	Last Year	Current Date
Earnings per share	$3.50	$3.50
Market price per share	$43.75	$21.88
Capitalization rate	8%	16%

The rapid drop in stock price has doubled the capitalization rate of Atlas over the past year, which makes this a reasonable investment opportunity that exceeds the investor's target rate of return.

Total Shareholder Return

When an investor buys the shares of a company, the return generated by the purchase will be derived from a combination of the change in the share price over the measurement period, plus any dividends paid by the company in the interim. The formula (on an annual basis) is noted in the following exhibit.

Total Shareholder Return Formula

	Ending stock price – Beginning stock price
+	Sum of all dividends received during the measurement period
=	Total shareholder return

The total return can then be divided by the initial purchase to arrive at a total shareholder return percentage.

This measurement can be skewed if a shareholder has control over a business. If this is the case and the company is sold, then the shareholder will likely be paid a control premium in exchange for giving up control over the entity.

EXAMPLE

An investor purchases shares of Albatross Flight Systems for $15.00 per share. One year later, the market value of the shares is $17.00, and the investor has received several dividends totaling $1.50. Based on this information, the total shareholder return is:

	$17.00 Ending stock price – $15.00 Beginning stock price
+	$1.50 Dividends received
=	$3.50 Total shareholder return

Based on the initial $15.00 purchase price, this represents a 23.3% total shareholder return.

Market Value Added

The market value added concept derives the difference between the market value of a business and its cost of invested capital. When market value is less than the cost of invested capital, this implies that management has not done a good job of creating value with the equity made available to it by investors. To derive market value added, follow these steps:

1. Multiply the total of all common shares outstanding by their market price.
2. Multiply the total of all preferred shares outstanding by their market price.
3. Combine these totals.
4. Subtract the amount of capital invested in the business.

The market value added formula appears in the following exhibit.

Market Value Added Formula

	(Number of common shares outstanding × Share price)
+	(Number of preferred shares outstanding × Share price)
-	Book value of invested capital
=	Market value added

This measurement should only be used if a company's stock is robustly traded on an established stock exchange. Otherwise, a few occasional trades could trigger substantial changes in the market price of the stock. It may be possible to derive the market value of shares by engaging an appraiser to provide an estimate.

Also, be aware that the current stock price may be based on changes in investor confidence in the market or industry as a whole, and do not relate to the performance (or lack thereof) of management in running a business.

EXAMPLE

The investor relations officer of Cud Farms is preparing a press release that reveals the increase in market value added since the new management team was hired. The analysis is based on the following information:

	Prior Year	Current Year
Number of common shares outstanding	5,000,000	5,700,000
Common stock price	$4.00	$4.20
Number of preferred shares outstanding	400,000	375,000
Preferred share price	$11.00	$11.30
Book value of invested capital	$18,000,000	$20,625,000

The market value added for the prior year is calculated as follows:

	(5,000,000 Common shares × $4.00 price)
+	(400,000 Preferred shares × $11.00 price)
-	$18,000,000 Equity book value
=	$6,400,000 Market value added

The market value added for the current year is calculated as follows:

	(5,700,000 Common shares × $4.20 price)
+	(375,000 Preferred shares × $11.30 price)
-	$20,625,000 Equity book value
=	$7,552,500 Market value added

Based on this analysis, the investor relations officer can highlight an increase of $1,152,500 in market value added since the new management team was hired.

Market to Book Ratio

A common measure of the value of a company's shares is the market to book ratio, which compares the market price of a company' stock to its book value per share. If the market price is well above the book value, this is said to be an indicator of the additional value that the investment community is placing on the ability of a company to earn a profit.

To calculate the market to book ratio, divide the ending price of the company's stock by the book value per share on the same date. The formula is:

$$\frac{\text{Ending market price of stock}}{\text{Book value per share}}$$

There are numerous problems with this measurement that limit its practical use. Consider the following issues:

- The comparison is of the market value of a business to the historical costs at which assets were recorded. There is no realistic reason why an asset base of any particular size should relate to a particular multiple of market price.
- Accounting standards mandate that some quite valuable intangible assets may not be recorded in the accounting records. In businesses where intangibles are the chief competitive advantage, this means that the market to book ratio will be inordinately high.
- Accounting standards mandate the use of accruals, reserves, and depreciation that can artificially alter the value of assets, irrespective of their real market value.
- The market price of the stock used in the numerator is as of a specific point in time, which may not closely relate to the average price of the stock in the recent past.

EXAMPLE

An analyst is reviewing the share performance of Failsafe Containment, which manufactures reactor vessels. The current market price of the company's stock is $20.00, and the book value per share is also $20.00, resulting in a market to book ratio of 1:1. However, further investigation reveals that the company has substantial real estate holdings, for which the recorded book value is substantially lower than their likely resale prices. Consequently, the analyst assigns a buy rating to the company's stock, which also attracts the attention of several corporate raiders that subsequently purchase the company and sell off the real estate for significant gains.

Insider Buy/Sell Ratio

In a publicly-held company, a large number of shares are typically held by corporate insiders. These insiders have the best access to information about the current and prospective performance of the business, and so are much more likely to sell their holdings when they believe the market price of the stock is likely peaking. Since these transactions must be reported to the Securities and Exchange Commission (SEC) and are therefore public knowledge, it is not especially difficult for an outside investor to obtain and analyze stock transactions by insiders. The logic followed by an analyst is that a high proportion of insider sales of company stock to insider purchases of stock is indicative of an insider belief that the stock price will go no higher. This information can be used by an investor to decide when to alter holdings of a company's stock.

To calculate the insider buy/sell ratio, aggregate the number of insider purchases of company stock over the measurement period, and divide by the aggregate amount of insider sales of company stock over the same period. The formula is:

$$\frac{\text{Aggregate insider stock purchases}}{\text{Aggregate insider stock sales}}$$

A ratio of less than one indicates that insiders believe that the price of the stock is peaking, while a ratio of greater than one indicates the reverse.

This is not an easy ratio to interpret, for corporate insiders may have excellent reasons for purchasing and selling company stock that have nothing to do with their perceptions of the company's prospects. Consider the following situations:

- A company recently went public, and many employees holding shares must wait six months before they are allowed to sell their shares. They will undoubtedly do so in six months.
- A newly-hired CEO is required to purchase $1 million of company shares as a condition of her employment.
- A CFO wants to purchase a new house, and sells enough shares to cover the purchase price of the home.
- Employees have such lucrative stock options pending that it would be foolish not to buy shares, irrespective of the future direction of the company's performance.

If the ratio is to be used as a valid indicator of the future direction in which the price of a stock may turn, consider the following situations that may be most applicable:

- There is a broad sell-off or purchasing pattern among multiple employees.
- Employees are incurring debt in order to buy shares.
- Employees in the accounting department, who presumably have the best understanding of company performance, are showing a decided buying or selling trend.

EXAMPLE

Six months have passed since Armadillo Industries went public. During the past week, Armadillo employees have finally had their shares registered, and have been actively liquidating their holdings in the company. An outside analyst reviews the following information to see if there is a discernible trend in insider activity:

Employee Title	Transaction Type	Number of Shares	Transaction Date
Engineering manager	Sell	300,000	November 3
Marketing director	Sell	185,000	November 3
Chief financial officer	Buy	25,000	November 4
Chief information officer	Sell	160,000	November 4
Production manager	Sell	325,000	November 5
Chief executive officer	Buy	15,000	November 6
Controller	Buy	5,000	November 6

The information in the table results in an overwhelmingly negative insider buy/sell ratio of 0.046. However, the analyst also notes that every one of the stock sale transactions involved a mid-level manager who might have simply been cashing in for the first time. All of the managers most closely associated with the company's finances are quietly buying up small blocks of shares. Based on his analysis of the information, and despite the outcome of the ratio, the analyst believes that the company will report above-average results when its next quarterly results are released.

Options and Warrants to Common Stock Ratio

A company may elect to pay third parties with warrants for various services, and compensate its employees with stock options. If the business does so extensively, this can create an inordinately large pool of options and warrants that could be converted to common stock in the near future, resulting in significantly reduced earnings per share, and therefore a possible reduction in the stock price. Because of this dilutive effect, outside analysts like to monitor the amount of outstanding options and warrants.

An analyst will not consider all options and warrants to be convertible into common stock. Instead, they will focus on just those instruments that are currently "in the money," which means that the designated exercise price is below the current market price of a company's common stock. In this case, someone could (for example) exercise a stock option at a designated price of $5.00 and immediately earn a profit of $1.00 if the market price is $6.00. Conversely, if the market price were $5.00 or less, no option or warrant holder would find it profitable to purchase common stock with their instruments, and so would let them expire unused.

Given the importance of being in the money, an analyst is only interested in these options and warrants, which may be far fewer than the total pool of options and warrants outstanding. Consequently, the calculation of options and warrants to common stock is to divide the grand total of in the money stock options and warrants by the total number of common shares currently outstanding. The formula is:

$$\frac{\text{Stock options in the money} + \text{Warrants in the money}}{\text{Total common shares outstanding}}$$

The measurement could be further refined to exclude those stock options that have not yet vested, since the holders of these options cannot yet exercise the options.

It may be useful to re-measure this ratio based on a modest prospective increase in the company's market price, rather than the current price. Doing so may significantly boost the number of shares beyond the level indicated by the initial measurement. This can warn outside investors that a run-up in the stock price could result in a large block of additional shares being issued.

EXAMPLE

Creekside Industrial has recently gone public through an initial public offering. An analyst is reviewing the information submitted by Creekside to the Securities and Exchange Commission to ascertain the extent to which existing stock options and warrants may trigger the issuance of additional shares in the near future, thereby watering down the price of Creekside's stock. The analyst finds the following information:

Common shares outstanding	50,000,000
Warrants in the money	1,000,000
Options in the money and vested	3,500,000
Options in the money and vesting in one year	750,000
Options in the money if price rises 20%	2,750,000
Options in the money if price rises 20%, and vesting in one year	10,000,000

The analyst converts this information into a series of ratios that compare the options and warrants under various circumstances to common stock, which is noted in the following table:

[cumulative] (000s)	In the Money Now	Vesting in One Year	In the Money with 20% Price Increase	In the Money with 20% Increase & Vesting in 1 Year
Options and warrants	4,500	5,250	8,000	18,000
Number of common shares	50,000	50,000	50,000	50,000
Ratio	9%	11%	16%	36%

The analyst notes that the amount of stock outstanding is likely to increase to a modest extent in the near future and in one year, but that the real risk is associated with a 20% increase in the price of Creekside's stock. If that happens, an additional 18,000,000 stock options will be in the money, which could result in a cumulative total of 36% of the existing balance of shares being issued. The analyst concludes that any run-ups in the price of Creekside stock should be closely monitored.

Short Interest Ratio

Short sellers profit from declines in the price of a company's stock. They do so by examining the financial statements and prospects of a company in great detail; if they find a business whose prospects appear poor, or which seems to be inflating its financial results, then they target this entity for short selling. Short selling involves the sale of borrowed stock, which a short seller expects to buy later on the open market at a lower price, earning a profit on the decline in price.

It can be useful to track the interest of short sellers in a company's stock, since this can presage an abrupt decline in the price of that stock, especially once the short sellers begin to publicize their findings in an effort to create bearish sentiments about the stock. The easiest way to track short seller interest is through the short interest ratio. To calculate it, obtain the aggregate amount of short interest (which is available from several websites) and divide by the average daily trading volume for the stock. Short interest is the number of shares that investors have sold short, and which they have not yet closed out. The formula is:

$$\frac{\text{Short interest}}{\text{Average daily trading volume}}$$

The outcome of this analysis is the number of days that it would take short sellers to cover their positions in the company's stock, which they would likely have to do if the price of the company's shares starts to rise (since an increase in price generates losses for a short seller).

There are several analyses that can be derived from the short interest ratio. Consider the following situations:

- A prolonged and significant short interest ratio reveals a great deal of downward pressure on a stock by short sellers; however,
- When the ratio exceeds 2:1, short sellers will likely need to start buying shares in order to cover their positions, which can create a short-term spike in the stock price.
- Also, the ratio can be applied to entire industries, to see if short sellers are bearish on the fundamentals of an industry. If so, this is a strong indicator that stock prices will be flat or fall across the sector.

Institutional Holdings Ratio

The investors in a publicly-held company are typically comprised of a small number of institutional investors, such as pension funds, and a large number of retail investors (i.e., individuals). It is generally considered good to have a large proportion of institutional shareholders, for the following reasons:

- They indicate that a sophisticated investor is willing to buy into the company
- The investor relations department can more easily sell shares in large blocks to a small number of these investors
- The investor relations staff can more efficiently concentrate its publicity efforts on a small group of shareholders

However, institutional investors are not always a benefit to a company, for the following reasons:

- They can cause a major decline in a company's stock price if they decide to sell off their holdings over a short period of time
- They can use the voting power conveyed by their share holdings to pressure management to take certain actions, such as issuing dividends
- Their holdings can represent such a large part of the total pool of stock that the number of shares readily available for trading is relatively small

In short, there is no optimum level of institutional holdings to target. Instead, be aware of long-term trends in the activity ratio, and how this activity may impact the company's position in the public markets.

To calculate the institutional holdings ratio, divide the total trading volume by the period-end holdings of institutional investors. The measurement period is three months, since the holdings information comes from the Form 13F filings that institutional investors must file on a quarterly basis. The formula is:

$$\frac{\text{Total trading volume}}{\text{Institutional investor stockholdings}}$$

EXAMPLE

The Excalibur Shaving Company recently went public, selling a massive number of its shares to a small group of institutional investors. The trouble is that there are so few remaining shares that retail investors are complaining of an inability to trade their shares. Accordingly, the investor relations department contacts several institutional investors to see if they will part with some of their holdings. The results appear in the following table:

	One Month After IPO	Six Months After IPO
Total trading volume	2,500,000	10,000,000
Institutional investor stockholdings	50,000,000	30,000,000
Institutional holdings ratio	5%	33%

The table reveals that the investor relations department has succeeded in convincing some of the institutional investors to part with their shares, since the total holdings of this group have markedly declined. The change has resulted in a significant benefit, as activity in the company's stock has quadrupled.

Summary

The measurements addressed earliest in this chapter, such as the price/earnings ratio, can certainly give an investor a general feel for whether the shares of a company are over or undervalued. However, the decision to invest in a company should not be based on just the measurements noted in this chapter. Instead, a comprehensive review of both the financial and operational condition of a business should be conducted, as well as of the industry in which it operates, to arrive at a complete set of information that can be used as the basis for an investment decision.

We also attempted to make it clear that the measures used to indicate the future value of shares are highly interpretive. The inputs to these measurements should be closely examined before relying upon the measurements themselves. Also, these leading indicators are no match for a detailed and ongoing review of a business, so that all factors impinging on the ability of an organization to provide shareholder value are fully understood.

There is some cross-over between the topic of this chapter and the measurements provided in other chapters. Book value per share and earnings per share are both included in the Return on Investment chapter.

Chapter 7
Growth Measurements

Introduction

One of the primary indicators of the value of a business is the rate at which it is growing. An investor is much more willing to pay a high price for a company's shares when there are strong indications of rapidly-increasing sales and profits. In this chapter, we focus on different ways to measure growth, taking into account such issues as inflation, the number of customers, and the results of core operations.

Overview of Growth Measurements

The most common indicators of the viability of a business are its reported sales and profits, and in particular the growth of these two figures over time. However, growth figures are subject to a certain amount of interpretation, sometimes resulting in reported figures that are misleading, if not downright fraudulent. In this chapter, we employ several concepts to yield more accurate views of growth. These concepts are:

- *Consistency*. Both sales and profits are subject to spikes and drops, especially when management focuses too much on the pursuit of a small number of large sale transactions. Tracking the consistency of sales and profits over time can put a spotlight on high levels of variability.
- *Core results*. A company may be involved in a variety of extraneous activities that either add to or detract from its results. We suggest stripping away these activities, and focusing instead on the results of only the core activities of a business.
- *Deflation*. The use of an inflation index can be employed to reduce the reported amount of sales, which is useful in a highly inflationary economy where prices must be continually raised to keep pace with inflation.

We also describe the affordable growth rate, which is the concept that a certain amount of assets are required to generate sales, and which therefore can be used to estimate the maximum rate of growth that a business can attain. While asset usage levels can be altered over time, thereby altering the ratio, we believe the underlying affordable growth rate concept to be sound, and recommend its use.

Sales Growth

Growth in sales is among the most highly-touted metrics of a business. Because of its popularity, sales growth is also subject to a certain amount of inflation. In this section, we propose several measures that can drill down to the underlying ability of an organization to generate sales. One concept is deflated sales growth, which is particularly useful in a high-inflation environment. Another option is sales growth consistency, where the focus is on the avoidance of sharp spikes and drops in sales over time. Yet another possibility is core sales growth, where the emphasis is on the ability of an entity's key operations to generate sales.

Deflated Sales Growth

In an inflationary environment, it is relatively easy for a company to report continually increasing sales, for it can routinely ratchet up its prices. It is possible to factor out this inflationary increase by deflating the reported sales level by the amount of the consumer price index, or some similar measure of inflation. To calculate deflated sales growth, follow these steps:

1. Determine which inflation index to use for the deflation calculation. The consumer price index is most commonly used.
2. Divide the price index for the preceding year by the price index for this year, and multiply the result by the net sales of the business for the current year. This yields the deflated sales for the current year.
3. Subtract the net sales for the preceding year from the deflated sales for the current year, and divide by the net sales for the preceding year.

The main issue with the measurement of deflated sales growth is to apply the same type of inflation index to the measurement from year to year, so that ongoing measurements are comparable.

EXAMPLE

Viking Fitness has opened a chain of health clubs in a country that is experiencing a high rate of inflation. In the preceding year, the country had a consumer price index of 132. In the current year, the index increased to 158. In the preceding year, Viking reported sales of 58,000,000 pesos. In the current year, the company reported sales of 73,000,000 pesos, with no additional health clubs having been opened. Based on this information, Viking's deflated sales growth is:

$$\frac{(73{,}000{,}000 \text{ Pesos} \times (132 \text{ CPI} \div 158 \text{ CPI})) - 58{,}000{,}000 \text{ Pesos}}{58{,}000{,}000 \text{ Pesos}}$$

$$= 5.2\% \text{ Deflated sales growth}$$

Thus, despite the high inflation rate, the company did indeed succeed in increasing its same-location sales by 5.2% during the current year.

Sales Growth Consistency

A sign of careful management is when sales grow at a consistent rate. This is indicative of a measured roll-out of new products, geographical sales regions, stores, and so forth. Sales growth consistency gives some indication of the ability of a business to continue growing at a reasonable pace into the future. The reverse situation, where sales continually spike and then crater, is indicative of a more opportunistic environ-ment where management pursues a small number of large sales transactions that may not be repeatable in the future.

To measure sales growth consistency, aggregate the number of consecutive re-porting periods over which net sales have exceeded the net sales from the prior period.

It is easier to report a high level of sales growth consistency if the measurement is tracked over longer reporting periods. For example, measuring consistency on an annual basis eliminates the impact of an occasional month during the year when sales might decline, which is particularly important if sales are seasonal. A common meas-urement interval for publicly-held companies is to report sales growth consistency on a quarterly basis, which matches the frequency with which these companies must re-port their financial results to the public.

An issue to be aware of is that a company might use an allowance for sales returns and accrue estimated sales returns that have not yet occurred. If this allowance were to be manipulated, it is possible to create an ongoing series of net sales increases, thereby allowing for the false reporting of a lengthy period of sales growth con-sistency. For example, a company could create a large sales return reserve in a month when gross sales are high, and cut back on the reserve in periods when gross sales are low; doing so has the net effect of creating artificially smooth sales growth.

EXAMPLE

The new president of Medusa Medical is devising an investor relations packet that highlights the company's ability to grow its sales in the crucial snake oil therapy market. The company routinely experiences large amounts of customer returns, based on their perceptions of the outcome of snake oil therapy, so net sales tend to be quite different from gross sales. Over the past six quarters, the company's net sales calculation has been:

	Gross Sales	Sales Returns	Net Sales
Quarter 1	$1,500,000	$275,000	$1,225,000
Quarter 2	1,600,000	240,000	1,360,000
Quarter 3	1,650,000	200,000	1,450,000
Quarter 4	2,000,000	570,000	**1,430,000**
Quarter 5	2,150,000	190,000	1,960,000
Quarter 6	2,190,000	205,000	1,985,000

Despite the ongoing increases in gross sales, the large amount of sales returns creates a decline in net sales in the fourth quarter. Accordingly, the president can only report sales growth con-sistency for the past two quarters.

Core Sales Growth

A large part of the sales increases reported by a business may be related to a variety of changes outside of the core operations of the organization. Examples of these changes are:

- Sales from acquired entities
- Sales due to changes in accounting standards
- Product price increases

Once these additional factors have been subtracted from the "additional" sales reported by a business, it is entirely possible that the underlying entity's sales have actually declined. The formula is:

$$\frac{\text{Change in sales from preceding year} - \text{Sales from acquired entities} - \text{Revenue recognition changes} - \text{Product price increases}}{\text{Sales in preceding year}}$$

This can be quite an illuminating measurement, since even management may have no idea that core sales growth is actually negative.

The main issue with the measurement is how long to continue excluding the various factors from the sales growth calculation. For example, the operations of an acquired entity may be fully integrated into the core operations of a business, at which point its revenues can also be considered part of core sales.

EXAMPLE

The senior management team of Pianoforte International has been boasting to investors that the company has achieved a massive 25% increase in sales during the past year, attaining a total of $18,750,000 in sales from the previous year's results of $15,000,000. At the beginning of the year, the company enforced a 5% price increase. There was also a one-time increase in revenue of $1,000,000 related to a change in revenue recognition policy. Finally, the company acquired a competitor, which added $3,000,000 in sales. Based on this information, the core sales growth of the company was:

$$\frac{\$3,750,000 \text{ Change in sales} - \$3,000,000 \text{ Acquired revenue} - \$1,000,000 \text{ Recognition change} - \$750,000 \text{ Price increase}}{\$15,000,000 \text{ Sales in preceding year}}$$

$$= -6.7\% \text{ Core sales growth}$$

Thus, the company actually experienced a decline in its core sales growth during the year, which was only evident once all the extraneous factors were eliminated from the total sales figure.

Customer Growth

If a company is to increase its sales over time, it will likely be mandatory to do so by increasing the number of customers. While it is possible to increase total revenue by increasing the volume of sales transactions with existing customers, this approach cannot be followed forever. Instead, management must focus on the continuing search for new customers. To measure customer growth, follow these steps:

1. Establish a minimum sales threshold, below which minor customers are ignored for the purposes of this calculation.
2. Aggregate the number of customers with which the company has had sales above the threshold level for the measurement period.
3. Aggregate the number of customers having had sales above the threshold level for the preceding period.
4. Subtract the number of customers above the threshold from the preceding period from the number of customers above the threshold for the current period, and divide by the number of customers above the threshold from the preceding period.

The calculation is:

$$\frac{\text{Number of customers above threshold in current period} - \text{Number of customers above threshold in preceding period}}{\text{Number of customers above threshold in preceding period}}$$

While useful, this measurement does not focus any attention on the profitability of customers. Thus, a company could go to great lengths to acquire certain customers, only to find that the incremental profit associated with these new customers is inconsequential or even negative. To monitor profitability, use profits above a predetermined threshold in the preceding formula, rather than sales.

EXAMPLE

Lethal Sushi is a chain of sushi restaurants that only sell exotic fish, some of which are poisonous. Lethal has a frequent customer program, and has found that these repeat customers generate the bulk of its business. However, given the nature of the food being served, the company has to keep locating new customers as its existing customer base dies off. In the most recent quarter, the marketing director initiated a new campaign to attract customers ("Want to take a chance?"). As a result, the number of people in the frequent customer program rose from 920 to 990. This results in a customer growth rate for the quarter of 7.6% (calculated as 70 new customers, divided by the preceding customer base of 920).

Expense Growth

Management should be extremely cognizant of any changes in expense levels over time, and promptly investigate the reason for any upward spikes. One tool for identifying these spikes is to measure expense growth. This can be done in aggregate for all expenses, but the result provides little actionable information. Instead, consider measuring expense growth for individual expense line items in the income statement. To calculate expense growth, subtract the prior period's expense from the current period's expense, and divide by the prior period's expense. The formula is:

$$\frac{\text{Current period expense} - \text{Prior period expense}}{\text{Prior period expense}}$$

This measurement works particularly well when tracked on a trend line over a number of reporting periods. By doing so, it is easier to spot situations where expenses are recorded twice in one period and not at all in another. This is a useful tool for spotting anomalies in expenses as part of the period-end closing process.

The main issue with the expense growth measurement is that it converts monetary changes into percentage changes, so that the user cannot see the size of any monetary changes over time. For example, compensation expense (typically a large line item) may increase by only a few percentage points, but the increase may represent a large monetary increase. Thus, a 1% increase in a baseline compensation expense of $10,000,000 is a $100,000 increase.

EXAMPLE

Henderson Industrial is in a flat growth industry, and so must maintain tight control over its costs in order to generate a profit. Accordingly, the key measurement followed by the management team is an expense growth trend line, stated as the percentage change in expense from period to period. The following table provides a sample of the expense growth trend line.

	Quarter 1	Quarter 2	Quarter 3	Quarter 4
Compensation	1%	1%	4%	1%
Depreciation	0%	0%	0%	10%
Maintenance	-3%	0%	8%	-3%
Travel	4%	-3%	5%	14%
Utilities	0%	20%	0%	-18%

The table reveals that several people were hired in the third quarter, thereby increasing the compensation expense. Also, new equipment was purchased in the fourth quarter, resulting in an increase in depreciation expense. The capital purchase was triggered by a large increase in maintenance expense in the third quarter, when a machine broke down. Travel costs increased because of the new hires in the third quarter. Finally, the company is located in a warm climate, so utility costs routinely increase during the summer months.

Profit Growth

A business is quite likely to trumpet high profit levels to its investors and the general public. However, profits tend to fluctuate a great deal over time, since they are impacted by swings in sales *and* expenses. In this section, we use the profit growth and profit growth consistency measurements to obtain a better understanding of the scale and long-term viability of the profits being reported.

Profit Growth

A company can have excellent sales growth, but unless that growth is combined with solid gross profit margins and expense controls, there may be no net profits. To monitor this most important area of the income statement, management should track profit growth over many periods.

To measure profit growth, subtract the net profits for the preceding period from net profits for the current period, and divide by net profits for the preceding period. The formula is:

$$\frac{\text{Net profits for current period} - \text{Net profits for preceding period}}{\text{Net profits for preceding period}}$$

There are several variations on this measurement. Consider running it for operating income, in order to focus on just the results of the core operations of the business. Another approach is to calculate the growth in before-tax income, which strips away any variability in income caused by tax planning.

In order to report more consistent profit growth, it helps to use a relatively broad measurement period, such as a quarter or year. Achieving consistent period-over-period growth on a monthly basis is quite difficult.

EXAMPLE

Nautilus Tours just spent $5,000,000 to purchase a submarine, with which it plans to take tourists to visit local marine reefs. Given the large expenditure, the owner of Nautilus wants to ensure that there is continual profit growth; otherwise, he will sell off the submarine to cut his losses.

In first two quarters since Nautilus acquired the new submarine, the company had profits of $50,000 and $32,000, respectively. This is negative profit growth of 36%, which is caused by an unusually high level of maintenance on the submarine. Given the negative trend, the owner promptly sells the submarine.

Profit Growth Consistency

It is quite difficult to achieve an ongoing increase in profits over time, since doing so requires the coordination of gradual increases in the customer base, new product rollouts, and tight expense control. Profit growth consistency is even more important than sales growth consistency, since it showcases the ability to manage all aspects of a business.

To measure profit growth consistency, aggregate the number of consecutive reporting periods over which net profits have exceeded the net profits from the prior period.

As was the case for the sales growth consistency measurement, it is easier to report a high level of profit growth consistency if the measurement is tracked over longer reporting periods, thereby avoiding seasonal profit declines. For this reason, the minimum comparison period that should be used is a quarterly period.

Unfortunately, there are many ways in which profit growth consistency can be fraudulently achieved. For example, the recognition of certain expenses could be delayed, or revenue recognition policies could be altered. Also, it is possible to delay expenditures on such discretionary expenses as employee training and advertising. In short, organizations can go to great lengths to report profit growth consistency, which may not reflect the true profitability of the entity.

EXAMPLE

The president of Logger Construction Company is determined to report profit growth consistency from year to year, no matter what actions must be taken. There has been consistent profit growth for the past four years. However, the initial indication of profits for the current year shows a decline of $150,000 from the preceding year's profits of $1,300,000. To boost reported earnings, the president requires the controller to alter the percentage of completion reported for several construction projects, resulting in a "revised" profit figure of $1,400,000, and therefore a fifth consecutive year of profit growth consistency.

During the annual audit, the auditors uncover the percentage of completion changes, and report their findings to the company's audit committee. The board of directors promptly fires the president.

Affordable Growth Rate

The central issue for many companies is the correct rate at which a business should grow, since growing too fast can strain the financial resources of an organization. This rate of growth can be estimated by assuming that a certain proportion of assets to sales must be maintained in order to fund future growth. The assumption is valid in most cases, since a certain amount of receivables, inventory, and fixed assets are required for each dollar of revenue generated. To calculate the affordable growth rate, follow these steps:

1. Subtract dividends paid from the amount of net profits reported for the year. The result should be an approximation of the cash generated by the business, and which is still available to fund future growth.
2. Divide this amount by stockholders' equity for the preceding year that was derived from tangible assets. In other words, aggregate all tangible assets listed on the balance sheet and subtract all liabilities to arrive at tangible

stockholders' equity. Intangible assets are excluded from the measurement, since these assets can be artificially manufactured through acquisitions.

The formula for the affordable growth rate is:

$$\frac{\text{Net profits} - \text{Dividends}}{\text{Tangible stockholders' equity in preceding year}}$$

The affordable growth rate is a useful metric, but must be considered in relation to several issues that could potentially vary over time, yielding different results. These issues are:

- *Asset usage.* A company may alter its business practices to reduce the amount of assets needed to support a given amount of sales. For example, production could be outsourced, thereby reducing the need for fixed assets. Similarly, a just-in-time production system could reduce the need for a large investment in inventory.
- *Borrowings.* The measurement assumes that lenders will continue to offer debt to the company in roughly the same proportion of debt to assets that they did in the past, which provides cash for growth. This assumption may be incorrect, based on the general availability of credit and the perceived ability of the company to support a certain debt load.
- *Cash flows.* Net profits are assumed to equate to cash flows, which may not be the case. The use of accrual-basis accounting may result in reported net profits that are significantly different from cash flows.
- *Dividends.* Dividends may be issued in the form of stock, which does not represent a cash outflow.
- *Equity.* The owners of the company may be willing to increase stockholders' equity by selling shares to additional investors, which gives the company a large amount of cash to use as the basis for a growth spurt.

Despite the issues noted here, the affordable growth rate is a reasonable tool for estimating the proper long-term rate of growth of a business.

EXAMPLE

The management team of Snyder Corporation is under pressure from the investment community to expand its sales in the coming year. To educate investors about the company's proper growth rate, the investor relations officer decides to formulate the affordable growth rate. Snyder's net profits for the current year were $12,000,000, dividends issued were $4,000,000, and the company's tangible net worth in the preceding year was $80,000,000. Based on this information, the company's affordable growth rate is:

$$\frac{\$12,000,000 \text{ Net profit} - \$4,000,000 \text{ Dividends}}{\$80,000,000 \text{ Tangible net worth in preceding year}}$$

$$= 10\% \text{ affordable rate of growth}$$

Summary

If any concept is to be gained from this chapter, it is to use trend line analysis for sales, expenses, and profits. By doing so, the reader can easily discern patterns in the ability of a business to generate adequate returns over the long term, and trace the causes of these returns to specific line items in the income statement.

Another issue related to growth measurements is changes in the ability of a business to generate cash flows over a long period of time. It can be argued that cash flows are more important than profits, since profit levels can be artificially increased through various types of accounting trickery. It is much more difficult to interfere with the proper reporting of cash flow information. For a full discussion of these measurements, see the Cash Flow Measurements chapter.

Chapter 8
Constraint and Throughput Measurements

Introduction

The constraint is one of the most poorly-understood concepts in business today, as well as the related concept of throughput. When a company is operating in accordance with the concepts of constraint management and throughput maximization, it may realize a substantial increase in profitability, as well as a reduced need for fixed assets. In this chapter, we explain the constraint and throughput concepts, and then present a number of measurements that can be used to monitor these items.

> **Related Podcast Episodes:** Episodes 43 through 47 of the Accounting Best Practices Podcast discuss constraint analysis. They are available at: **accountingtools.com/podcasts** or **iTunes**

Overview of Constraint Measurements

The measurements in this chapter are based upon the core underlying concept of the bottleneck – this is the chokepoint through which work must flow before a finished product can be delivered to the customer. The bottleneck concept is more formally known as the constraint. Examples of constraints are:

- A production workstation that must process some aspect of the work flowing through a production facility
- A raw material that is in short supply
- A highly-skilled salesperson who is responsible for most incoming orders

Constraints are usually difficult to eliminate. For example, a production workstation might be extremely expensive, or there is no alternative source of raw materials, or the level of training required to develop another salesperson is excessive. For these reasons, it makes more sense to tightly manage a constrained resource to maximize its usage. There are several ways to measure a constrained resource, including its overall level of utilization, the operator's ability to fulfill the assigned production schedule, and the nature of any downtime.

Constraint maximization means that a bottleneck should never be allowed to run out of work. This is a particularly important notion if the bottleneck is located in the production area, where it is likely to be a work center. A constrained work center should always have a buffer of inventory in front of it that can be drawn upon if the upstream workstations stop sending materials to the bottleneck. The buffer should be especially large if the flow of goods into the bottleneck operation is highly variable. Clearly, the amount of usage of this buffer should be measured.

Another concept is throughput, which is revenues minus all totally variable expenses. Throughput must be maximized at all times in order to pay for the fixed costs of a business and generate a profit. More specifically, the amount of throughput that flows through the constrained resource must be maximized, since the bottleneck controls the ability of a business to generate profits. Throughput can be monitored through a combination of measurements, including bottleneck schedule fulfillment, manufacturing effectiveness, and delayed throughput.

Bottleneck Utilization

In most production operations, there is a particular work station that is perpetually overworked, and which keeps the rest of the facility from maximizing its production potential – this is the bottleneck operation. A key focus of the manufacturing manager is to ensure that this work station is fully supported and utilized at all times, which makes the bottleneck utilization metric one of the more important performance measures that a company can track.

To calculate bottleneck utilization, divide the actual hours of usage of the operation by the total hours available. Depending on how closely management watches this metric, you may want to re-calculate it every day. The formula is:

$$\frac{\text{Actual hours of bottleneck usage}}{\text{Total hours in the measurement period}}$$

While important, the bottleneck utilization metric does not track the profitability of the work being run through the bottleneck operation. Thus, it could be utilized nearly 100% of the time, but with only low-profit items being manufactured, the company's profitability would still be low. Thus, this metric should be used in combination with an analysis of the profitability of products being scheduled for production.

EXAMPLE

Mole Industries runs a small production line that creates motorized tunneling devices for cable laying operations. The bottleneck in the production line is the paint booth. The paint booth runs for three shifts, seven days a week, while the rest of the production line runs for a standard eight-hour day, five days a week. Management is concerned that the paint booth will limit the production line's ability to expand, and wants to know what bottleneck utilization it has. The calculation is:

$$\frac{152 \text{ Actual hours of operation}}{168 \text{ Hours in a week}}$$

$$= 90\% \text{ Bottleneck utilization}$$

The calculation shows that there are only 16 additional hours of bottleneck time available, and it is likely that the paint booth staff will have a difficult time making those few additional hours available, given ongoing maintenance requirements. Thus, the management team needs to discuss whether it should invest in an additional paint booth or outsource some painting to a supplier. It may make more sense to build a new paint booth if there is an expectation of a large and permanent increase in sales (which would pay for the investment in a new paint booth), whereas outsourcing may be the better option if sales are not expected to increase much beyond the current level.

Bottleneck Effectiveness

The classic measure of the bottleneck is the utilization measurement described in the last section. However, bottleneck utilization only addresses the efficiency of an operation – the amount of time during which it is in operation. What is of just as much importance is the effectiveness of the operation, which is the amount of throughput generated per hour of bottleneck time. Ideally, the bottleneck should have both a high utilization rate *and* high effectiveness, in order to maximize the total amount of throughput generated.

To calculate bottleneck effectiveness, divide the total amount of throughput dollars generated by the number of hours that the bottleneck was in operation. The formula is:

$$\frac{\text{Total throughput dollars generated}}{\text{Total hours of bottleneck operation}}$$

Note that the throughput figure used in the numerator is not just the throughput passing through the bottleneck, but rather the throughput of the *entire* production operation. We use this more expansive figure in order to account for the ability of the logistics staff to route work around the bottleneck, such as through outsourcing. This means that bottleneck effectiveness can be improved in multiple ways, such as:

- Shifting work away from the bottleneck to increase throughput without using the bottleneck
- Improving the speed of operation of the bottleneck, so that more units can be processed per hour
- Increasing product prices to increase throughput per unit
- Reducing the cost of materials to increase throughput per unit

EXAMPLE

Horton Corporation's management team recently bought the company in a leveraged buyout, and needs to reconfigure the company to generate more cash, so that the debt used to purchase the company can be paid off. The company's widget splicing operation is the constrained resource in the production area. The industrial engineering staff concludes that the best way to increase throughput per hour is to shorten the changeover time for new widget jobs at the splicing operation. The current changeover time for the splicer is 15% of its total operational time. The splicer currently generates $100 of throughput per minute of operating time, and the machine operates for an average of 35,000 minutes per month.

After two months of effort, the engineering staff succeeds in shortening the 15% changeover time to 10% of operating time. Doing so frees up an additional 1,750 minutes per month, which represents an increase in throughput of $175,000. Following this engineering work, the company's bottleneck effectiveness is:

$$\frac{\$3,675,000 \text{ Throughput}}{36,750 \text{ minutes}}$$

$$= \$100 \text{ per minute}$$

Interestingly, the bottleneck effectiveness of the company in the preceding example did not increase. Instead, it stayed the same, despite an increase in the number of minutes available for operation. The reason for the lack of change was that the operation became more *efficient* (with more operating time available for use), but the amount of throughput generated for each hour of use did not change.

A common side-effect of an increased level of bottleneck utilization is that bottleneck effectiveness *declines*. The reason is that the highest-throughput jobs are presumably already being processed through the bottleneck, so increasing its efficiency only makes room for the processing of jobs that presumably have lower throughput levels.

Bottleneck Schedule Fulfillment

We noted in a prior section that it is possible to completely fill the time of a bottleneck operation without generating any profit. This situation arises when the bottleneck is filled with low-profit or no-profit work. Someone attempting to report a high level of bottleneck usage could do so by working on a large-volume, low-throughput job, without generating any benefit for the company as a whole. To detect this situation, consider measuring how well the bottleneck operation completes its assigned work schedule.

To measure fulfillment of the bottleneck schedule, aggregate the number of jobs completed at the bottleneck operation by the number of jobs scheduled for the operation. The ratio is:

$$\frac{\text{Number of scheduled bottleneck jobs fulfilled}}{\text{Total number of scheduled bottleneck jobs}}$$

This measurement works best when there are a large number of jobs scheduled at the constrained operation. If there are just a few massive jobs during the measurement period, then this measurement could vary wildly from period to period. For example, if there are only two long-duration jobs scheduled in the measurement period and one job is still ongoing at the end of the month, then the measurement will result in a paltry 50% fulfillment rate.

Of course, if the contents of the work schedule contain minimal amounts of throughput, then even fulfilling the schedule will not generate much profitability for a business. Thus, use of this measurement should be coupled with an examination of the throughput associated with each job assigned to the bottleneck operation. If the assigned throughput is low, then the company has pricing problems with the products it is selling.

EXAMPLE

Oberlin Acoustics builds concert-grade guitars. The sound board construction facility is the bottleneck of the company, since this area requires detailed work with expensive hardwoods, such as Brazilian Rosewood and Tasmanian Blackwood. Recently, this area has been experiencing problems with the completion of the more dense wood sound boards, which require the attention of the most experienced craftsmen. Consequently, the sound board manager has been bolstering his bottleneck utilization measurement by spending more time on spruce sound boards, which are easier to complete.

To ensure that the sound board facility spends more of its time on the higher-throughput hardwood sound boards, the CFO mandates that the bottleneck schedule fulfillment measurement be tracked. The results for the past three months are as follows:

Month	Scheduled Hardwood Sound Boards	Completed Hardwood Sound Boards	Bottleneck Schedule Fulfillment
September	200	84	42%
October	210	97	46%
November	190	93	49%

The measurement indicates that the sound board manager is slowly ramping up the staffing needed to complete the hardwood sound boards in a more timely manner. It appears that this measurement should continue to be tracked over a long period of time, to ensure that the facility is appropriately staffed.

Buffer Penetration

As noted earlier, an inventory buffer is positioned in front of the bottleneck machine in the production area, which is used to ensure a steady flow of work into the bottleneck. By doing so, utilization of this work station is maximized. However, there is a cost of funds associated with maintaining too large a buffer, so there is a countervailing incentive to keep this buffer at a modest size. Consequently, a reasonable management task is to fine-tune the size of the inventory buffer by tracking buffer penetration. Buffer penetration is the proportion of the buffer that is used up at any point in time. It is never acceptable to allow the buffer to reach zero, since this implies that the bottleneck operation is being starved of resources. Instead, the level of buffer penetration must be examined continually to determine how close it has come to being eliminated, possibly resulting in some adjustment to the size of the buffer.

To calculate buffer penetration, divide the number of jobs at the bottleneck for which materials had to be accessed from the buffer by the total number of jobs at the bottleneck. The calculation is:

$$\frac{\text{Number of job requiring buffer usage}}{\text{Total number of jobs at the bottleneck}}$$

It is particularly important to look at the trend line of this measurement, to see if an increasing proportion of jobs are accessing the buffer. If so, it may be necessary to increase the size of the buffer. Conversely, if the buffer is rarely or never accessed, it may be possible to reduce the size of the buffer.

The buffer penetration report can also be used to evaluate the performance of the upstream workstations that are feeding jobs to the bottleneck operation. If the buffer is routinely being penetrated, it is quite likely that the cause is production or raw materials sourcing issues somewhere in front of the bottleneck.

Bottleneck Maintenance to Operating Ratio

When the constrained resource in a business is a work center within the production department, the bottleneck likely involves equipment that must be properly maintained. This can be a significant problem when the maximization of profits mandates that this work center be operated 100% of the time, three shifts per day, 365 days per year. Given the need to maximize profits, the maintenance work associated with a bottleneck should be carefully planned in advance, practiced, and then executed at the highest possible speed. This high degree of preplanning is rewarded by increased throughput, which generates more profitability. Thus, when it comes to maintaining the bottleneck operation, time is money.

A good way to measure the amount of downtime associated with maintenance is to compare maintenance time to the amount of time that the bottleneck operation is functioning. Doing so emphasizes to the maintenance staff the importance of minimizing the time that the bottleneck is not available for production purposes. The calculation is:

$$\frac{\text{Bottleneck downtime caused by maintenance}}{\text{Total bottleneck operating time}}$$

While this measurement does a good job of focusing attention on maintenance, it could promote the use of short-term fixes, rather than more extensive overhauls that could reduce the long-term amount of maintenance required. For example, if a bearing is wearing out on a machine, the maintenance staff could conduct a minor lubrication fix in a few minutes, or break down the machine and replace the bearing. The latter solution is the best solution over the long term, but a maintenance manager focusing too closely on the maintenance to operations ratio might opt for the reduced short-term amount of downtime offered under the first option.

The measurement of this ratio should be modified if the bottleneck operation is not being operated on a 24 × 7 basis, but rather on a reduced schedule. In this situation, the maintenance staff should always be encouraged to engage in maintenance operations outside of the core operating hours of the bottleneck operation. The recordation of bottleneck downtime caused by maintenance should therefore only be recorded if the downtime occurs within the regularly scheduled working hours of the bottleneck.

EXAMPLE

Bland Cabinets makes mass-produced cabinets for apartment buildings. Nearly all of its products are run through a high-speed drum sander. Given the cost of this equipment, management is reluctant to purchase an additional unit, so the single sander is operated around the clock in order to handle the volume of cabinet components. The drum sander must be disassembled at regular intervals for maintenance, as well as to replace the sanding drum. The average amount of maintenance time per month is currently 12 hours, while the sander is fully operational for the remaining 228 hours. This results in a bottleneck maintenance to operations ratio of:

$$\frac{12 \text{ Maintenance hours}}{228 \text{ Operating hours}} = 5.3\%$$

While the 5.3% result initially appears acceptable, the production manager realizes that the amount of throughput passing through the drum sander is $6,000 per hour. Consequently, the 12 maintenance hours per month when the sander is not operational is costing the company $72,000 per month of lost throughput. Given the amount of money involved, a consultant is hired at a cost of $1,000 per day to examine the time required to conduct maintenance, and arrives at a time-compressed alternative procedure that reduces maintenance to six hours per month. This expenditure reduces lost throughput by half, to $36,000 per month.

Bottleneck Rework Processing

There may be instances where a job is processed through the bottleneck operation, only to find that a product requires refinishing work at the bottleneck. Such rework has a negative impact on the bottleneck in two respects, which are:

- The bottleneck was already used to process the product, so any additional work on the product is a waste of bottleneck time that could have been used to generate throughput via some other product.
- Rework is typically presented to the bottleneck operation in small quantities or even as single units. This may call for a time-consuming equipment changeover to process the units, and if the changeover is lengthy, this represents an additional expensive use of bottleneck time.

To measure the amount of bottleneck rework processing, divide the total amount of rework time at the bottleneck by the total hours of operation of the bottleneck. The calculation is:

$$\frac{\text{Hours of rework time consumed by bottleneck}}{\text{Total operating hours of bottleneck}}$$

The amount of bottleneck rework processing is a valuable measure to track, especially when the cause of the rework is also noted. Management can use this information to track down what caused the out-of-specification condition that requires re-use of the bottleneck operation, and ensure that the condition does not happen again. However, the staff that operates the bottleneck is likely to under-report rework time, especially if they believe the amount of rework is immaterial. Thus, this is one of the more difficult measures to derive, despite being one of the more useful constraint measurements.

EXAMPLE

Spade Designs manufactures chrome-plated trowels for the fine art of digging up potatoes. The chrome plating process is the bottleneck of the company's production facility, since a large number of trowels are discovered to have non-uniform coatings in their electroplating. When this happens, the Spade staff must run them through the chrome-plating process again. In the most recent month, the chrome plating operation spent 72 hours on rework issues, as compared to 650 hours of total operation. The bottleneck rework processing percentage is calculated as follows:

$$\frac{72 \text{ Hours rework time at the bottleneck}}{650 \text{ Hours total bottleneck operating time}}$$

$$= 11.1\% \text{ Bottleneck rework processing}$$

Post-Bottleneck Scrap

In a prior section, we addressed how maintenance activities interfere with the amount of time available at the bottleneck operation. The same logic applies to any scrap that occurs downstream from the bottleneck. Anything processed at the bottleneck that is subsequently scrapped represents a loss of bottleneck time that cannot be recovered.

The amount of bottleneck time lost through scrap can be calculated by aggregating the bottleneck time consumed by each item scrapped, and multiplying by the average amount of throughput per minute generated by the constraint. The calculation is:

$$\sum (\text{Bottleneck minutes used to process scrapped items}) \times \text{Average throughput/minute}$$

The amount of scrap that occurs *after* the bottleneck is not to be confused with scrap that occurs *before* the bottleneck. When scrap is flushed out of the system before the bottleneck, this is actually a benefit to the company, since these items are being spotted and removed before they waste precious bottleneck time.

The main problem with the measurement is building a system to track scrap throughout the production area and then discern the amount of bottleneck time used by these items. A considerable amount of manual effort may be required to collect the information. However, given the benefit of knowing the lost amount of throughput caused by post-bottleneck scrap, it may be worth the effort.

EXAMPLE

Radiosonde Corporation fabricates weather balloons that are sent into the upper atmosphere with attached instrument packages. The constrained operation of the business is the extrusion work station, which creates the material used in the balloons. The average throughput generated by this machine is $50 per minute.

A downstream operation from the extruder is the attachment work station, where the straps for the instrument package are bonded to the balloon. The bonding process tends to overheat, causing the balloon to melt at the attachment points and rendering the entire balloon unusable. Though this problem is infrequent, the production manager wants to highlight the problem by quantifying the post-bottleneck scrap. In the past month, four balloons were scrapped at the attachment work station. Each of these balloons required 100 minutes of processing time at the extrusion work station. The resulting post-bottleneck scrap figure is derived as follows:

$$4 \text{ Units} \times 100 \text{ Minutes} \times \$50 \text{ Throughput/minute} = \$20,000$$

Even though only four units are being scrapped per month, the throughput lost from the melting problem is costing Radiosonde $20,000 per month.

Manufacturing Effectiveness

The bottleneck portion of a production facility may involve quite a small part of the total manufacturing operation, and so is strongly influenced by how well it is integrated into and supported by the surrounding operations. Consequently, it is useful to apply the throughput and constraint concepts to these surrounding operations, using the following measurements.

Manufacturing Productivity

The entire manufacturing function should be able to generate the largest possible amount of throughput at the lowest possible cost, which is known as manufacturing productivity. A well-run operation should be able to reduce the cost of operations while maintaining or increasing the level of throughput generated. The calculation is:

$$\frac{\text{Throughput generated}}{\text{Production expenses recognized}}$$

Ideally, manufacturing productivity should be tracked on a trend line, to see if continual improvements are being made. However, be aware of the following issues:

- Half of this measurement is throughput, which is dependent on prices charged – and over which the manufacturing department has no control.
- Production expenses can be reduced by maintaining tight control over labor costs. However, doing so may drive away the most experienced staff, which eventually can impact the overall productivity of operations.

- Management could manipulate the measurement by shifting some production expenses into the administrative area. If so, consider adding administrative expenses to the denominator, which reduces the ability of anyone to hide expenses.
- Some expenditures may be recorded as assets, so that they do not appear in the denominator. If so, impose tight controls over which expenditures can be capitalized.
- The production manager may be tempted to cut back on the production capacity of the business in order to reduce production expenses. Doing so may impede the ability of a business to keep the bottleneck operation fully fed with incoming jobs. Consequently, be sure to pair this measurement with an analysis of when the bottleneck is starved of incoming work.

In short, the manufacturing productivity measurement can be used to model how changes in production expenses incurred will alter the amount of throughput generated. The following example illustrates the concept.

EXAMPLE

The industrial engineering manager of Grubstake Brothers wants to install an automated metal stamping operation with the company's backhoe production facility. The net additional cost of doing so will be $100,000, on top of the current monthly production expense of $900,000. The production facility currently generates $1,400,000 of throughput, which is expected to increase to $1,700,000 as a result of the automation. The before-and-after manufacturing productivity resulting from this change is as follows:

	Before	After
Throughput generated	$1,400,000	$1,700,000
Production expenses recognized	$900,000	$1,000,000
Manufacturing productivity	1.56x	1.7x

Since manufacturing productivity is expected to increase as a result of the automation project, the requested investment should be approved.

Manufacturing Effectiveness

The preceding discussion of manufacturing productivity focused on the ability of the entire production area to reduce operating costs in relation to the amount of throughput generated. Manufacturing effectiveness focuses on the amount of throughput generated, rather than the cost of creating the throughput. In effect, the focus shifts from expenses to revenue.

To determine the level of manufacturing effectiveness, divide the total amount of throughput generated during the measurement period by the number of hours during which the bottleneck operation was in use. The calculation is:

$$\frac{\text{Throughput generated}}{\text{Number of bottleneck hours used}}$$

The ability to increase throughput can hinge upon a number of activities, such as:

- Reduce scrap levels occurring after the constrained resource, so that more net throughput makes its way through the entire production process.
- Enhance the processing speed of the bottleneck operation, such as through faster equipment changeovers or an investment in higher-speed equipment.
- Reconfigure products so that they use less processing time at the bottleneck.
- Outsource work so that a job requires no bottleneck time at all.

However, a change in manufacturing effectiveness may not be caused by the production staff at all. Instead, it is quite possible that the mix of products sold has changed, so that the amount of throughput generated is varying even in the absence of any process enhancements by the production staff. For example, if the engineering department creates a hot new product that is in great demand, the marketing department will set a high price point for it that results in a massive boost in throughput – which has nothing to do with production. Conversely, a discount offered to customers by the sales department could lower throughput to the point where manufacturing effectiveness looks catastrophically bad.

EXAMPLE

New Centurion Corporation translates Latin texts to English for its university customers. This task is done by the company's new TransSCRIBE machine, which automates much of the translation process, leaving a staff of trained scholars to verify the resulting texts. The machine is the constrained resource in the company, since the conversion process is extremely slow, even for a computer.

The translation manager of New Centurion has found that the effectiveness of the TransSCRIBE machine can be greatly enhanced by having the staff clean up incoming texts, deleting stray marks on the documents and ensuring that they are properly positioned for scanning. Doing so also reduces the amount of review time by the scholars, since the translations are cleaner when the inputs are better (thereby validating the concept of garbage in, garbage out).

The translation manager institutes these input changes, with the following results in the manufacturing effectiveness of the operation:

	Before	After
Throughput generated*	$375,000	$460,000
TransSCRIBE hours used*	240	240
Manufacturing effectiveness	$1,563/hour	$1,917/hour

 * Measurement period is one month

Manufacturing Throughput Time

Manufacturing throughput time is the amount of time required for a product to pass through a manufacturing process, thereby being converted from raw materials into finished goods. The concept also applies to the processing of raw materials into a component or sub-assembly. The time required for something to pass through a manufacturing process covers the entire period from when it first enters manufacturing until it exits manufacturing – which includes the following:

- *Processing time.* This is the time spent transforming raw materials into finished goods.
- *Inspection time.* This is the time spent inspecting raw materials, work-in-process, and finished goods, possibly at multiple stages of the production process.
- *Move time.* This is the time required to move items into and out of the manufacturing area, as well as between workstations within the production area.
- *Queue time.* This is the time spent waiting prior to the processing, inspection, and move activities.

The concept of manufacturing throughput time is primarily oriented toward the reduction of time required by the manufacturing process, so that you can increase the amount of throughput flowing through the system and thereby boost profitability. The bulk of the time spent in manufacturing tends not to be in processing, but rather in inspection, moves, and queues. Thus, it is easiest to reduce manufacturing throughput time by eliminating as much inspection, move, and queue time as possible.

EXAMPLE

The production manager of Mole Industries wants to calculate the manufacturing throughput time for the Ditch Digger Mini product. He accumulates the following information:

Processing time	3.0 hours
Inspection time	0.5 hours
Move time	1.0 hour
Queue time	12.0 hours

The total manufacturing throughput time for the Ditch Digger Mini is 16.5 hours. The production manager has a golden opportunity to reduce the throughput time, since the amount of queue time is almost three-quarters of the total throughput time, and can probably be reduced without too much trouble.

Delayed Throughput

An intense focus on throughput should not end at the constrained resource. It is entirely possible that the amount of throughput passing through the bottleneck is greater than the amount actually shipped to customers. This problem arises when there are problems in the production process downstream from the bottleneck operation that delay shipments. This can be a particular problem when the bottleneck is early in the production process, so that work must still pass through a number of work stations before a finished product can be shipped. Conversely, it is less of an issue if the bottleneck is one of the last processes before shipment.

If there appears to be a significant shortfall in the amount of recognized throughput, measure it with the following steps:

1. At the end of the period, compile the total amount of throughput dollars actually shipped and recognized as income.
2. Compile the total throughput dollars scheduled to be shipped in the period, as per the production schedule.
3. Subtract the amount of throughput actually shipped from the total amount scheduled.
4. Divide by the total throughput dollars scheduled to be shipped in the period.

The calculation is:

$$\frac{\text{Scheduled throughput dollars} - \text{Actual throughput dollars shipped}}{\text{Scheduled throughput dollars}}$$

This is not one of the easier measurements to compile, since there may be many shipments during the reporting period. The best approach is to use a report writing package and a standard costing system to create a computerized report that matches the price of each product shipped to its standard variable cost; the report writer then states the difference between the two as throughput, and aggregates throughput for the period to arrive at total throughput shipped.

EXAMPLE

Giro Cabinetry produces western-style cabinets, which require a heavy coat of lacquer as the final production step. Though not the bottleneck, flaws in the finish caused by dirt particles have delayed the delivery of multiple orders, resulting in a decline of monthly throughput of $50,000 from the scheduled $800,000. The effect of this delayed throughput is as follows:

$$\frac{\$800,000 \text{ Scheduled throughput} - \$750,000 \text{ Actual throughput shipped}}{\$800,000 \text{ Scheduled throughput}}$$

$$= 6.25\%$$

Since the company usually only earns about $40,000 per month, the monthly delay of $50,000 in recognizing throughput threatens to have a major effect on the company. Accordingly, management implements a crash program to locate the source of the dirt particles, resulting in the installation of a close-grained air filtration system to screen out dirt.

Summary

The focus in this chapter has been on the concepts of constraints and throughput. These concepts can apply to multiple functional areas within a business, including sales (because of price points), procurement (because of material costs) and production (since this is where bottlenecks are commonly found). Given their universal usage, we have created a free-standing chapter for these concepts, so that you may be encouraged to apply them to many parts of a business. Bottlenecks are particularly prevalent in the sales area, where it can be difficult to develop enough fully-trained staff to locate new sales and properly bid on work and complete product demonstrations in a timely manner. Nevertheless, you will find that many of the concepts discussed in this chapter carry over into the Production Measurements chapter.

Chapter 9
Cash Management Measurements

Introduction

The cash management function is separate from the normal operational part of a company, where goods are produced and sold. Most measurements are designed to monitor the performance of these other operational areas, since that is where most company profits and losses are generated. Nonetheless, the cash management function should be monitored with a small group of metrics. By doing so, the treasurer can gain insights into how well the cash management staff can predict cash flows, the earnings generated on invested funds, and similar matters. In this chapter, we describe a variety of cash management metrics that can be of use to the treasurer.

Overview of Cash Management Measurements

At first glance, the cash management area might appear resistant to the use of any ongoing, standardized metrics to measure its performance. After all, we are merely finding a home for excess cash. In reality, there are a number of areas in which metrics can be profitably employed. Consider the following conceptual areas for measurement:

- *Cash forecasting.* The treasurer needs to know how well future projections of cash positions are matching actual outcomes, so that investments can be properly planned. Also, the ability of the company to apply incoming payments to receivables should be noted, so that actual cash receipts can be compared to cash projections.
- *Cash at work.* The treasurer should be fully informed of those pockets of cash not being put to good use earning income for the business, as well as the extent of the returns on invested funds.
- *Cash at risk.* If the company has extensive positions in foreign currencies, there should be a measurement system in place that tracks unhedged gains and losses on those positions, thereby clarifying the extent of the risk to which the company is subjected.

In short, there are a number of areas in which metrics can provide valuable information for the cash management function. In the following sections, we discuss specific metrics that address all of the conceptual areas just noted.

Auto Cash Application Rate

In a larger organization that has many cash receipts from customers, it can be cost-effective to install a system that automatically sorts through the various receipts and applies them to open accounts receivable. This is of use to the cash management function, since cash appears in the accounting system more quickly than would be the case with a manual application process. These "auto cash" systems are not very effective initially, based on the generic application logic provided by the system supplier. As a result, a large percentage of cash receipts are rejected, and must be manually applied to open receivables. However, fine-tuning the system with additional cash application logic for each individual customer will gradually improve the auto cash application rate, to the point where very few cash receipts require manual processing. Thus, continuing attention to the application rate of such a system is of some importance from the perspective of cash management.

To calculate the auto cash application rate, divide the number of check payments automatically applied by the auto cash system by the total number of check payments received. All up-front payments received (i.e., not involving receivables) should not be included in the measurement. The ratio is:

$$\frac{\text{Number of check payments automatically applied in full}}{\text{Total number of check payments received}}$$

Consider running this measurement every day during the early stages of an auto cash installation. This is needed to focus attention on the constant updating of system logic to accommodate the payment foibles of individual customers. Once a high application rate has been achieved, the measurement frequency can be reduced.

EXAMPLE

Cud Farms bills its thousands of retail customers once a week for milk deliveries, and is usually paid by check about one week later. Cud installs an auto cash system to handle this incoming blizzard of payments. The treasury department tracks the performance of the system using the auto cash application rate. In the first week, auto cash applications were made for 5,100 out of 8,300 check receipts. A month later, the rate is 5,350 applications out of 8,900 check receipts. The target application rate advertised by the auto cash system provider is 80%. Since the initial application rate was 61% and the following rate was 60%, Cud is clearly not going to achieve the target rate without additional assistance from the system provider.

Suspense to Receivables Ratio

When payments are received from customers, some are so poorly documented that it can be quite difficult to apply them to open accounts receivable. To ensure that these payments are at least recorded *somewhere* in the accounting system, they are assigned to a suspense account. By doing so, the cash balance is increased by the amount of these payments, even if no specific receivable accounts are impacted. However, this means that the cash management staff cannot determine the accuracy of its cash forecasts, since it does not know which customers have submitted payments. Thus, there is a need to resolve the contents of the suspense account as soon as possible.

The suspense account can be a quagmire of old and poorly-documented receipts, and so tends to be avoided by the accounting staff. To focus attention on this area, consider measuring the suspense to receivables ratio, which is a simple comparison of the total balance in the suspense account to the total amount of trade receivables. The ratio is:

$$\frac{\text{Suspense account balance}}{\text{Trade accounts receivable balance}}$$

The main problem with this measurement is that the suspense account may be relatively small in comparison to the total balance of trade receivables, so the resulting ratio may not generate much attention from the controller. There are two variations on the concept that might trigger more vigorous attention:

- Use only the overdue receivables balance in the denominator of the ratio, since this is probably the group of receivables related to the payments stored in the suspense account. Since the denominator will be smaller, the suspense account balance will appear comparatively larger.
- Track the average age of the payments stored in the suspense account, rather than the suspense to receivables ratio. Many older payments will be more likely to trigger additional clerical support.

EXAMPLE

Colossal Furniture hired a relatively inexperienced cash receipts clerk one year ago, and the treasury staff is complaining that it can no longer accurately track cash receipts against its cash forecast, since so many payments are sitting in the suspense account. To verify this allegation, the controller assembles the following information about the contents of the suspense account from just before the clerk was hired and from the preceding day:

	Suspense Account Balance	Total Receivables > 30 Days	Suspense to Receivables Ratio
One year ago	$250,000	$25,000,000	1%
Yesterday	2,100,000	26,250,000	8%

The suspense to receivables ratio in the table indicates that there is indeed a problem, so the controller assigns additional staff to investigate and resolve the contents of the suspense account.

Actual Cash Position versus Forecast

It is of some importance to maintain a cash forecast that is as accurate as possible, so that investments can be properly managed. If there are any variations in actual cash flows from forecasted results, the treasury staff must investigate them and use the resulting knowledge to improve the forecasting model.

An excellent way to monitor cash forecast accuracy is to routinely compare the company's actual cash position, prior to financing activities, to the forecasted amount. The main point of this metric should be to note the size of the difference from the expected result. An unusually large variance, whether positive or negative, should be grounds for a review. Thus, the calculation should be on an absolute basis, rather than showing a negative or positive variance.

For example, the treasurer of a company compares actual to forecasted results for the last six weeks, and obtains the following information:

Week	Actual Ending Cash	Forecasted Ending Cash	Variance	Absolute Variance	Percent Variance
1	$1,237,000	$952,000	-$285,000	$285,000	23%
2	1,080,000	1,274,000	194,000	194,000	18%
3	1,591,000	1,846,000	255,000	255,000	16%
4	826,000	727,000	-99,000	99,000	12%
5	739,000	658,000	-81,000	81,000	11%
6	2,803,000	3,083,000	280,000	280,000	10%

The actual versus forecast information in the table reveals that the treasury staff is rapidly improving its ability to accurately forecast cash flows.

Average End of Day Available Balance

The treasurer should be aware of the average end of day available balance in each of a company's bank accounts. This information is useful for determining the amount of funds being left in non-interest-bearing accounts. It is particularly helpful for those businesses where no attempt is made to shift funds into investments, since management can then discern the approximate amount of lost interest income. This information can be transformed into a ratio, by comparing the average end of day available balance to the total amount of invested cash. The measurement is:

$$\frac{\text{Average end of day available cash balance}}{\text{Total amount of invested cash}}$$

The ratio is intended to bring clarity to the level of effort being expended on the investment of excess cash.

The metric can also be of use in companies where the cash balances in accounts are being routinely swept into investment accounts. Theoretically, the average end of day available balance should be zero for all accounts other than the investment account into which cash is being swept. In reality, the treasurer may have set up target balances that leave certain cash balances in outlying accounts. Further, it may have been deemed too difficult to include some accounts in a cash sweeping arrangement, perhaps due to an obstreperous local manager or currency restrictions in an account held in a different country. By tracking the average end of day available balance for each account on a trend line, the treasurer can see if some accounts are retaining excessively large balances. At a minimum, the result is a useful reminder to periodically examine target balances and ensure that they are still valid.

Earnings on Invested Funds

The treasurer is not being paid to put a company's cash at risk in equity investments, which usually leaves only interest income as the type of income generated by invested cash, not changes in the market value of equity investments. Nonetheless, there may be cases where management is willing to put some cash at risk in an equity investment, which can generate equity gains or losses. Consequently, the following formula for earnings on invested funds includes market value changes:

$$\frac{\text{Interest income} + \text{Market value changes}}{\text{Average funds invested}}$$

Note that the calculation uses average funds invested, not the amount of cash invested as of the end of a reporting period. The amount of cash invested can change substantially by day, so the average investment figure in the denominator should be based on an average of the invested balance in every business day of a reporting period.

EXAMPLE

A treasurer is authorized to invest in both short-term debt instruments and stocks. As a result, the business earns $45,000 in interest income and $15,000 from an increase in the market value of its equity holdings. During the measurement period, the company had average investments of $3,000,000. The company's earnings on invested funds is calculated as:

$$\frac{\$45{,}000 \text{ Interest income} + \$15{,}000 \text{ Market value changes}}{\$3{,}000{,}000 \text{ Average funds invested}}$$

$$= 2.0\% \text{ Earnings on invested funds}$$

In many organizations, a much higher premium is placed on risk avoidance than on investment earnings, so it is fairly common to downplay this metric. If it is used, the board of directors should confine the cash management staff to specific types of conservative investment choices, so there is no temptation to earn outsized returns by making risky investments.

Unhedged Gains and Losses

There may be circumstances where the cash management staff chooses not to create a hedge against a foreign exchange position, and the company subsequently incurs a gain or loss on that position. It is also possible that the company does not have an adequate foreign exchange forecasting system, and so does not know that it even has unhedged positions, which will most certainly result in unhedged gains or losses.

In either case, it is extremely useful to keep track of gains or losses arising from unhedged foreign currency positions, so that the treasurer can estimate when the size of these gains or losses warrants the imposition of a more extensive hedging program. The simplest form of metric is a trend line analysis. This trend line will likely yield results that routinely bounce between gains and losses. The key issue to watch for is an increasing trend in the *size* of the gains or losses over time. When they become large enough to seriously impact the company's reported results from operations, it is time to consider a combination of a better forecasting system and a more active hedging program.

Summary

In this chapter, we addressed ratios and other measurements that are used to monitor the accuracy of cash forecasting, how cash is used, and risk related to cash positions. The frequency of measurement varies substantially for each of these classifications. Cash forecasting ratios are typically run once a week, to coincide with the generation of weekly cash forecasts. Cash usage measurements can be limited to just once a month, especially in economic environments where the return on invested funds is quite low, and therefore of lesser importance. The most critical area from a measurement frequency perspective is the risk associated with unhedged cash positions, which may require daily reporting; this is the case only when the amount of cash at risk is substantial.

Chapter 10
Credit and Collection Measurements

Introduction

The credit and collection functions deal with large numbers of customers and invoices on an ongoing basis. Given the high volume, this environment is suitable for a variety of measurements that can be used to monitor and manage the credit and collection functions. In this chapter, we begin with discussions of measurements related to collections, since most measurements are concentrated in this area, and not in the credit area.

Overview of Credit and Collection Measurements

The credit and collection functions deal with very large numbers of customers and their invoices. On a day to day basis, it is easy to be lost in the minutiae of granting credit and collecting receivables, without giving consideration to the overall result of these efforts. The measurements described in this chapter can be used to monitor performance, which is useful for deciding whether sufficient resources are being allocated to the department, or if action should be taken to improve efficiency. Some of the measurements can also be used to drill down to the specific issues causing certain types of collection problems.

At a minimum, there must be a measurement that compares the amount of accounts receivable to credit sales, in order to roughly estimate the average period over which receivables are outstanding. The classic measure of this type is days sales outstanding (DSO), as described in a later section. In addition, consider using other measurements to obtain additional information about different aspects of the credit and collection functions. Ideally, such a system begins with a high-level DSO measurement and then drills down into the various components of the credit and collection functions to give the user additional information about why receivables are not being collected. For example, a manager may have an interest in the following additional measurements:

- The gross amount of receivables in each time bucket on the aged accounts receivable report, to determine the age range in which most overdue receivables are clustered
- The average number of days to pay, sorted by collector, which can be used to identify the most effective collectors
- The time required to settle payment disputes, which can be used to improve the deduction management process

When reviewing the results of a measurement system, keep in mind that the liquidity of customers, and therefore their ability to pay, varies somewhat from month to month, in a recurring cycle. For example, a partnership may pay out cash to its partners at the end of the calendar year, and so may delay some payments at the end of the year. Similarly, corporations may make estimated tax payments on a quarterly basis, which may impinge upon their accounts payable at the times when these payments are made. Further, there is a certain amount of seasonality in many industries, which can impact cash flows. For all of these reasons, a system of measurements will likely reveal that collection results differ from month to month, and quite possibly through no fault of the credit and collection employees. To filter out the effects of customers' ability to pay, compare the results of a particular month with the same month in the preceding year. For example, the DSO for this February may bear more resemblance to the DSO for the preceding February than to the DSO calculations for the adjacent January period in the current year.

The end result of a credit and collection measurement system should be specific actions to reduce the amount of overdue accounts receivable, such as:

• Adding credit and/or collection staff
• Adjusting the method for dealing with payment deductions
• Altering the policy for granting credit
• Altering the procedure for contacting customers
• Curtailing management overrides of credit decisions

In short, a system of measurements is only as good as the actions that result from its use. If measurements are routinely calculated and no action results, then the system has failed.

Days Sales Outstanding

When evaluating the amount of accounts receivable outstanding, it is best to compare the receivables to the sales activity of the business, in order to see the proportion of receivables to sales. This proportion can be expressed as the average number of days over which receivables are outstanding before they are paid, which is called days sales outstanding, or DSO. DSO is the most popular of all collection measurements.

Days sales outstanding is most useful when compared to the standard number of days that customers are allowed before payment is due. Thus, a DSO figure of 40 days might initially appear excellent, until you realize that the standard payment terms are only five days. A combination of prudent credit granting and robust collections activity is the likely cause when the DSO figure is only a few days longer than the standard payment terms. From a management perspective, it is easiest to spot collection problems at a gross level by tracking DSO on a trend line, and watching for a sudden spike in the measurement in comparison to what was reported in prior periods.

To calculate DSO, divide 365 days into the amount of annual credit sales to arrive at credit sales per day, and then divide this figure into the average accounts receivable for the measurement period. Thus, the formula is:

$$\frac{\text{Average accounts receivable}}{\text{Annual sales} \div 365 \text{ days}}$$

EXAMPLE

The controller of Oberlin Acoustics, maker of the famous Rhino brand of electric guitars, wants to derive the days sales outstanding for the company for the April reporting period. In April, the beginning and ending accounts receivable balances were \$420,000 and \$540,000, respectively. The total credit sales for the 12 months ended April 30 were \$4,000,000. The controller derives the following DSO calculation from this information:

$$\frac{(\$420{,}000 \text{ Beginning receivables} + \$540{,}000 \text{ Ending receivables}) \div 2}{\$4{,}000{,}000 \text{ Credit sales} \div 365 \text{ Days}}$$

$$=$$

$$\frac{\$480{,}000 \text{ Average accounts receivable}}{\$10{,}959 \text{ Credit sales per day}}$$

$$= 43.8 \text{ Days}$$

The correlation between the annual sales figure used in the calculation and the average accounts receivable figure may not be close, resulting in a misleading DSO number. For example, if a company has seasonal sales, the average receivable figure may be unusually high or low on the measurement date, depending on where the company is in its seasonal billings. Thus, if receivables are unusually low when the measurement is taken, the DSO days will appear unusually low, and vice versa if the receivables are unusually high. There are two ways to eliminate this problem:

- *Annualize receivables.* Generate an average accounts receivable figure that spans the entire, full-year measurement period.
- *Measure a shorter period.* Adopt a rolling quarterly DSO calculation, so that sales for the past three months are compared to average receivables for the past three months. This approach is most useful when sales are highly variable throughout the year.

Whatever measurement methodology is adopted for DSO, be sure to use it consistently from period to period, so that the results will be comparable on a trend line.

Tip: If DSO is increasing, the problem may be that the processing of credit memos has been delayed. If there is a processing backlog, at least have the largest ones processed first, which may reduce the amount of receivables outstanding by a noticeable amount.

Best Possible DSO

After running the DSO calculation, it may be useful to establish a benchmark against which to compare the DSO. This benchmark is the best possible DSO, which is the best collection performance that can be expected, given the existing payment terms given to customers. The calculation is:

$$\frac{\text{Current receivables}}{\text{Annual credit sales}} \times 365$$

The key element in this formula is the *current* receivables. The calculation is essentially designed to show the best possible level of receivables, based on the assumption that DSO is only based on current receivables (i.e., there are no delinquent invoices present in the calculation).

EXAMPLE

The collections manager of the Red Herring Fish Company has established that the company's DSO is 22 days. Since the company requires short payment terms on its short-lived products, the question arises – is 22 days good or bad? At the end of the current period, Red Herring's current receivables were $30,000, and its trailing 12-month credit sales were $1,000,000. Based on this information, the best possible DSO is:

$$\frac{\$30,000 \text{ Current receivables}}{\$1,000,000 \text{ Credit sales}} \times 365$$

$$= 11 \text{ Days}$$

In short, actual DSO is running at a rate double that of the company's best possible DSO, and so should be considered an opportunity for improvement.

Collection Effectiveness Index

The days sales outstanding measurement operates at a relatively high level, and only gives a general indication of the state of receivables in comparison to sales over a fairly long period of time. An alternative that yields a somewhat higher level of precision is the collection effectiveness index (CEI). This measurement compares the amount that was collected in a given time period to the amount of receivables that were available for collection in that time period. A result near 100% indicates that a collection department has been very effective in collecting from customers.

The formula for the CEI is to combine the beginning receivables for the measurement period with the credit sales for that period, less the amount of ending receivables, and then divide this number by the sum of the beginning receivables for the measurement period and the credit sales for that period, less the amount of ending *current*

122

receivables. Then multiply the result by 100 to arrive at a CEI percentage. Thus, the formula is stated as:

$$\frac{\text{Beginning receivables} + \text{Credit sales for the period} - \text{Ending total receivables}}{\text{Beginning receivables} + \text{Credit sales for the period} - \text{Ending current receivables}} \times 100$$

A collections manager can attain a high CEI number by focusing on the collection of the largest receivables. This means that a favorable CEI can be generated, even if there are a number of smaller receivables that are very overdue.

The CEI figure can be calculated for a period of any duration, such as a single month. Conversely, the DSO calculation tends to be less accurate for very short periods of time, since it includes receivables from prior periods that do not directly relate to the credit sales figure in that calculation.

EXAMPLE

Milagro Corporation, maker of espresso coffee machines, has been relying on DSO to measure its collection effectiveness, but wants to supplement it with a measurement designed for a shorter period of time. The collection effectiveness index is selected as that measure. For the most recent month, the company had $400,000 of beginning receivables, $350,000 of credit sales, $425,000 of ending total receivables, and $300,000 of ending current receivables. The calculation of its CEI reveals the following information:

$$\frac{\substack{\$400,000 \text{ Beginning receivables} + \$350,000 \text{ Credit sales for the period} \\ - \$425,00 \text{ Ending total receivables}}}{\substack{\$400,000 \text{ Beginning receivables} + \$350,000 \text{ Credit sales for the period} \\ - \$300,000 \text{ Ending current receivables}}} \times 100$$

$$= 72\% \text{ Collection effectiveness index}$$

Thus, Milagro was able to collect 72% of the receivables that were available for collection in that month.

Measurements Based on Time Buckets

After calculating total collection effectiveness, it is useful to drill down at the time bucket level to see how old the clusters of overdue receivables are that are impacting collection effectiveness. A time bucket is a time period listed on the aged accounts receivables report, where each time bucket is in 30-day increments. Thus, the usual increments are:

- 0 to 30 days
- 31 to 60 days
- 61 to 90 days
- 90+ days

Many reporting packages allow users to alter the duration of time buckets, so these standard periods may not be reflected in all aging reports. For example, a company that has 15-day payment terms may set its first time bucket to be 0 to 15 days, the next time bucket at 16 to 45 days, and so on.

Usually, the amount of receivables in a time bucket is relatively consistent from period to period, unless a disproportionately large receivable is creating a bulge in a certain time bucket. Consequently, it is useful to calculate the percentage of total receivables in each time bucket, and monitor these percentages on a trend line. The following trend analysis for a six-month period illustrates the concept.

Sample Time Bucket Analysis

	January	February	March	April	May	June
0 to 30 days	58%	53%	49%	47%	45%	43%
31 to 60 days	30%	35%	34%	27%	29%	30%
61 to 90 days	10%	10%	15%	19%	10%	11%
90+ days	2%	2%	2%	7%	16%	16%
Totals	100%	100%	100%	100%	100%	100%

The sample time bucket analysis reveals a disturbing trend, where one or more large receivables have shifted out of the shortest time bucket near the beginning of the period, and gradually worked their way through the time buckets until they are now firmly parked in the oldest bucket. In short, there appears to be a cluster of uncollectible receivables burdening the aging report.

Some collection managers prefer to focus particular attention on the 90+ day time bucket, since it contains the most intractable collection problems. The formula for calculating the percent of receivables over 90 days past due is:

$$\frac{\text{Receivables} > 90 \text{ days past due}}{\text{Total receivables}}$$

We do not advocate focusing on the 90+ day time bucket to the detriment of the earlier time buckets, since receivables are much more likely to be collected during the earlier stages of their existence. Once a receivable reaches the 90+ time bucket, the probability of its collection, simply due to the passage of time, has declined. If anything, the collection manager should focus on the 31 - 60 day time bucket, where collection problems first make their appearance and are most likely to be resolved.

Days Delinquent Sales Outstanding

Rather than focusing on the entire set of accounts receivable, consider focusing the measurement only on those receivables that are overdue, and ignoring those invoices that are currently within terms. This measurement is called the days delinquent sales outstanding (DDSO), for which the measurement is:

$$\frac{365}{\text{(Annualized credit sales from delinquent customers} \div \text{Average delinquent receivables)}}$$

When deriving this calculation, the main factor is defining at what point a receivable is considered delinquent. Setting the threshold at 30 days when the payment terms are net 30 days will likely catch a large proportion of customers that pay on time, but whose payments have not yet arrived in the mail. Consequently, a somewhat higher threshold should be set, such as 10 days past terms.

EXAMPLE

New Centurion Corporation translates Latin texts for a variety of educational institutions. Most customers pay on time or early, but a small number of underfunded colleges pay quite late. The collections manager of New Centurion decides to focus attention on this small group by implementing the measurement of DDSO. She sets the delinquent account threshold at 40 days, and finds that the annualized credit sales to the resulting group of customers is $600,000, and the related average receivables are $150,000. The DDSO calculation is:

$$\frac{365}{(\$600,000 \text{ Annual credit sales} \div \$150,000 \text{ Average receivables})}$$

$$= 91 \text{ Days delinquent sales outstanding}$$

Average Days to Pay per Collector

When investigating the reasons for a lengthy DSO, one possibility is to subdivide the measurement by collector, to see if any collectors are unusually efficient or inefficient at collecting from overdue accounts. The result may be retraining of some collectors to enhance their collection skills, or perhaps shifting the more difficult accounts to those collectors who are more adept at collecting funds.

A caution when using average days to pay at the collector level is that some customers are more difficult to collect from than others, irrespective of who is handling the account. Thus, an excellent collections person may have been assigned several customers who simply are not going to pay anywhere near the date mandated by their collection terms. Also, if collectors are being evaluated based on this measurement, there may be infighting over who is assigned certain accounts, or perhaps a rush to write off the more difficult receivables. Because of these issues, it may not be wise to rely on measurements at the collector level, at least when making determinations about changes in compensation or promotions.

Collection Dispute Cycle Time

While the days sales outstanding measurement provides a good overview of how long receivables are outstanding, it does little to provide additional detail about why the receivables are outstanding for so long. The next level of detail below DSO is to track the time required to resolve collection disputes. This measurement is called the *collection dispute cycle time*; when applied just to the resolution of payment deductions, it is called *days deduction outstanding*, or DDO. The simplest approach is to use the same case tracking system used by the customer support function, and record within it the beginning and ending dates for each dispute, as well as the amount in dispute, the cause of the problem, and who is handling its disposition. When summarized over a large number of disputes, this information gives management a good idea of the average time required to settle a dispute, as well as which customers are repeatedly involved with the longest-running disputes, what root problems caused them, and which collections staff have the best (and worst) ability to resolve disputes within a short period of time.

When used properly, an ongoing examination of the collection dispute cycle time can result in decisions to eliminate more difficult customers, provide training to those employees who have problems resolving disputes in a timely manner, and correct the underlying causes of disputed payments.

The measurement can be deliberately skewed by altering the recorded beginning and ending dates of dispute cases. To keep this from happening, do not tie any reduction in the dispute duration period to a bonus plan; this ensures more honest record keeping.

Deduction Turnover

If the company deals with a large number of deductions on an ongoing basis, consider calculating the rate of turnover in deductions. This approach is useful for tracking the ability of the collections staff to rapidly settle deductions. The formula is:

$$\frac{(\text{Number of deductions outstanding at beginning of the period} + \text{Number of new deductions created in the period})}{\text{Number of deductions at end of the period}}$$

EXAMPLE

Milford Sound routinely deals with a large number of customer payment deductions related to its ongoing marketing cost reimbursement programs. The controller wants to know if the collections staff is keeping up with the volume of these deductions, and so compiles the following information for each of the past three months:

	January	February	March
Beginning deductions outstanding	300	325	340
New deductions in period	1,200	1,250	1,280
Ending deductions outstanding	325	340	350
Deduction turnover	4.6x	4.6x	4.6x

The table reveals that the number of new deductions is rising through the period, as is the number of unresolved deductions at the end of each period. However, in comparison to the total volume of deductions under review, turnover has remained the same throughout the period. Thus, if the controller uses a turnover rate of 4.6x as an acceptable standard, then no operational changes are required.

Average Time to First Contact

If a company uses a computerized collection tracking system, the computer should be able to track all collection actions taken through the system, such as issuing dunning letters or autodialing a customer. If so, have the system compare the date when an invoice came due and when the first collection contact related to that invoice was first made. When aggregated, this should result in a fairly consistent average time to first contact.

It is not always a good use of staff time to accelerate the average time to first contact, since many payments really *are* in the mail, and will be received shortly. Thus, a close examination of cash receipts will probably suggest a certain number of days past the due date when it is most cost-effective to contact a customer.

Bad Debt Percentage

The end result of the credit and collection process is the proportion of accounts receivable that cannot be collected – the bad debt percentage. Ultimately, the bad debt percentage, combined with days sales outstanding, are the core measurements of the credit and collection function.

The bad debt percentage is a simple calculation, just the bad debt expense for the year, divided by credit sales. However, be aware that the reported amount can be "adjusted," sometimes by a significant amount. Under the accrual basis of accounting, bad debts are estimated and charged to the allowance for doubtful accounts, which is a reserve against which actual bad debts are later charged. If the collections manager wants to present a somewhat lower bad debt percentage at the end of the year, he or she can simply underestimate the amount of bad debts expected to be incurred, and reduce the size of the allowance for doubtful accounts. This issue can be mitigated by adopting a standard procedure for calculating the amount of the allowance, and rigidly adhering to that procedure.

EXAMPLE

Quest Adventure Gear, maker of rugged travel clothing, has been experiencing increasing difficulty in collecting from its retailer base of customers over the past few years despite growing sales, which has triggered a discussion to only sell through a website where customers must pay in advance. The controller of Quest accumulates the following information about the company's bad debts to prove the case that collecting from retailer customers is not going well:

	20X1	20X2	20X3	20X5	20X6
Bad debt expense	$35,000	$47,000	$68,000	$130,000	$176,000
Credit sales	2,900,000	3,100,000	3,250,000	3,500,000	3,900,000
Bad debt percentage	1.2%	1.5%	2.1%	3.7%	4.5%

Collection Performance Report

If a manager wants to monitor the daily performance of the collection staff, the following report format can be used, subdivided by individual collector:

+	Funds collected for the period to date
+	Cash expected from post-dated checks in the period
+	Promised funds expected by the end of the period
=	Total expected collections
	Total projected collections ((collections to date per day × days remaining in period) + funds already collected)
	Total period collection goal (for comparison purposes)
	Proportion of goal achieved to date

The total projected collections number in the preceding list is particularly important, since it is used to estimate, based on the historical collection rate, how much cash a collector is likely to take in by the end of the period. This number is usually less than the amount indicated by the promised funds line item, which tends to be overly optimistic.

An example of the collection performance report is shown next, and is stated for a single collector. There are 20 business days in the reporting period shown, of which 15 days have been completed.

Sample Collection Performance Report

Collector: Edith Wharton	
$140,000	Funds collected for the period to date
20,000	Cash expected from post-dated checks in the period
<u>82,000</u>	Promised funds expected by the end of the period
<u>$242,000</u>	Total expected collections
<u>$220,665</u>	Total projected collections (($16,133 collections/day × 5 days remaining in period) + $140,000 funds already collected)
$240,000	Total period collection goal
58%	Proportion of goal achieved to date

In the example, note that both the total projected collections figure and the proportion of goal achieved to date indicate that the collector may have difficulty in achieving her collection targets for the period.

Average Time to Establish Credit

If a company wants to complete a sale to a new customer, it has to complete the credit analysis process quickly and assign credit to the customer. Consequently, the speed with which the credit department can process requests for credit is of some importance. The calculation is based on an internal database of when requests are logged in, and when the corresponding credit decisions are also logged in. The aggregation of these processing time periods results in an average time to establish credit. The same database could then be used to investigate those outlier credit decisions that took much longer than the median time requirement.

Unfortunately, this measurement can be easily manipulated by adjusting the dates and times when credit requests and credit decisions are logged in. Some of the problem can be eliminated by having the sales department log in credit requests, rather than the credit department.

General Management Measurements

There are a variety of additional measurements that can be used to monitor the costs incurred within the department, the performance of employees, and the proportion of costs incurred as a percentage of total credit sales. Consider the following possibilities:

- Employee turnover
- The number of accounts assigned to each credit employee
- The number of accounts assigned to each collection employee
- The average rate of pay as compared to the median pay rate in the area for similar jobs

- The total cost of the credit and collection functions as a percentage of sales
- The amount of credit sales divided by the full-time equivalent number of credit and collection employees

Most general measurement systems in the credit and collection area should focus on the employees, since they comprise nearly all of the expenses incurred in these functional areas, and their effectiveness is central to the success of the company.

Summary

It is by no means necessary to use all of the measurements described in this chapter. Only calculate and report a measurement if it will be used. Thus, if there is no interest in reducing the amount of time taken to resolve payment disputes, do not measure the collection dispute cycle time. It may be that management attention will shift in the future, at which point the mix of measurements will change, and a measurement that was previously ignored is now in vogue. Conversely, if no action is now being taken in regard to a measurement that was actively followed in the past, it may be time to discontinue that measurement, and let managers focus on a different aspect of the credit and collection functions.

Chapter 11
Customer Service Measurements

Introduction

At the core of a company's profitability is the satisfaction of its customers with the goods and services provided. A high level of satisfaction equates to higher customer retention, as well as more willingness to pay higher prices. In this chapter, we address a variety of measurements for those aspects of a business that most directly impact the satisfaction of customers, with particular emphasis on deliveries and call center capabilities.

Overview of Customer Service Measurements

The measurements in this chapter fall into several major areas. The first classification addresses the ability of a business to provide the correct goods in a timely manner. We note the on-time delivery percentage as being the most important, though the order cycle time should be monitored at the same time to ensure that employees are not altering the measurement information to improve the on-time percentage. We also advocate using the order fill rate and orders damaged in transit measurements to provide a complete picture of the ability of a business to provide a complete, undamaged order to a customer.

These measures are followed by the customer turnover metric, which can be used to generally estimate how many customers are not returning to place repeat orders. This measurement concludes the basic set of measurements that most businesses should use to monitor customer service.

We then turn to more specialized measurements that are intended for inbound call centers (where customers are calling the company with problems). The first contact resolution measurement is used to monitor the ability of the call center staff to resolve customer issues on the first call, with no additional follow-up needed. An ancillary measurement is the escalation rate, which is the proportion of customer contacts requiring more in-depth contacts with additional company personnel. From the perspective of the customer, these are the most important measurements.

We also note the caller abandonment rate, which is the proportion of callers dropping their calls before getting in touch with a call center employee. This measurement is used to monitor how well the call center manager matches staffing with the volume of calls. A closely-related measurement is incident volume, which is the number of calls received by time and date. Incident volume is used to estimate the number of employees to have on hand to answer calls.

The remaining call center measurement is inbound caller retention, which is a specialized metric that examines the ability of employees to persuade customers not to cut off whatever service the company is providing.

Finally, we describe two measurements that track customer opinions, which are the customer satisfaction ratio and the net promoter score. We take the unusual step of using sales returns and allowances as the basis for tracking customer satisfaction, since it is the most easily quantifiable way to do so. The net promoter score is only applicable under limited circumstances, but can be useful for focusing company attention on increasing the number of actively delighted customers, as well as reducing the number of distinctly unhappy customers.

On-Time Delivery Percentage

The first component of customer service is the ability to ship goods to customers by the requested date and time. Customers may even request that goods not be shipped early, which leaves a company with a relatively narrow time slot in which to make a delivery. If a delivery is not made in a timely manner, then the customer could be seriously inconvenienced, and might even reject a delivery or refuse to pay the full billed amount. Given these issues, it is critical for management to understand how many orders are delivered on time.

The on-time delivery percentage is calculated as a binary result – that is, either a delivery is made within a designated time slot, or it is not. For the measurement, aggregate all on-time deliveries and divide by the total number of deliveries made. The formula is:

$$\frac{\text{Total number of deliveries made within requested time slot}}{\text{Total number of deliveries made}}$$

While this is an excellent measure, be aware of several issues that can arise from its use:

- *Rush delivery fees*. A company may rely too much on expensive overnight delivery services to deliver goods to customers, resulting in an excellent on-time delivery percentage, but no profits. Watch for this issue by examining freight costs in conjunction with the measurement.
- *Rescheduling*. The customer service staff might contact customers and convince them to accept a later delivery date. Doing so might make it look as though delivery dates are still being met, even though the point of the measurement – satisfying customers – is not being met. This issue can be detected by having internal auditors compare initial order dates to revised dates for a selection of customer orders. Also, see the following order cycle time measurement.
- *Buffer time*. The order entry staff may insert a generous buffer into quoted delivery dates, to ensure that orders will be delivered on time. While this can be a reasonable way to manage customer expectations, it might also drive away some customers who require delivery within a shorter period of time than what is being quoted to them.

If it proves to be exceptionally difficult to attain a high on-time delivery percentage for all customers, consider instead using the percentage for only those core customers with which the company does the bulk of its business.

EXAMPLE

The Red Herring Fish Company has been troubled by late deliveries for many months. This is a problem, since the fish must be delivered fresh to the company's restaurant clients around town. If deliveries are even a few hours old, there is a significant risk of rejection. To reduce the extent of this issue, the company president mandates that the on-time delivery percentage be tracked on a daily basis. The initial percentage is only 42%, so the president authorizes the purchase of several additional delivery vans and the installation of a delivery routing system. After a three-month implementation period, the company is routinely making a minimum of 32 deliveries per day on-time out of 35 total customers, which is an on-time delivery percentage of 91%.

At this point, the president is considering the cost-benefit of additional capital purchases in order to overcome the issues delaying the last few deliveries.

Order Cycle Time

We have just noted that an issue with the on-time delivery percentage is that the order processing department could convince customers to delay their requested delivery dates, thereby making it appear as though the company is shipping goods on time. We can measure the propensity to have customers delay their requested delivery dates by tracking the average time required to process an order (the order cycle time). If the on-time delivery percentage goes up while the order cycle time also goes up, this is an indicator that there is not really an improvement in the rate of on-time delivery.

To measure the order cycle time, subtract the original order placement date from the order shipping date, and average this figure for all orders shipped in a period. The formula is:

$$\frac{\text{Sum of (Order shipping date – Original order placement date)}}{\text{Number of orders shipped}}$$

There are two considerations to be aware of when using this measurement, which are:

- *Multi-line orders.* If some line items on an order are shipped and some are not, assume that the entire order has not shipped until the last line item has been shipped.
- *Orders not shipped.* An order that is extremely delayed will not appear in the measurement, which only tracks orders that have been shipped. It may be necessary to track these items separately.

EXAMPLE

The human resources manager of Treasure Trove International has recently advocated the use of a bonus plan that pays employees a percentage of company profits if the on-time delivery percentage can be maintained at a level of at least 95% for the entire year. Strangely enough, the on-time delivery percentage for the company's sales of designer jewelry jump from 65% to 95% almost immediately. Suspecting employee manipulation, she conducts a comparison of the on-time delivery percentage and the order cycle time, creating the following table for the past few months (the new bonus plan went into effect in January):

	December	January	February	March
On-time delivery percentage	65%	92%	95%	97%
Order cycle time	11 days	17 days	18 days	19 days

The table reveals that employees have been persuading customers to adjust their requested delivery dates outward, thereby making it easier for the company to achieve its on-time delivery goal. The human resources manager promptly scraps the bonus plan.

Order Fill Rate

We have just noted the on-time delivery percentage, which is perhaps the most sensitive issue for customers. The second most critical issue, once an order has been received, is whether everything ordered has been delivered. This issue can be monitored by the order fill rate. To calculate the order fill rate, follow these steps:

1. Aggregate all customer orders within the measurement period that were delivered by the requested receipt date *and* for which all order line items were filled.
2. Aggregate all customer orders that were scheduled for delivery within the measurement period.
3. Divide the first item (filled orders) by the second item (total orders).

The formula is:

$$\frac{\text{Orders completely filled and delivered on time}}{\text{Orders scheduled to be delivered}}$$

This measurement is essentially a subset of the on-time delivery percentage, since an order must be on-line *and* completely filled to qualify for inclusion in the numerator. Thus, the order fill rate will always be equal to or less than the result for the on-time delivery percentage.

This percentage is subject to manipulation, especially if it is being used to track employee performance. If so, employees have an incentive to ship substitute items if certain items are not in stock, or to alter the promised delivery date in customer order records. Employees may also be tempted to fill simpler one-item orders first, since it is easier to bolster the results of the measurement by ensuring that these orders are completed, rather than highly-complex, multi-line orders.

EXAMPLE

Smithy Ironworks sells iron garden curios to distributors and direct to individuals. The orders from distributors are massive documents, routinely containing several hundred line items. Orders from individuals usually contain only a single line item. The president is reviewing complaints received from customers, and notes that most of the distributors have issues about the ability of the company to fill orders on a timely basis, resulting in stockout conditions.

The president has a financial analyst develop the order fill rate for different classes of customers, which results in the following measurement:

	Distributors	Individuals
Orders completely filled on time	140	780
Orders scheduled to be delivered	320	800
Order fill rate	44%	98%

The information in the table clearly shows that the warehouse staff is easily filling one-line customer orders, but is struggling with the massive distributor orders. The president decides to launch a major project that focuses on ways to improve order fulfillment rates for large multi-line orders.

Orders Damaged in Transit

A company may think that it has done an excellent job of shipping on time and fulfilling every line item in an order. However, these activities mean little if a customer finds that the goods have been damaged in transit. The result is a flurry of activity to issue a credit to the customer or to deliver a replacement (possibly using an overnight delivery service). The end result is more expense incurred by the seller and an unhappy customer.

To calculate the proportion of orders damaged in transit, divide the number of complaints received regarding damaged goods by the total number of orders shipped. The formula is:

$$\frac{\text{Number of customer complaints regarding damaged goods}}{\text{Total number of orders shipped}}$$

There is generally little time delay between when an order is shipped and when a customer complains about damage, since damage is usually observed as soon as a delivery is opened and inspected. Nonetheless, it is possible that an order recorded at the end of one measurement period will not experience a complaint until the beginning of the next period. To mitigate this issue, use a relatively wide measurement period, such as three months, and adopt it on a rolling basis.

This measurement is only the starting point for a considerable amount of analysis into the reasons for product damage. Here are several possible areas in which damage can occur:

- *Product design.* A product may not have been designed in a sufficiently robust manner to withstand the rigors of transport.
- *Components.* Parts included in a product may be failing, which may require re-sourcing the part with a different supplier.
- *Packaging.* The packaging in which a product is shipped may not provide a sufficient buffer from transport movement.
- *Transport.* The transport company may be handling goods excessively, stacking them inappropriately, or using the wrong form of transport.
- *Receiving.* The handling by the customer's receiving department may be damaging goods before they are opened.

In short, damage in transit has a multitude of causes, and so it can require a prolonged amount of effort to understand and correct problems.

EXAMPLE

Country Figurines produces ceramic, hand-painted figurines from the 1800s era. These figurines are fragile, and require special handling. The company suffers from an inordinately high damage rate for shipped goods. A special task force has concluded that there is nothing wrong with the company's packaging or third-party shippers, and turns its attention to the sole remaining issue that could impact damage – the quality of the production process. The team finds that the temperature at which the glaze on the figurines is fired is inconsistent. A temperature that is 30 degrees or more too high makes the ceramic brittle, rendering it five times more likely to break in transit. After a new temperature control system is installed in the company's firing ovens, the before-and-after results of the damage in transit measurement are as follows:

	Before Temperature Control Fix	After Temperature Control Fix
Damaged goods complaints	360	32
Total orders shipped	4,200	4,450
Proportion of orders damaged in transit	8.6%	0.7%

The temperature control issue has eliminated the bulk of the problem, though there appear to still be some residual issues causing a small number of breakage problems.

Customer Turnover

It is usually much less expensive to retain existing customers than to acquire new ones, so companies typically go to great lengths to retain existing customers. However, this logic is not entirely correct, for some customers order in such low volume or require so much maintenance that a business should be indifferent to their departure. Only the core group of customers that buy in volume or yield significant profits should be encouraged to remain. For this select group, a company should track the customer turnover rate.

To calculate the customer turnover rate, divide the number of customers not having placed orders within a set time period by the total number of customers. The set time period should be an interval judged sufficiently long that a customer is likely not planning to place an order if they have not done so within this time period. The formula is:

$$\frac{\text{Number of core customers} - \text{Number of these customers placing orders}}{\text{Number of core customers}}$$

There are two elements of this measurement that are subject to interpretation. The first issue is which customers to include in the core group being tracked. One possible threshold for this group is to use the 20% of customers that comprise 80% of the company's profits (i.e., pareto analysis). The second issue is the time period within which orders must be placed in order to be considered a current customer. This latter issue could be defined by individual customer, based on their ordering history, or as an average ordering interval with an additional buffer period added.

EXAMPLE

The owners of Ambivalence Corporation sell various potions and brews to self-styled witches around the world. An in-depth customer analysis finds that the company receives 90% of its sales from just 10% of its customers. To ensure that the company retains these customers, the president decides that customer turnover for this key group will be the number one metric followed by the measurement team. Over the past three quarters, the turnover rate has been as follows:

	Quarter 1	Quarter 2	Quarter 3
Customers not ordering	6	9	37
Total core customers	320	314	305
	2%	3%	12%

Further investigation of the sudden decline in the third quarter reveals that all of the lost customers are based in Jamaica, where a new competitor has opened a warehouse and is offering same-day delivery. The management team decides to do the same, and notifies its former customers of an impending plan to deliver within two hours of order placement.

First Contact Resolution

The ultimate goal of the customer service function is to resolve a customer's problems on the first contact between the customer and the company. This means that the customer service staff is allowed to stay on the phone with callers for as long as it takes to resolve an issue, and escalate issues on the spot. Though it may take more time to resolve issues on the first contact, customers are much more satisfied, and the support staff does not have secondary and tertiary callers clogging the queue.

To calculate the first contact resolution, aggregate the number of customer interactions that are resolved on the first contact, and divide by the total number of contacts received from customers. The calculation is:

$$\frac{\text{Number of contacts resolved on initial engagement}}{\text{Total number of customer contacts}}$$

This measurement can be falsely altered by the customer service staff, so it can be useful to occasionally audit calls to see if the number of initial resolutions is being correctly recorded.

EXAMPLE

Milagro Corporation sells an espresso machine for home use. The device is so complicated that many users must call the customer support line and be walked through the process. The initial engagement is considered to be resolved if a customer can produce a cup of espresso by the end of a call. In the most recent month, the first contact resolution rate is as follows:

$$\frac{247 \text{ Initial contacts resolved}}{311 \text{ Total customer contacts}} = 79\% \text{ First contact resolution}$$

This outcome means that 21% of all customers must call back to be walked through the process again. Based on this result, the engineering manager decides to design a simpler product for the next generation of the machine.

There are several variations on the first contact resolution that may be considered. Here are two alternatives:

- *Average resolution time.* This is the amount of operator time required to completely resolve a customer issue. While there should not be a focus on requiring shorter calls, it can be instructive to learn why certain calls require much more time than normal. Investigation of these calls may indicate the need for additional employee training, or perhaps the presence of an unusual customer problem for which the entire support staff should receive training.
- *Incidents resolved in one day.* Some customer issues cannot be resolved in a single phone call. If so, it behooves a company to research and correct these issues as fast as possible, or risk customer disaffection. Thus, if there are a number of calls that cannot be resolved on the first contact, create a second measurement that tracks the resolution speed for the residual items.

One customer service measurement that we have elected not to feature is the average call time, since it is counterproductive to the concept of customer service. The intent of average call time is to reduce the amount of time spent on the phone with customers, in order to reduce labor costs. However, doing so may mean that customers do not feel that their issues have been completely resolved, which may lead to additional calls to the company. Consequently, we suggest downplaying this measurement in favor of the first contact resolution measurement.

Escalation Rate

The most difficult customer contacts are those that cannot be resolved by the customer service staff, requiring special handling. These cases are of particular concern, because they fall outside of the normal training of the customer service staff. These cases could represent outlier issues that will rarely be encountered, but they may also be early contacts concerning major issues that the main customer service staff must be trained to deal with.

To calculate the escalation rate, divide the total number of calls shifted to a second party by the total number of calls received. The formula is:

$$\frac{\text{Number of calls escalated}}{\text{Total number of calls received}}$$

How the escalation rate is handled is of some importance. The management team must sort through the detailed list of escalated contacts to determine which calls are related to rarely-encountered outlier issues, and which are the precursors to major issues. When the latter items are noted, an escalated call becomes a major management focus, not only to correct the underlying issue, but also in regard to public relations activities and customer service staff training.

EXAMPLE

The Crumb Cake Café sells a variety of cakes through its website that are packaged in frozen containers. Most customer service calls involve allegedly wrong items being shipped to customers, with few calls requiring escalation. However, two calls are escalated in May that involve alleged issues with allergic reactions to delivered cakes. The management team decides that there could be a major issue, and authorizes a detailed investigation of the baking process; it appears that a pan lubricant containing peanut oil was mistakenly used for one batch of cakes. The company authorizes an immediate product recall, and issues warnings and an apology through its public relations department.

Caller Abandonment Rate

When customers are calling the support line for a business, a certain percentage of them will abandon the calls if they cannot get in touch with a company representative within a certain period of time. Thus, as the hold time increases, so too does the caller abandonment rate. Abandonment is a more comprehensive measure than average hold time, since it can be mitigated by the types of messages being sent to callers who are on hold (such as the estimated remaining wait time). A high abandonment rate can be avoided through proper staffing of the call center, especially during periods that have historically proven to have high call volumes. Otherwise, customers are more likely to buy from competitors in the future, and may also complain about the company's poor service on social media sites.

To calculate the caller abandonment rate, divide the number of callers in queue that abandon their calls prior to speaking with a company representative (usually obtained from the company's call management system) by the total number of calls to the company's customer service line. The formula is:

$$\frac{\text{Callers abandoning their calls prior to contact with the company}}{\text{Total number of calls received}}$$

The caller abandonment rate may increase as a result of messages sent to waiting callers, informing them of alternative sources of information that may be of use (such as the company's web site). This is clearly a good way to expedite the handling of customers, and yet may worsen the measurement.

EXAMPLE

Thimble Clean sells concentrated detergents. Caller volumes have proven to be extremely difficult to predict, with call volumes spiking at numerous times of the day. Management has elected to staff the customer support function for the average call volume, which routinely results in lengthy wait times and customers abandoning their calls. The current call abandonment rate is 20%. To improve the results, the company includes in a pre-recorded message to callers a web page on which the answers to the most frequently asked questions are noted. Of more importance, the company includes the phone number for a poison control center, which is needed for those callers concerned about their children ingesting detergent. Once these messages are included, the caller abandonment rate actually *increases* to 40%, since many callers find that their questions are being dealt with by the messages.

Incident Volume

A key element of customer satisfaction is the speed with which customers are put in touch with customer representatives. This can be a prolonged period of time if the inbound call center is not properly staffed to handle the maximum number of calls during peak periods. For most businesses, incident volume follows the same historical pattern by time of day and day of the week. Thus, examining a trend line of incident volume is a crucial requirement for obtaining high customer satisfaction levels.

To calculate incident volume, aggregate the number of calls initiated on the company's customer support line. This is not a ratio, but rather a simple aggregation. Do not measure the number of calls answered, since this figure is capped by the number of customer support people on hand.

It can require a lengthy analysis to properly interpret incident volume. For example, there may be an initial spike in calls immediately after a new product is released, after which calls decline. Or, there may be specific events during the year that only occur once, and which cause unusual spikes in demand that are well beyond the usual weekly pattern (such as calls to pizza delivery services during the Super Bowl).

EXAMPLE

Clinician Reps, Inc. is a 24-hour call center service that takes calls on behalf of independent doctors, and schedules appointments based on the severity of the conditions reported by callers. Compensation is by far the largest cost for the company, so there is a strong incentive to manage the staff size. However, the nature of the business is such that calls must be answered as quickly as possible. Consequently, the key metric for the business is incident volume. The manager of the call center reviews incident volume for each hour of the past 24 hours, as well as on a trend line for the past month. Based on the resulting information, she increases the call center staffing based on the following factors:

- Add staff for the period 6 a.m. to 9 a.m. on Mondays, when callers are more likely to want appointments for illnesses or injuries occurring over the weekend.
- Add staff for the 4 p.m. to 6 p.m. time slot during weekdays, for children injured during after-hours school sports events.
- Add staff for the 10 a.m. to 3 p.m. time slot during weekdays, when most industrial accidents occur.

Inbound Caller Retention

In some industries, it is customary to require customers to call the company in order to cancel service. Doing so allows a business one last chance to convince a customer to remain active. Examples of such businesses are anything involving a subscription, a credit card operation, or a utility (such as cell phone coverage or home security monitoring). Given the ability to earn a profit from these types of customers over a long period of time, it is of considerable interest to try to retain them, perhaps with special offers or other discounts. Accordingly, it can be useful to track the number of inbound callers who are persuaded not to cancel service.

To calculate the number of callers who are persuaded not to cancel service, divide the number of initial cancellation requests that were reversed by the number of initial cancellation requests. The formula is:

$$\frac{\text{Number of initial cancellation requests reversed}}{\text{Number of initial cancellation requests}}$$

This measurement should be matched against the reduced profitability associated with offering customers special discounts in order to continue buying from the company. It may turn out that the cost of retaining customers is greater than the profits lost by letting them go.

Another issue with retaining customers is their high propensity to quit again, once the special offer used to retain them has expired. If a customer wants to cancel service immediately after a retention deal expires, it is likely that the company will be continually subjected to this behavior. If so, it may be more profitable for the company over the long term to let these customers go, despite the resulting negative impact on the retention ratio.

EXAMPLE

Fire Alert Corporation sends an alert to the nearest fire station as soon as its detectors find evidence of excessive heat in a residence. The company owns the detectors and offers installation for free, in exchange for a $20/month fee. The company's costs to maintain service are entirely fixed, other than the occasional detector that must be swapped out due to incorrect readings. In short, all of the proceeds from monthly fees drop straight to the company's bottom line.

There is a massive layoff by a major employer in the area serviced by Fire Alert, and the company is inundated with calls from customers, saying that they can no longer afford the service. The company decides to allow free service for six months, in hopes that laid off employees will be able to afford the service again, once they find work with new employers. Since there is no cost associated with these deals, the management team does not believe there is any downside to offering free service.

Customer Opinions

We complete this chapter with a discussion of the less quantitative area of customer opinions. One possible measurement is an estimation of customer satisfaction, while the net promoter score focuses on that subset of customers actively engaged in promotion on behalf of the company.

Customer Satisfaction Ratio

Customers may be asked to complete a satisfaction survey, in which they select a numerical score in regard to several aspects of how they were treated by a seller. These scores tend to be inordinately high or low, and so only give a general view of how customers actually view a company. A more robust measurement is to compare net sales to gross sales; if there are few product returns or requests for sales allowances, this is a good indicator that customers are happy with what they have purchased from the company. The formula is:

$$\frac{\text{Net sales}}{\text{Gross sales}}$$

This measurement is only useful for businesses that sell tangible goods; other measurements will be required for a business that provides services. Also, if a company has an extremely restrictive returns policy, this measure does not work well, since there will be little evidence of sales returns or allowances.

For this type of customer satisfaction ratio to work properly, there must be a separate account in which sales returns and allowances are recorded. If these transactions are instead grouped into the sales account, there will be no way to differentiate between net sales and gross sales.

This ratio is essentially a "back door" approach to discerning customer opinions of a company. For information about specific issues, it is necessary to investigate each individual sales return or allowance transaction, to see why there was a problem. For example, goods may have been damaged in transit, an order was filled improperly, there was a pricing dispute, and so forth.

The result of this measurement is likely to be an apparently high level of customer satisfaction. However, many customers never take action to contact the company about a return or allowance, and instead just decide to buy from a different supplier in the future. This latter group is typically larger than the more vocal group that contacts the company, so even a high apparent satisfaction rate could really represent a much lower level of customer satisfaction.

EXAMPLE

Lowry Locomotion manufactures toy cars and trucks, which it sells exclusively to retail stores. It is difficult to discern customer satisfaction levels, since the retailers stand between the company and its ultimate customers. The company elects to use a net sales to gross sales comparison to estimate customer satisfaction levels. The results for the past four quarters are noted in the following table.

(000s)	Quarter 1	Quarter 2	Quarter 3	Quarter 4
Net sales	$13,500	$14,200	$12,800	$15,100
Gross sales	$13,600	$14,300	$14,500	$15,500
Customer satisfaction ratio	99.2%	99.1%	88.4%	97.3%

Upon further inquiry, the company finds that the reason for the large spike in returns and allowances in the third quarter was a problem with the company's new line of metal sports cars, which broke more easily than expected.

> **Tip:** An alternative way to measure customer satisfaction that avoids surveys is to measure the volume and type of field service calls.

Net Promoter Score

Some products, usually of the consumer variety, are enthusiastically endorsed by customers to friends and family through their social networks. These small clusters of avid customers can play a major role in expanding the sales of a business. Consequently, it is useful to understand what proportion of the total customer base is considered to be actively promoting the company's products. The related measurement is called the net promoter score.

To develop the net promoter score, conduct a survey of customers that only asks them whether they would recommend the company's offerings to others, using a scale of 1 to 10. Only those customers ranking the company as a 9 or 10 on this scale are considered to be promoters. Anyone scoring the company in the range of 1 to 6 are considered to be people who might actively persuade others *not* to buy from the company. Anyone submitting a score of 7 or 8 is considered to be satisfied with the company, but is not likely to go out of their way to promote the company. Next, divide the number of customers scoring either 9 or 10 by the group that scored the company in the range of 1 to 6. The calculation is:

$$\frac{\text{Customers scoring 9 or 10 on survey}}{\text{Customers scoring 1 through 6 on survey}}$$

A company can improve the score either by increasing the number of promoters or decreasing the number of detractors. In many cases, the amount of negative publicity can outweigh the amount of positive publicity, so it can make more sense to address the needs of those scoring the lowest before working on the development of a core group of delighted customers.

As noted earlier, the net promoter score is only useful for certain types of goods, such as consumer electronics. However, it may be possible to provide outstanding service for more pedestrian products. For example (and keeping with the pedestrian theme), a company selling paving stones could focus on outstanding delivery and installation service that might garner the company (rather than its products) outstanding net promoter scores.

EXAMPLE

Treadway Corporation has sold paving stones in bulk for many years, and has managed to not create a distinct market position during that time. The next generation of the owner's family takes over, and wants to create a distinctive image for the company that will allow it to increase recognition among customers and thereby generate a high net promoter score. An initial measurement reveals that the entire customer base is completely indifferent, and would not detract from or recommend the company to anyone.

The new management team decides to create an installation service that specializes in designing paving stone layouts for home patios, as well as conducting the actual installation. The before-and-after net promoter score is as follows:

	Before New Installation Service	After New Installation Service
Customers scoring 9 or 10	0	16
Customers scoring 1 through 6	0	4
Net promoter score	0	4:1

The scoring reveals a growing number of enthusiastic customers, but some detractors are also appearing, probably due to improper installations. The management team focuses on more installation training to eliminate the lower scores.

Summary

This chapter has only addressed those factors most commonly associated with customer satisfaction, which are the timely and complete delivery of goods, as well as the ability to respond to direct customer contacts. In reality, there are several other issues that can impact customer satisfaction. Product quality and the ability of its design to meet customer expectations are crucial, as well as after-market servicing, instruction manuals, and the price charged. These issues are tangentially addressed in other chapters, particular the Product Design and Pricing chapters.

Chapter 12
Facility Measurements

Introduction

The cost of the facilities in which a business operates is typically among the largest expenditures incurred, and so is worthy of a detailed review. Management should have a complete understanding of the cost of company facilities, and how well those facilities are being utilized. Accordingly, we address a number of measures of facility cost and usage.

Overview of Facility Measurements

One focus in this chapter is on the cost of facilities. There are two ways in which facility costs can be measured, both of which are comparative in nature. One choice is to measure cost per square foot, which is the classic measurement when space is being leased. Another option is to compare total occupancy cost to sales, which can apply to owned or leased facilities. Both measurements can be used to compare facility costs to those of competitors or nearby companies.

Our other focus is on the usage of facilities. There are a number of ways to measure usage. A common choice is square feet per person, which works well in an employee-intensive environment, such as an office building. This measure can be refined to focus on the percentage of storage in high-cost locations, which can be used to shift stored items to less-expensive facilities.

If a company's facilities are mostly related to production, then the floor space utilization measurement could be a better choice than square feet per person. If there is a warehouse facility, then the measurement should instead focus on the cubic volume of space utilized, the percentage of storage bins utilized, and the honeycombing percentage.

It may not be necessary to use all of the measurements noted in this chapter, but a selection of them will focus management's attention on a major expense category.

Cost per Square Foot

An excellent way to measure the cost of any facility is to aggregate all rent, maintenance, and utility costs for it and then divide by the square footage of the facility to derive the cost per square foot. This information can be used to compare the cost of the facility to alternative forms of housing elsewhere in the area. The result may be a switch to a facility with a lower aggregate cost per square foot.

This measurement does not track the usage level of a facility, only its total cost. Thus, even an inexpensive facility could be shut down if its usage level is minimal.

EXAMPLE

Kelvin Corporation's CFO is reviewing information regarding the possible lease of replacement office space for the company. The company's current facility contains 20,000 square feet, and the company pays its share of utility and maintenance costs, as well as for the rental of parking spaces for employees. The proposed replacement facility contains 25,000 square feet and has the same cost sharing arrangement, except that parking is free. The relevant information is noted in the following table:

	Current Facility	Proposed Facility
Square footage	20,000	25,000
Total rent	$340,000	$400,000
Utilities and maintenance cost	52,000	60,000
Parking fees	28,000	0
Total cost	$420,000	$460,000
Cost per square foot	$21.00	$18.40

Based on the total cost of these facilities, it initially appears that the company should retain the current facility. However, the lower cost per square foot of the larger facility could make it more attractive if the company expects to add staff during the lease term, or can sublease the excess space.

This measurement does not factor in the duration of a lease agreement, which could be a critical issue. For example, if there is a choice between a long-term lease at a very low rate per square foot and a short-term lease at a much higher rate, it may still make sense to enter into the short-term lease, to give the company the option in the near term to shift its operations elsewhere.

Occupancy Cost Ratio

The cost of company facilities is one of the higher expenditures made, usually in third place after the cost of goods sold and compensation costs. Given its size, it makes sense to track occupancy cost as a percentage of net sales, and see if this percentage is reasonable in comparison to the same measurement for competitors and nearby companies.

To calculate occupancy cost, aggregate all costs of a facility, such as rent (or depreciation, if the business owns a facility), maintenance, insurance, real estate taxes, and utilities, and divide by net sales. The formula is:

$$\frac{\text{Rent expense} + \text{Depreciation} + \text{Utilities} + \text{Maintenance} + \text{Insurance} + \text{Real estate taxes}}{\text{Net sales}}$$

There is no ideal occupancy cost ratio. A company may have an inordinately high ratio, but chooses to incur this expense because its target pool of employees is located within a major metropolitan area, or because the facility must be located next to a key customer. Conversely, a company's strategic vision might require that the occupancy cost be as low as possible, irrespective of whether qualified employees live nearby, and so a facility is located in a rural area.

EXAMPLE

Big Data Corporation builds and leases out enormous server farms. The key cost of these farms is the availability of cheap electricity, so all of the company's locations are situated near hydroelectric or geothermal generating stations, usually deep in the countryside. In this case, utilities are the key element of the occupancy cost ratio.

Big Apple Produce sells its organic food products to restaurants in the New York City area. Because of high property taxes, Big Apple's facilities are always located just outside of the property lines of the incorporated areas near New York.

The Twister Vacuum Company elects to move to Arizona from its current location near Oklahoma City. The reason is the insurance component of the company's occupancy cost. The weather damage insurance associated with being located in Tornado Alley in Oklahoma is too much for the company, so moving to the more benign environment in Arizona allows the company to reduce its occupancy cost.

Square Feet per Person

The measurement of square feet per person places an emphasis on arranging a work space to maximize space utilization, especially during the initial layout phase for a facility. Likely outcomes of using this measurement are shifting storage space offsite, increased use of cubicles, and the reduction of "dead space" that serves no useful purpose. The following issues can impact the measurement:

- *Hoteling.* If a company transitions some staff to common-usage areas that they are assigned upon arrival, there is an open question regarding how to incorporate what may be quite a large number of hoteling employees into the calculation.
- *Part time staff.* A part-time staff person still fills a cubicle, so unless several people are using the same office space in sequence, it is probably best to consider a part-time person a full-time employee for the purposes of calculating square feet per person.
- *Work at home part time.* Many employees work from home for a portion of the week, but still retain their office space. If so, continue to count anyone as a full-time, on-site employee if he or she retains exclusive use of a work space.

Based on these issues, we suggest the following measurement for square feet per person:

$$\frac{\text{Total facility square footage} - \text{Hoteling square footage}}{\text{Total number of employees} - \text{Hoteling employees}}$$

In essence, that portion of the facility used for hoteling is stripped away from the calculation, leaving only the portion of the facility that is regularly used by non-hoteling employees.

EXAMPLE

New Centurion Corporation translates Latin texts for its university clients. There is an on-site staff of translators that work primarily from cubicles, while a number of visiting scholars are assigned space in a common area under a hoteling arrangement. There are also part-time translators that are assigned their own office space on a permanent basis. Management wants to understand the space utilization of the facility, and so compiles the following information:

Total square footage	20,000
Square footage of hoteling common area	5,000
Number of on-site full-time staff	38
Number of on-site part-time staff	12

Based on this information, square feet per person is calculated as:

$$\frac{20,000 \text{ Total square footage} - 5,000 \text{ Hoteling square footage}}{38 \text{ Full-time staff} + 12 \text{ Part-time staff}}$$

$$= 300 \text{ Square feet per person}$$

This measurement is most useful in an employee-intensive environment, and much less so where most of the square footage is taken up by retail, production, training, or storage space.

Percent of Storage in High-Cost Locations

The most expensive facility space is invariably used by office staff, such as corporate and administrative personnel. The cost per square foot for production and warehousing space is typically lower, because it is located in a lower-rent area, and may be a more simple structure on a concrete slab, and which is not air conditioned. Given the higher cost of office square footage, it is not economical to set aside much of this space for storage purposes. However, many offices are extremely cluttered with files and other items that could be shifted to a lower-cost facility.

The percent of storage in high-cost locations highlights the amount of space that could be eliminated or put to other uses if stored items are moved. To calculate this ratio, divide the number of square feet set aside for storage by the total number of square feet of office space. The formula is:

$$\frac{\text{Number of square feet set aside for storage}}{\text{Total number of square feet of office space}}$$

Active use of this measurement should result in a reduced retention of files on-site, along with an archiving program that shifts all other files to an off-site (and lower cost) location. It may also trigger the use of a document imaging system that eliminates the need for on-site paper documents.

EXAMPLE

The CFO of Tsunami Products notes a wide disparity between the rental rate for the company's corporate headquarters, at $35 per square foot, and the $5 rate for its production facility. The company has 20,000 square feet in its corporate headquarters, of which 8,000 is taken up by a file storage area for product designs and accounting records. Since storage constitutes 40% of the total office space, the CFO decides to institute an off-site storage program; doing so will open up space for an upcoming hiring campaign intended to bolster the corporate staff.

Floor Space Utilization

The traditional layout of a production facility uses a great deal of space, since production lines tend to be long and straight, with lots of space nearby for the materials handling staff to move with their forklifts and deposit stacks of inventory near operator workstations. This is not an efficient use of space, since a more compressed environment can eliminate the need for buffer inventory that would otherwise pile up next to work stations. Also, production lines are more effective when set up in a serpentine configuration, since people working on the line can more easily communicate with each other. For these reasons, a high degree of floor space utilization is to be encouraged.

To calculate floor space utilization, measure the footprint of existing equipment, as well as the space required by machine operators, the storage of inventory next to the equipment, and the travel lanes needed by the materials handling staff. Then divide this aggregate square footage used by the total square footage of the facility. The formula is:

$$\frac{\text{Square footage required for machinery, personnel, inventory, and transport}}{\text{Total square footage}}$$

If this measurement is used as the basis for a reduction in square footage used, be aware that there is likely to be an optimal layout that will still require a certain amount of space. Any layout that uses an even more compressed footprint may have safety issues, or not involve the best materials flow. Also, the cost of reconfiguration can be substantial, especially if a company has invested in very large machinery that cannot be easily moved; in these situations, it may not be cost-effective to pursue the compression of floor space used.

EXAMPLE

The management of Hodgson Industrial Design is interested in combining facilities for its aerospace widget manufacturing operations, which currently occupy an aggregate total of 25,000 square feet of production space in two buildings. By centralizing in a single building, the company can sell off the other building. A consultant who specializes in manufacturing cells is brought in to examine the current layout, and issues the following report:

	Two Facility Layout (sq. ft.)	One Facility Layout (sq. ft.)
Machinery footprint	4,500	4,500
Operator working space	1,750	1,500
Inventory storage	4,000	500
Materials handling travel lanes	14,000	2,000
Total space required	24,250	8,500

The analysis reveals that a more compressed layout is possible that will allow the company to eliminate one of its production facilities. However, the compression can only be accomplished if the traditional materials handling system is eliminated, in favor of conveyor belts that move parts from one machine to the next. Management must consider the cost of the reconfiguration and the investment in conveyor belts when deciding whether to eliminate a building.

Cubic Volume Utilization

The warehouse is the only location in a business where storage space can go up into the rafters, rather than being used on a single level. In this area, it makes sense to maximize the entire cubic volume of the storage space, which may call for the use of multi-level storage racks.

To calculate the utilization of cubic warehouse volume, determine the cubic volume of the storage systems currently in use, and divide by the entire cubic volume of the warehouse. The formula is:

$$\frac{\text{Cubic volume of storage racks}}{\text{Cubic volume of warehouse area}}$$

There are some issues with forcing too much storage space into a warehouse. Consider the following issues:

- Storage racks may be so high that they are unstable when fully loaded.
- Aisles must have sufficient space for forklifts and other materials handling equipment to safely navigate without running into the storage racks.
- Overhead sprinkler systems may limit the extent to which rack height can be increased.

In short, there will be an optimum usage percentage that is notably less than the actual cubic volume of available warehouse space, due to the restrictions imposed by safety issues, travel lanes, and building obstructions.

EXAMPLE

The Terminal Cow Company runs a slaughterhouse, and stores the resulting cuts of beef in a nearby deep-freeze warehouse. The plant manager wants to take advantage of the full cubic space afforded by the storage facility, and so commissions a study of how to maximize the space. The resulting report contains the following points:

Current space usage	62%
Required for travel lanes	18%
Required for refrigeration units	6%
Required for building supports	4%
Residual space available	10%
Total cubic volume	100%

The analysis reveals that the facility is quite well utilized already, with only 10% of the space available for the installation of additional storage racks.

Percentage of Storage Bins Utilized

A company may do an excellent job of setting up racking systems within a warehouse, and yet not maximize the use of those racks. For example, the materials handling staff may not want to use the uppermost bins, or those located furthest from the receiving docks. If so, this represents space that could be more fully utilized, and is a concern if the warehouse manager is instead paying for third party storage or storage in trailers. The measure is also useful for budgeting purposes, since the materials manager can use it to estimate when the warehouse will be completely filled, based on budgeted sales volumes and production rates. Management can then estimate when to purchase or rent additional warehouse space.

To calculate the percentage of storage bins utilized, count the number of bins currently in use (this may be available through a report generated by the warehouse management system), and divide by the total number of bins. The formula is:

$$\frac{\text{Number of storage bins in use}}{\text{Total number of storage bins}}$$

The measure is somewhat flawed, in that storage bins may vary greatly in size, where some can accept fully-loaded pallets, and others are essentially drawers in storage cabinets. If this is the case, consider using one measurement for large-size bins and another measurement for all other sizes. Another issue is that some bins may only be partially filled, and so can still accept additional inventory.

EXAMPLE

Mole Industries requires a large amount of storage space for the raw materials needed to construct its ditch digging and tunneling products. The CFO is trying to estimate when the company will need to construct an extension to the warehouse. Currently, 80% of all storage bins are being utilized, leaving 500 bins still open. The marketing manager is pushing for an entirely new product line of digging machines that are targeted at the retail market, and which would be rented from local home supply stores. These machines will require the storage of 300 additional stock keeping units of various kinds, which will leave only 200 unused bins. The remaining bins will likely be required to store the finished goods related to this product line.

Based on the addition of the new product line, the CFO begins to make arrangements for a small amount of rented storage space to be used for overflow situations.

Honeycombing Percentage

Honeycombing is the amount of space in a warehouse that is not being properly utilized. It can be triggered by a variety of issues, including the following:

- Assigning a specific rack location to goods, but not having any goods to store in that location.
- Creating a long stacking lane but having insufficient pallets to fill the lane.
- Putting just one pallet in a double-deep storage rack.
- Incorrectly storing cases, so there is not sufficient room to store adjacent cases.

There are two ways to calculate the amount of honeycombing, either as a proportion of storage locations or as a percentage of cubic warehouse storage space. The calculation of the first method is as follows:

Empty storage locations ÷ Total storage locations = Honeycombing percentage

This calculation is imperfect, for it does not account for those storage locations that are partially filled, assumes a single stacking lane is one storage location (despite its considerable size), and also assumes that all storage locations have roughly the same footprint. Nonetheless, it is easily calculated from a warehouse report of storage bin locations, or simply by walking through the warehouse and counting empty storage locations.

The more accurate honeycombing measurement is to track the percentage of unused cubic warehouse storage space. This approach requires that you divide the warehouse into locations of varying sizes, and then estimate the cubic volume of each location size. The cubic volume of empty spaces can then be calculated and compared to the total volume of storage spaces. The calculation is:

Cubic volume of empty storage locations ÷ Cubic volume of total storage locations

= Honeycombing percentage

The second calculation is still not perfect, for it does not account for partially-filled storage locations. This issue can be corrected by conducting a manual walk-through of the warehouse and adjusting the calculation for these partially-filled locations, but doing so is quite labor intensive.

EXAMPLE

Entwhistle Electric operates a warehouse for its battery manufacturing facility, which houses raw materials for battery construction, as well as finished goods for a variety of cell phone battery products. It is becoming increasingly difficult to putaway goods in the warehouse, so the warehouse manager wants to determine the effects of honeycombing to see if additional storage space can be found. He accumulates the following information about the storage locations in the facility:

Location Type	Number of Locations	Cubic Feet per Location	Total Cubic Feet	Empty Locations	Empty Cubic Feet
Pallet storage	600	100	60,000	80	8,000
Case storage	350	50	17,500	50	2,500
Broken case storage	150	40	6,000	20	800
	1,000		83,500	150	11,300

The warehouse manager first calculates honeycombing based just on the number of empty locations, which yields the following result:

150 Empty locations ÷ 1,000 total locations = 15.0% Honeycombing

The warehouse manager then runs the calculation based on cubic feet of storage space, with the following result:

11,300 Empty cubic feet ÷ 83,500 Total cubic feet = 13.5% Honeycombing

Summary

When using measurements to judge facilities, it is useful to keep in mind the alternative uses to which excess space can be put. In some situations, it is possible to sublease space that is made available through the concentration of existing operations. In other cases, subleasing is not an option. Thus, facility measurements may indicate that space is being poorly used, but the presence of a long-term lease liability and the absence of alternative uses may mean that a business has no ability to reduce its costs in this area. Even if this is the case, the measurements described in this chapter should still be followed, so that management understands the real usage requirements of the business when it is time to search for new facilities.

Chapter 13
Financing Measurements

Introduction

A company may have an interest in obtaining debt to fund its operations or pay for asset purchases or acquisitions. If so, there are a number of measurements available that can be used to estimate the amount of debt that a company can safely take on. In this chapter, we focus primarily on the ability of a borrower to repay its debts, with some additional attention to measures of risk, debt usage levels, and the cost of debt.

Overview of Financing Measurements

Debt is usually the lowest-cost form of funding that a business can obtain, so there is a natural interest in using debt funding when a business needs additional cash. However, there is a limit to the amount of debt that a business can safely take on. Above that level, the fixed cost of interest expense, as well as the obligation to pay back debt, makes it increasingly risky to commit to more debt. From the perspective of the borrower, it is useful to examine the Ability to Pay measurements noted in this chapter, particularly in regard to the variability of earnings. If a business is subject to seasonal or cyclical variations in earnings, then the ability to pay for debt should be based on one of the following concepts:

- The worst-case cash flows of the business at the bottom of the business or seasonal cycle; or
- Variable debt levels that are paid off during periods when the company is flush with cash, in preparation for an expected decline in cash flows.

The first of these variations is recommended for modeling the correct level of debt to take on, for the second variation can be quite difficult to predict. A company may maintain a high debt load too far into a business cycle, and then see its cash flows decline precipitously before it has a chance to pay off the debt.

A lender will look at the same ratios, but will also consider the proportion of debt to equity, to see if the owners of a business have contributed a sufficient amount of funds to the business. If not, a lender may curtail additional lending until such time as a borrower can obtain additional equity financing.

Debt to Equity Ratio

The debt to equity ratio of a business is closely monitored by the lenders and creditors of the company, since it can provide early warning that an organization is so overwhelmed by debt that it is unable to meet its payment obligations. This may also be triggered by a funding issue. For example, the owners of a business may not want to contribute any more cash to the company, so they acquire more debt to address the cash shortfall. Or, a company may use debt to buy back shares, thereby increasing the return on investment to the remaining shareholders.

Whatever the reason for debt usage, the outcome can be catastrophic, if corporate cash flows are not sufficient to make ongoing debt payments. This is a concern to lenders, whose loans may not be paid back. Suppliers are also concerned about the ratio for the same reason. A lender can protect its interests by imposing collateral requirements or restrictive covenants; suppliers usually offer credit with less restrictive terms, and so can suffer more if a company is unable to meet its payment obligations to them.

To calculate the debt to equity ratio, simply divide total debt by total equity. In this calculation, the debt figure should also include all lease obligations. The formula is:

$$\frac{\text{Long-term debt} + \text{Short-term debt} + \text{Leases}}{\text{Equity}}$$

EXAMPLE

An analyst is reviewing the credit application of New Centurion Corporation. The company reports a $500,000 line of credit, $1,700,000 in long-term debt, and a $200,000 operating lease. The company has $800,000 of equity. Based on this information, New Centurion's debt to equity ratio is:

$$\frac{\$500,000 \text{ Line of credit} + \$1,700,000 \text{ Debt} + \$200,000 \text{ Lease}}{\$800,000 \text{ Equity}}$$

$$= 3:1 \text{ debt to equity ratio}$$

The debt to equity ratio exceeds the 2:1 ratio threshold above which the analyst is not allowed to grant credit. Consequently, New Centurion is kept on cash in advance payment terms.

Supplier Financing of Assets

It can be quite a struggle for a business to obtain debt financing, in which case it should make an effort to extract as much financing as possible from its suppliers in the form of trade credit. In some cases where the supply of cash is extremely tight, the managers of a firm may shift their purchases to those suppliers most willing to provide it with longer-term financing. By doing so, they are gaining interest-free lines of credit from their suppliers.

The supplier financing of assets measurement can be used to determine the success of these efforts. This measurement is derived by dividing accounts payable by total assets and then multiplying the result by 100. The calculation is:

$$\frac{\text{Accounts payable}}{\text{Total assets}} \quad \times \quad 100$$

A smaller company with poor financing prospects may consider its supplier financing arrangements to be absolutely essential, and so will take great care to only grow if it can obtain sufficient supplier financing to do so.

EXAMPLE

Ruff'n Tumble makes boat shoes for fishermen. It has no access to a traditional line of credit, and so bases its expansion decisions on the willingness of its leather and sole suppliers to provide it with credit. Over the past year, the company has averaged total assets of $3.6 million and accounts payable of $1.2 million. This results in the following measure of supplier financing of assets:

$$\frac{\$1,200,000 \text{ Accounts payable}}{\$3,600,000 \text{ Total assets}} \quad \times \quad 100 \quad = 33\%$$

The company has received an order for an additional $600,000 of sales from an overseas distributor. Accepting the order will cause an increase of $400,000 in its assets. Since the company is currently unable to obtain any additional financing from its suppliers, the outcome of the sale would be the following change in the measurement:

$$\frac{\$1,200,000 \text{ Accounts payable}}{\$4,000,000 \text{ Total assets}} \quad \times \quad 100 \quad = 30\%$$

Since accepting the order will result in a 9% drop in the proportion of supplier financing of assets, the company's managers decide to turn down the offer.

Ability to Pay Measurements

When estimating the correct amount of debt burden to maintain, it is useful to measure the ability of a business to pay its fixed costs, which include interest expenses. The following four measurements can be employed, beginning with the narrowly-focused interest coverage ratio, and then expanding the focus of the measurement in the debt service coverage ratio to include principal, and to other fixed costs in the fixed charge coverage ratio. Also, the cash coverage ratio looks at the ability to pay from the perspective of available cash, rather than earnings as reported under the accrual basis of accounting.

Interest Coverage Ratio

The interest coverage ratio measures the ability of a company to pay the interest on its outstanding debt. A high interest coverage ratio indicates that a business can pay for its interest expense several times over, while a low ratio is a strong indicator that an organization may default on its loan payments.

It is useful to track the interest coverage ratio on a trend line, in order to spot situations where a company's results or debt burden are yielding a downward trend in the ratio. An investor would want to sell the equity holdings in a company showing such a downward trend, especially if the ratio drops below 1.5:1, since this indicates a likely problem with meeting debt obligations.

To calculate the interest coverage ratio, divide earnings before interest and taxes (EBIT) by the interest expense for the measurement period. The formula is:

$$\frac{\text{Earnings before interest and taxes}}{\text{Interest expense}}$$

EXAMPLE

Carpenter Holdings generates $5,000,000 of earnings before interest and taxes in its most recent reporting period. Its interest expense in that period is $2,500,000. Therefore, the company's interest coverage ratio is calculated as:

$$\frac{\$5,000,000 \text{ EBIT}}{\$2,500,000 \text{ Interest expense}}$$

$$= 2:1 \text{ Interest coverage ratio}$$

The ratio indicates that Carpenter's earnings should be sufficient to enable it to pay the interest expense.

A company may be accruing an interest expense that is not actually due for payment yet, so the ratio can indicate a debt default that will not really occur, or at least until such time as the interest is due for payment.

Debt Service Coverage Ratio

The debt service coverage ratio measures the ability of a revenue-producing property to generate sufficient cash to pay for the cost of all related mortgage payments. A positive debt service ratio indicates that a property's cash outflows can cover all offsetting loan payments, whereas a negative ratio indicates that the owner must contribute additional funds to pay for the annual loan payments. A very high debt service coverage ratio gives the property owner a substantial cushion to pay for unexpected or unplanned expenditures related to the property, or if market conditions result in a significant decline in future rental rates.

To calculate the ratio, divide the net annual operating income of the property by all annual loan payments for the same property, net of any tax savings generated by the interest expense. The formula is:

$$\frac{\text{Net annual operating income}}{\text{Total of annual loan payments net of tax effect}}$$

There may be no tax effect associated with debt, if a company has no taxable income. Otherwise, the tax effect is based on the income tax rate expected for the year.

EXAMPLE

A rental property generates $400,000 of cash flow per year, and the total annual loan payments of the property are $360,000. This yields a debt service ratio of 1.11, meaning that the property generates 11% more cash than the property owner needs to pay for the annual loan payments.

A negative debt service coverage ratio may result when a property is transitioning to new tenants, so that it is generating sufficient cash by the end of the measurement period, but was not doing so during the beginning or middle of the measurement period. Thus, the metric can yield inaccurate results during transition periods.

Fixed Charge Coverage Ratio

A business may incur so many fixed costs that its cash flow is mostly consumed by payments for these costs. The problem is particularly common when a company has incurred a large amount of debt, and must make ongoing interest payments. In this situation, use the fixed charge coverage ratio to determine the extent of the problem. If the resulting ratio is low, it is a strong indicator that any subsequent drop in the profits of a business may bring about its failure.

To calculate the fixed charge coverage ratio, combine earnings before interest and taxes with any lease expense, and then divide by the combined total of interest expense and lease expense. This ratio is intended to show estimated future results, so it is acceptable to drop from the calculation any expenses that are about to expire. The formula is:

$$\frac{\text{Earnings before interest and taxes} + \text{Lease expense}}{\text{Interest expense} + \text{Lease expense}}$$

EXAMPLE

Luminescence Corporation recorded earnings before interest and taxes of $800,000 in the preceding year. The company also recorded $200,000 of lease expense and $50,000 of interest expense. Based on this information, its fixed charge coverage is:

$$\frac{\$800,000 \text{ EBIT} + \$200,000 \text{ Lease expense}}{\$50,000 \text{ Interest expense} + \$200,000 \text{ Lease expense}}$$

$$= 4{:}1 \text{ Fixed charge coverage ratio}$$

Cash Coverage Ratio

The cash coverage ratio is useful for determining the amount of cash available to pay for interest, and is expressed as a ratio of the cash available to the amount of interest to be paid. This is a useful ratio when the entity evaluating a company is a prospective lender. The ratio should be substantially greater than 1:1. To calculate this ratio, take the earnings before interest and taxes (EBIT) from the income statement, add back to it all non-cash expenses included in EBIT (such as depreciation and amortization), and divide by the interest expense. The formula is:

$$\frac{\text{Earnings before interest and taxes} + \text{Non-cash expenses}}{\text{Interest expense}}$$

There may be a number of additional non-cash items to subtract in the numerator of the formula. For example, there may have been substantial charges in a period to increase reserves for sales allowances, product returns, bad debts, or inventory obsolescence. If these non-cash items are substantial, be sure to include them in the calculation. Also, the interest expense in the denominator should only include the actual interest expense to be paid – if there is a premium or discount to the amount being paid, it is not a cash payment, and so should not be included in the denominator.

EXAMPLE

The controller of Currency Bank is concerned that a borrower has recently taken on a great deal of debt to pay for a leveraged buyout, and wants to ensure that there is sufficient cash to pay for its new interest burden. The borrower is generating earnings before interest and taxes of $1,200,000 and it records annual depreciation of $800,000. The borrower is scheduled to pay $1,500,000 in interest expenses in the coming year. Based on this information, the borrower has the following cash coverage ratio:

$$\frac{\$1,200,000 \text{ EBIT} + \$800,000 \text{ Depreciation}}{\$1,500,000 \text{ Interest expense}}$$

$$= 1.33 \text{ Cash coverage ratio}$$

The calculation reveals that the borrower can pay for its interest expense, but has very little cash left for any other payments.

Average Cost of Debt

A company that uses a large amount of debt financing may not be aware of the average cost of the debt load that it has incurred. If so, consider deriving the average cost of debt, which could lead to an investigation of the more expensive tranches of debt, and possibly their payoff or refinancing with less-expensive types of debt.

The calculation of the average cost of debt should encompass all types of debt, which includes the costs of bonds, bank loans, and capital leases. The calculation is:

$$\frac{\text{Annual cost of interest on loans, bonds, and capital leases}}{\text{Average amount of bonds, loans, and leases outstanding}}$$

It may be easier to calculate the average cost of debt on a monthly basis, rather than an annual basis, if the amount of debt varies considerably over the one-year measurement period.

There are several issues with the collection of information for the average cost of debt, which are:

- *Lease rate.* It can be difficult to determine the interest rate contained within a lease. If the amount of a lease is quite small, its inclusion in the average cost of debt may be immaterial, and so it can be excluded. Otherwise, contact the lessor to obtain the rate.
- *Bond rate.* The effective interest rate should be used as the interest rate for a bond, rather than the stated interest rate. When a bond is sold for an amount other than its face amount, this means the associated interest rate varies from the stated interest rate. For example, if a company sells a bond for $95,000 that has a face amount of $100,000 and which pays interest of $5,000, then the effective interest rate being paid is $5,000 ÷ $95,000, or 5.26%. Thus, if a company sells a bond at a discount from its face value, the effective interest

162

rate is *higher* than the stated interest rate. If the company sells a bond at a premium from its face value, the effective interest rate is *lower* than the stated interest rate.

- *Other expenses.* There may be several additional expenses associated with debt, such as an annual audit required by the lender, and an annual loan maintenance fee. If these expenses would not be incurred in the absence of the debt, include them in the interest cost of the debt.

The interest rate paid does not reveal a complete picture of the borrowing instruments employed by a business. There may be restrictive covenants or conversion clauses built into these instruments that are of more importance than the interest rates being paid. For example, a covenant not to pay dividends could be of concern to a family-held business, while a conversion clause could allow debt holders to convert their debt to equity at extremely favorable rates.

EXAMPLE

Puller Corporation, maker of plastic and wooden doorknobs, has acquired a considerable amount of debt while acquiring competitors that make other door fittings. The CEO is concerned about the cost of this debt, and asks for a derivation of the average cost. The resulting report contains the following information:

	Annual Interest Cost	Principal Outstanding	Interest Rate	Other Features
Factory lease	$280,000	$2,300,000	12.1%	No early payment clause
Senior bank loan	1,200,000	15,000,000	8.0%	Balloon due in 24 months
Junior bank loan	975,000	6,500,000	15.0%	Risk of acceleration
Bonds	1,680,000	24,000,000	7.0%	Convertible into common stock
	$4,135,000	$47,800,000		

Based on the table, Puller's average cost of debt is:

$$\frac{\$4,135,000 \text{ Annual interest cost}}{\$47,800,000 \text{ Principal outstanding}}$$

$$= 8.65\%$$

Overall, the interest rate being paid by Puller is acceptable. However, the interest rate on the junior bank loan is quite high, since the lender is unlikely to have access to the company's assets in the event of a default. There are also covenants associated with this loan that Puller could breach, resulting in loan acceleration. Consequently, the junior bank loan is clearly the loan to be paid off or refinanced, if the opportunity to do so is available.

Borrowing Base Usage

If a company does not have large cash reserves, it must rely upon a line of credit to provide it with sufficient cash to keep the company operational. Lenders almost always insist upon using a company's accounts receivable and inventory as the collateral basis (or *borrowing base*) for a line of credit. The amount loaned to a company under a line of credit agreement cannot exceed the borrowing base. Consequently, a critical financing metric to follow is borrowing base usage. This is the amount of debt that has been loaned against the collateral provided by a company.

EXAMPLE

A business has $1,000,000 of accounts receivable and $600,000 of inventory on hand. Its lender will allow a line of credit that is based on 75% of all accounts receivable less than 90 days old, and 50% of inventory. $20,000 of the accounts receivable are more than 90 days old. This means that the applicable borrowing base for the company is:

Applicable Assets		Discount Rate		Allowable Borrowing Base
Accounts receivable of $980,000	×	75%	=	$735,000
Inventory of $600,000	×	50%	=	300,000
		Total	=	$1,035,000

The unused amount of the borrowing base is crucial, since it must be compared to any cash shortfalls projected in the cash forecast to see if a business has sufficient available and unused debt to offset negative cash positions.

Borrowing base usage requires continual analysis, since the amount of receivables and inventory to be used as collateral is constantly changing. This is a particular concern in seasonal businesses, since they tend to build inventory levels prior to the sales season, followed by a build in accounts receivable levels during the sales season, followed by a quiet period when assets are liquidated and debts are paid off. The continual changes in debt needs and asset levels make borrowing base usage perhaps the most important metric for the CFO of a seasonal business.

Summary

A lender or prospective lender is likely to use several measures to quantify the ability of a borrower to repay its debts. The situation is considerably easier for the borrower, which must focus its attention on borrowing base usage and the debt service coverage ratio. These two metrics focus attention on the ability to maximize borrowings and then pay back the debt. In addition to these measurements, the borrower should pay particular attention to the maturity dates of loans and the status of projected cash flows, to see if the business can indeed repay its liabilities. If not, the CFO or treasurer should prepare to roll over loans as far in advance as possible.

Chapter 14
Fixed Asset Measurements

Introduction

Fixed asset measurements are used to obtain a general understanding of the adequacy of a company's investment in fixed assets. Fixed asset ratio analysis is not typically used within a business, since employees instead use detailed asset-specific records to evaluate replacement, usage, and maintenance issues. However, ratios are quite useful for an outsider who is investigating the investment in and usage of fixed assets by a company. With this latter audience in mind, we present several measurements in this chapter that relate to fixed assets.

Overview of Fixed Asset Measurements

An outsider who is reviewing the financial statements of a company can discern a large amount about the efficiency with which a business employs its fixed assets, how frequently those assets are replaced, and the state of the maintenance of that equipment. Asset efficiency can be explored by measuring the proportion of the carrying amount of fixed assets to annualized sales, and especially when this figure is then compared to the same figure for other firms in the same industry. Asset replacement speed can be estimated by comparing the amount of accumulated depreciation to the carrying amount of fixed assets. Finally, equipment maintenance can be tracked by comparing the reported amount of repairs and maintenance expense to the carrying amount of fixed assets. In brief, there are several excellent ratios available that can be used to extract crucial fixed asset information from the financial statements of a business. These and other ratios are enumerated in the following sections.

Sales to Fixed Assets Ratio

It requires a large amount of fixed assets to compete in some industries, such as computer chips and automobiles. The sales to fixed assets ratio can be used to determine how a company's expenditures for fixed assets compare to those of other companies in the same industry, to see if it is operating in a more lean fashion than the others, or if there may be opportunities to scale back on its fixed asset investment. This is quite useful to track on a trend line, which may show gradual changes in expenditure levels away from the historical trend. The ratio is most useful in asset-intensive industries, and least useful where the required asset base is so small that the ratio would be essentially meaningless.

The ratio can also be misleading in cases where a company must invest in an entire production facility before it can generate any sales; this will initially result in an inordinately low sales to fixed assets ratio, which gradually increases as the company maximizes sales for that facility, and then levels out when it reaches a high level of asset utilization.

To calculate the sales to fixed assets ratio, divide net sales for the past twelve months by the book value of all fixed assets. The formula is:

$$\frac{\text{Trailing 12 months' sales}}{\text{Book value of all fixed assets}}$$

The fixed asset book value listed in the denominator is subject to some variation, depending on what type of depreciation method is used. If an accelerated depreciation method is used, the denominator will be unusually small, and so will yield a higher ratio.

EXAMPLE

Mole Industries manufactures trench digging equipment. It has a relatively low sales to fixed assets ratio of 4:1, because a large amount of machining equipment is needed to construct its products. Mole is considering expanding into earth-moving equipment, and calculates the sales to fixed assets ratio for competing companies, based on their financial statements. The ratio is in the vicinity of 3:1 for most competitors, which means that Mole will need to invest heavily in fixed assets in order to enter this new market. Mole estimates that the most likely revenue level it can achieve for earth moving equipment will be $300 million. Based on the 3:1 ratio, this means that Mole may need to invest $100 million in fixed assets in order to achieve its goal.

Mole's CFO concludes that the company does not currently have the financial resources to invest $100 million in the earth moving equipment market, and recommends that the company not enter the field at this time.

Accumulated Depreciation to Fixed Assets Ratio

If a company is not replacing its fixed assets, then the proportion of accumulated depreciation to fixed assets will increase over time. The ratio is quite useful for analyzing prospective acquisitions, since it is an easy way to see if an acquiree is not reinvesting in its business. This information is especially useful when tracked on a trend line, since it shows gradual changes in the ratio that might not otherwise be immediately apparent.

There are several situations where this ratio is not useful. For example, a business may be using accelerated depreciation, which results in a large amount of accumulated depreciation despite having relatively new assets. The ratio can also be problematic if a company is not removing assets and accumulated depreciation from its books as soon as it disposes of them. It is also possible that a company has chosen to switch to leased assets under operating leases, where the fixed assets do not appear on the company's balance sheet. Finally, a company may acquire assets that have very long useful lives (such as hydroelectric facilities), where the gradual accumulation of depreciation is a natural part of the business. Be aware of these situations when deciding whether to use the ratio.

To calculate the accumulated depreciation to fixed assets ratio, divide the total accumulated depreciation by the total amount of fixed assets (before depreciation). The formula is:

$$\frac{\text{Accumulated depreciation}}{\text{Total fixed assets before depreciation deduction}}$$

EXAMPLE

Mole Industries is conducting an investigation of Vertical Drop, a heavy-lift helicopter company that installs cell towers and power poles, with the intent of buying the company. The primary asset of Vertical Drop is its fleet of Sikorsky helicopters, which must be properly maintained and replaced at regular intervals. Mole collects the following information about Vertical Drop's fixed assets:

	20X1	20X2	20X3	20X4
Accumulated depreciation	$4,900,000	$6,000,000	$9,400,000	$10,450,000
Fixed assets	$32,700,000	$33,400,000	$31,350,000	$29,875,000
Accumulated depreciation to fixed assets ratio	15%	18%	30%	35%

The ratio calculation in the table indicates that Vertical Drop essentially stopped purchasing replacement helicopters two years ago, which means that Mole may be faced with large-scale replacements if it buys the company.

Cash Flow to Fixed Asset Requirements Ratio

Does a company have sufficient cash to pay for its upcoming fixed asset purchases? The cash flow to fixed asset requirements ratio is useful both as a general internal analysis of a company's future prospects, and also as a means for determining the health of a possible acquisition. The ratio must be greater than 1:1 for a company to have sufficient cash to fund its fixed asset needs. If the ratio is very close to 1:1, then a company is operating near the edge of its available cash flows, and should consider bolstering its cash position with a line of credit. The ratio is less useful if the company in question has substantial cash reserves, since it can always draw upon these reserves to fund its fixed asset requirements, irrespective of short-term cash flows.

To calculate the cash flow to fixed asset requirements ratio, divide the expected annual cash flow by the total expenditure that has been budgeted for fixed assets for the same period. The cash flow figure in the numerator can be calculated by adding non-cash expenses (such as depreciation and amortization) back to net income, and subtracting out any non-cash sales (such as sales accruals). Also subtract from the numerator any dividends and principal payments on loans. The formula is:

$$\frac{\text{Net income} + \text{Noncash expenses} - \text{Noncash sales} - \text{Dividends} - \text{Principal payments}}{\text{Budgeted fixed asset expenditures}}$$

EXAMPLE

Mole Industries has just compiled the first iteration of its budget for the upcoming year, which reveals the following information:

Budget Line Item	Amount
Net income	$4,100,000
Depreciation and amortization	380,000
Accrued sales	250,000
Dividend payments	100,000
Principal payments	800,000
Budgeted fixed asset expenditures	3,750,000

Based on this information, Mole's controller calculates the ratio of cash flow to fixed asset requirements as:

$$\frac{\$4,100,000 \text{ Net income} + \$380,000 \text{ Depreciation and amortization} - \$250,000 \text{ Accrued sales} - \$100,000 \text{ Dividends} - \$800,000 \text{ Principal payments}}{\$3,750,000 \text{ Budgeted fixed asset expenditures}}$$

$$=$$

$$\frac{\$3,330,000 \text{ Cash flows}}{\$3,750,000 \text{ Budgeted fixed asset expenditures}}$$

$$= 89\%$$

The ratio is less than one, so Mole will either need to draw upon its cash reserves to pay for the fixed assets, cut back on its fixed asset budget, or revise other parts of the budget to increase cash flow.

Repairs and Maintenance Expense to Fixed Assets Ratio

When reviewing the potential acquisition of a product line or entire company, it is useful to review the target company's ratio of repair and maintenance expense to fixed assets, especially on a trend line. If the ratio is increasing over time, there are several ways to interpret it:

- *Old assets.* The acquiree is relying on an aging fixed asset base, since it must spend more to keep them operational. This is the worst-case scenario, since the buyer may be faced with a wholesale replacement of the acquiree's fixed assets.
- *High utilization.* The acquiree is experiencing very high asset usage levels, which calls for higher maintenance costs just to keep the machines running fast enough to meet demand. This condition can be spotted by looking for a high sales to fixed assets ratio (see the prior ratio). A high profit level is also likely.
- *Preparing for sale.* If there is a sudden spike in the ratio in the recent past, it may be because the owner of the acquiree is simply preparing it for sale, and so is either catching up on delayed maintenance or is bringing machinery up to a high standard of performance.
- *Accounting changes.* It is possible that the repairs and maintenance expense has been moved among different accounts, such as from the cost of goods sold account or an overhead cost pool to its own account, which means that there could appear to be a sudden jump in expenses that is not really the case.

This ratio is least useful when the bulk of the repairs and maintenance expense is comprised of salaries paid to a relatively fixed group of repair technicians. In this case, the expense is essentially a fixed cost, and cannot be expected to vary much over time.

A problem that this ratio does *not* reveal is when an acquiree simply lets its machinery decline by not investing in repairs and maintenance; this means that the ratio would remain flat or could even decline over time. In this case, look elsewhere for an indicator, such as declining sales or an inability to meet customer delivery schedules.

To calculate the repairs and maintenance expense to fixed assets ratio, divide the total amount of repairs and maintenance expense by the total amount of fixed assets before depreciation. The amount of accumulated depreciation that may have built up on older assets would otherwise bring the denominator close to zero for some acquirees, so it is better not to use depreciation at all. The formula is:

$$\frac{\text{Total repairs and maintenance expense}}{\text{Total fixed assets before depreciation}}$$

EXAMPLE

Mole Industries is investigating the purchase of Grubstake Brothers, a manufacturer of back-hoes. Its acquisition analysis team uncovers the following information:

	20X1	20X2	20X3	20X4
Sales	$15,000,000	$14,500,000	$13,200,000	$12,900,000
Profit	$1,000,000	$200,000	$(150,000)	$(420,000)
Repairs expense	$400,000	$240,000	$160,000	$80,000
Fixed assets	$5,400,000	$6,000,000	$6,050,000	$6,100,000
Repairs to fixed assets ratio	7%	4%	3%	1%

The information in the table strongly indicates that the decline in Grubstake's profitability over the past few years has led its management to cut back on repair and maintenance expenditures. Thus, if Mole elects to buy Grubstake, it can expect to invest a large amount to replace fixed assets.

Summary

The determination of the adequacy of an investment in fixed assets is a difficult one to make just from ratio analysis. An analyst really needs to examine the capacity level of each machine, its age and maintenance record, and how it relates to the production flow to see if new equipment is needed. Also, the ratios enumerated in this chapter are only as good as the quality of the reported information. For example, if the accounting staff does not remove old assets from the accounting records when the assets are disposed of, the amount of accumulated depreciation reported in the balance sheet will be too high, leading to the false perception that a company's asset base is aging. In short, there are limitations on the use of fixed asset ratios. Nonetheless, the ratios are still useful for forming an overall impression of the fixed asset base used by a business.

Chapter 15
Human Resources Measurements

Introduction

Measurements can be applied not only to the performance of the human resources department in particular, but also to the productivity and cost of employees throughout an organization. In this chapter, we explore a number of measurements that can reveal hiring efficiency, as well as the ability of employees to generate income in a cost-effective manner. The measurements discussed here are particularly relevant in a labor-intensive business where the productivity of employees represents the primary driver of profits.

Overview of Human Resources Measurements

There are several areas in which the human resources function can be measured. The ability to fill job requisitions in a timely manner is the most obvious and measurable function directly associated with this area. The concept can be further refined into the speed with which positions are filled, which positions continue to *not* be filled, the effectiveness of recruiters, and the proportion of interns hired into full-time positions. All of these measurements are addressed in the following sections.

Human resources measurements can also be expanded to cover an entire business. For example, a company in the service industry or which employs a large number of skilled positions (or both) needs to understand the amount of employee turnover, since this issue directly impacts its ability to compete. Also, if labor and related costs are high, management needs to have a clear understanding of the total cost of employees, which includes all forms of compensation, such as commissions, stock, overtime, bonuses, and so forth. This total cost concept can be expanded to address the net benefits cost per employee, which encompasses every type of benefit paid, less employee deductions. The association between the number of employees and revenue can also be explored with the sales per person measurement, and refined further by calculating profit per person. There are other ways to delve into specific aspects of employee costs, such as the ratio of administrative staff employed by a business, and the effectiveness of a decision to outsource in-house labor to a supplier. While it may not be necessary to track all of these measurements, a selection of those most applicable to a company's operations can yield insights into where costs are being incurred, and whether those costs are appropriate.

Position Fulfillment Speed

When an organization is attempting to grow at a fast rate, the main restriction on growth may well be the speed with which positions are filled. This is a particular concern for skilled positions, such as programmers, where there may be competition from other employers. Alternatively, it can be an issue even for lower-skilled positions when hiring must be completed in bulk, such as when the staff for an entire hotel must be hired within a short period of time. In these cases, it can make sense to measure the success of the human resources team by tracking position fulfillment speed.

To track position fulfillment speed, calculate the difference between the date of offer acceptance and the original job posting date, aggregated for all jobs posted, and divide by the total number of jobs posted. The measurement is:

$$\frac{\sum (\text{Offer acceptance date} - \text{Original job posting date})}{\text{Total number of jobs posted}}$$

The calculation of this ratio can lead to incorrect results, since the underlying information may be skewed in several ways. Consider the following issues:

- A job posting may have been frozen for some time due to a funding constraint or other reasons, resulting in a longer measurement interval than is really the case. These postings should not be included in the measurement.
- Some positions are informally posted without notifying the human resources department, with formal notice only being given at the same time that an offer is extended to a recruit. This usually happens when a position is being advertised informally among other employees and their friends.
- Some positions may have been open for some time and continue to be unfilled on the measurement date. These positions can be reported separately as a total number of unfilled job postings. See the measurement described in the next section.

In short, some positions will be excluded from the measurement, while problems with the job posting system may cause others to appear to be instantaneous hires. These issues can cause difficulty in developing the measurement.

An additional problem is that position fulfillment speed can be impacted by factors that are outside of the control of the human resources department. For example:

- The department managers who are approving hires may be inordinately picky for certain positions.
- The company's finances do not allow for offers to be extended at pay rates at or above the industry median.
- The company has a reputation for laying off employees that reduces the interest of recruits in being hired.

The reasons noted here are caused by the entire company, so position fulfillment speed can be considered a measurement for the entire business, rather than just the human resources department.

EXAMPLE

Cupertino Beanery is planning to open a large number of coffee shops in the current fiscal year. Fifty shops are planned, each of which requires 20 employees, for a total of 1,000 new hires. The president knows that recruiting for these positions has interfered with the rate at which Cupertino has been able to open shops in the past. She assembles the following information for the last three months of hiring:

> Aggregate days to fill all positions = 4,025 business days
>
> Total number of positions filled = 175
>
> Position fulfillment speed = 23 business days

Since it currently takes the company more than a month to hire an employee, the president hires a consultant to review alternative hiring practices, and also doubles the size of the human resources department (which, unfortunately, requires 23 days to complete!).

Unfilled Requisitions Ratio

We noted in the preceding measurement that position fulfillment speed does not include any job postings that continue to be unfilled. These postings can be addressed in a different ratio, called the unfilled requisitions ratio, which should accompany the position fulfillment speed measurement to give a complete picture of how well the human resources department is filling posted job requisitions.

The concept behind the unfilled requisitions ratio is to set a threshold number of days, above which all unfilled job requisitions are counted. The threshold is set at a level designed to capture requisitions that have been open for an inordinately long period of time. For example, if the average position is filled in 30 days, then set the threshold at more than 30 days, and only count open requisitions exceeding that figure. Then divide by the number of job requisitions opened over a sufficiently long period of time to give a sense of scale to the number of unfilled requisitions. A smaller organization with minimal hiring needs could use the annual number of job requisitions posted, while a larger organization with massive hiring needs could set the figure at just the last few months. The calculation is:

$$\frac{\text{Number of job requisitions open more than designated threshold}}{\text{Number of job requisitions opened during past \_\_ months}}$$

There is no standard format for this measurement, so the calculation of the numerator and denominator can be set to whatever figures give management the best feel for how well the company is filling positions. However, once set, the format should be locked in, so that performance can be reliably compared over multiple periods.

Though useful as a general measure of hiring difficulties, the unfilled requisitions ratio suffers from a few underlying problems, which are:

- *Threshold manipulation.* It can be manipulated by setting a threshold for the numerator that is just high enough to keep most unfilled positions from being listed. The issue can be avoided by having a senior manager review and approve the threshold being used, and having the calculation periodically examined by the company's internal audit staff.
- *Closed postings.* Someone could continually close old job postings and reestablish them as new postings to keep old postings from being incorporated into the ratio. This is a difficult issue to remedy.
- *Position importance.* The measurement includes all unfilled requisitions, some of which may be for inconsequential positions that can be filled at leisure without damaging the business. This issue can be avoided by only calculating the ratio for specific departments, such as engineering, where filling positions in a timely manner may be more important.

EXAMPLE

Luminescence Corporation is greatly expanding its research lab for LED lighting, and is continually on the hunt for more electrical engineers to fill a number of positions for the lab. In light of the great demand for these positions, Luminescence has been unable to fill positions within a reasonable period of time. The following table illustrates the growing problem, with the hiring threshold set at 45 days:

	Quarter 1	Quarter 2	Quarter 3	Quarter 4
Requisitions open > 45 days	17	23	29	37
Annual requisitions opened*	81	82	91	109
Unfilled requisitions ratio	21%	28%	32%	34%

* The annual requisitions opened is derived on a rolling 12-month basis.

The measurements reveal that the company's problem is worsening, so management may need to take additional steps to accelerate its recruiting efforts, such as bringing in recruiting firms, raising pay rates, and offering signing bonuses.

Recruiter Effectiveness Ratio

When a company employs an outside recruiting firm to locate prospective recruits, the assumption is that the recruiter will do an effective job of screening candidates before sending them on to the company for interviews. If not, company personnel will end up spending an inordinate amount of time conducting pointless interviews of underqualified candidates.

The measurement is a simple one: divide the number of recruits eventually hired by the number forwarded to the company from a recruiter. The calculation is:

$$\frac{\text{Number of recruits hired}}{\text{Number of recruits forwarded by recruiting firm}}$$

Though the measurement is simple, its interpretation is not. There are several factors that can play a role in legitimately shifting the blame for ineffective recruiting away from a recruiter. Consider the following issues:

- *Job description.* The company may not have done an adequate job of defining the position for which it is hiring. This can be an iterative process, where the initial job description is continually modified, based on the qualifications of the candidates being forwarded from a recruiter.
- *Company reputation.* If the company is known for low pay, poor benefits, continual layoffs, and so forth, then recruits are much less likely to accept an offer from the company.
- *Pickiness.* The people assigned by the company to interview candidates sent from recruiters may be extraordinarily picky in recommending who should be hired. Thus, the ratio could be skewed for a particular recruiter because it is unfortunate enough to have its candidates be screened by a particular inter-viewer.
- *Regional demand.* The ability of a company to attract recruits may be impaired by supply and demand in the region. If there are few candidates available, then recruiters may be forced to suggest only partially-qualified recruits that are more likely to be rejected.

Despite these issues, it should still be possible to detect significant differences in the effectiveness of different recruiting agencies, when multiple agencies are being used at the same time.

EXAMPLE

The Atlas Machining Company routinely uses a group of three outside recruiting firms to locate software engineers. The human resources manager wants to reduce the time spent by company employees in the interviewing process, and so measures the recruiter effectiveness ratio for each of the recruiting firms. The results are as follows:

Recruiter Name	Number Hired	Number Forwarded	Effectiveness Ratio
Heroes for Hire	11	41	27%
Rocket Recruiters	14	117	12%
Simple Staffing	16	52	31%

The analysis reveals that the number of recruits hired through each firm is roughly the same, but that Atlas' employees must expend much more interviewing effort to sort through the recruits forwarded from Rocket Recruiters. The human resources manager concludes that it is time to terminate the services of Rocket, and shift more business to the other two firms.

Intern Conversion Ratio

Some organizations like to bring in interns from local universities during the summer months, with the intent of allowing both parties to review each other and see if long-term employment is a viable possibility. This concept is useful for the human resources department, which views it as a relatively low-cost way to evaluate possible recruits.

To measure the success of the program, divide the number of interns hired full-time by the number of interns from which the full-time hires were drawn. The calculation is:

$$\frac{\text{Number of interns hired full-time}}{\text{Number of interns employed by the company}}$$

There can be some variation in the derivation of the denominator. Interns who are hired full-time are typically drawn from the pool of interns used by a company during the preceding summer, so the total number of interns from the prior summer is typically used as the denominator. However, if the company continually brings in interns throughout the year, then a revised figure may be needed.

The intern conversion ratio should not necessarily be considered a goal, such as increasing it to 100%. Doing so might result in the hiring of interns who do not meet the company's minimum performance criteria. Instead, the measurement can be considered an historical benchmark to be used for planning purposes. For example, the human resources manager can derive an annual hiring plan that is based on an assumption of 50% of all interns being hired.

EXAMPLE

Franklin Drilling typically hires a number of geology interns from the local school of mines, evaluates them over the summer, and offers a certain percentage of them jobs before they graduate from school the following year. The human resources department incorporates an estimate of the intern conversion ratio into its hiring plans for the upcoming year. In the past three years, the intern conversion ratio was 55%, 62%, and 58%. Franklin currently employs 18 interns. The human resources department has been told to hire a total of 16 geologists for the upcoming year. Based on the historical conversion ratio, the human resources manager can expect to hire about 60% of the 18 interns, which fills 11 of the 16 positions. She must therefore plan to use alternative methods to hire five additional geologists.

Cost per Hire

The real effectiveness of a hiring program is the quality of the recruits hired, especially when highly-skilled employees are needed. However, even in these situations, the human resources manager should pay attention to the average cost required to hire employees. The issue is of considerably more importance in situations where a business must hire in bulk, and expects to continue doing so over a long period of time. In the latter case, paying close attention to the cost per hire can have a major impact on the reported level of profitability of a business.

The essential cost per hire calculation is to compile all hiring costs and then divide by the total number of employees hired in the measurement period. A refinement of the calculation is to only divide by the number of employees who have passed a probationary period, thereby stripping away those hires that have clearly been proven to not be suitable. The calculation is:

$$\frac{\text{Total cost of hiring}}{\text{Number of new hires}}$$

When deriving the cost per hire calculation, be sure to include all hiring costs, which may be substantially greater than is initially apparent. The following costs should be included:

- Administrative cost of new employee set up
- Advertising cost
- Assessment testing fees
- Drug testing fees
- Fees paid to outside recruiters
- Wages paid to all employees associated with the hiring process
- Wages paid to in-house recruiting staff

A portion of the salaries paid to interviewers working outside of the human resources department should not be assigned to the cost per hire, since a salary is paid irrespective of the specific activities on which these employees are engaged.

EXAMPLE

New Centurion Corporation translates Latin texts on behalf of major universities and libraries. It is exceedingly difficult to hire fully-qualified Latin scholars, so the company engages in a broad range of recruitment activities, including advertising in the *Latin Scholar Daily*, underwriting translator conferences, and reviewing citations in scholarly texts.

In the most recent quarter, New Centurion hired five new translators and incurred the following hiring costs:

Hiring Cost	Amount
Newsletter advertising	$3,000
Conference fees	12,000
Recruiter fee	9,000
Recruit entertainment expense	2,500
Total	$26,500

The cost per hire is $5,300, which is calculated as $26,500 total hiring costs incurred, divided by five new hires.

Employee Replacement Cost

The cost to replace an employee can be exceedingly high, but the cost is so dispersed that management is not usually aware of it. To bring replacement cost to their attention, consider reporting the average employee replacement cost on a periodic basis. The result may be greater attention to those factors that are causing employees to leave the company, such as improved benefits or a more spacious work environment.

Employee replacement cost can be derived at an aggregate level by compiling all replacement costs and dividing by the number of replacements hired. A refinement of the calculation is to only divide by the number of replacement employees who have passed a probationary period, thereby stripping away those hires that have clearly been proven to not be suitable. The calculation is:

$$\frac{\text{Total cost of replacing positions}}{\text{Number of replacement hires}}$$

The total cost of replacing positions includes all of the hiring costs just noted for the cost per hire measurement. In addition, include the following costs:

- Lost productivity cost
- New hire training cost
- Overtime cost for employees filling in for missing employees
- Temporary replacement cost

The cost of lost productivity can be difficult to quantify. Depending on the situation, possible costs that can be classified as due to lost productivity are an increased error rate that requires additional staff time to fix, and lost customer sales that result in reduced gross margins.

EXAMPLE

Lethal Sushi provides sushi to customers that is derived from the most toxic fish in the sea. Customers pay a high price for properly-prepared sushi, since they might otherwise die. Accordingly, the loss of a sushi chef is a major blow to the company. In the past year, Lethal lost four sushi chefs who needed to be replaced. The costs of doing so were as follows:

Replacement Cost	Amount
Recruiting fees	$20,000
New hire training	40,000
Overtime costs	12,000
Insurance settlement	100,000
Total	$172,000

The insurance settlement was with the next of kin of a customer who died from consuming improperly-prepared sushi that was prepared by a temporary hire who was not properly trained by the company.

The average replacement cost is $43,000, which is calculated as $172,000 total replacement costs incurred, divided by four new hires.

There can be a striking difference between the replacement costs for certain positions. For example, replacing a qualified software developer with someone of equal skill may be inordinately expensive, while replacing someone working on a production line may require a considerably lower expenditure. Given this disparity, it can make sense to separately report on the average employee replacement cost for those job classifications that are exceptionally difficult to hire.

Accession Rate

In situations where a large number of new employees are being hired, the human resources staff may have to engage in extensive planning for how the new employees are to be properly trained and assimilated into the organization. This issue can be discerned using the accession rate, which measures the proportion of new employees hired to the total base of existing employees. When the proportion is quite high, or is projected to be quite high in the future, the need for additional training activities becomes more critical. The calculation is:

$$\frac{\text{Total number of new employees}}{\text{Number of employees at end of previous measurement period}}$$

The measurement is usually derived on an annual basis. If there is a need to track it more frequently, a rolling annual derivation is acceptable. If the calculation is made over a short time period, such as one month, and then annualized, there is a danger that a one-time surge in hiring will be annualized, resulting in a much higher calculated accession rate than is really the case.

EXAMPLE

The human resources manager of Nefarious Industries is anticipating a massive increase in staffing in states where marijuana use has been legalized, especially in the company's farming operations. In farming operations, the company is expecting an increase of 100 employees over the existing staff of 40, which is a 250% accession rate. This calls for the design of a detailed farm operations training program in anticipation of the hiring activities.

Employee Turnover

When an employee leaves a company, the cost of replacing that person is extremely high. The business must pay for recruiting and training, and also endure a period of reduced efficiency before the replacement person is as efficient as the person who departed. For these reasons, a close examination of employee turnover is a key management task in almost any company.

To calculate employee turnover, obtain the number of full-time equivalent employees who left the business during the measurement period, and divide it by the average number of employees on the company payroll during that period. The calculation is:

$$\frac{\text{Number of departed FTE employees}}{(\text{Beginning FTEs} + \text{Ending FTEs}) / 2}$$

An issue to consider is the time period over which employee turnover is measured. In a larger company with thousands of employees, a single month may be an adequate time period. However, in a smaller firm, it may be necessary to use the preceding 12 months on a rolling basis in order to collect sufficient information to derive a measurement.

EXAMPLE

Crosswind Tours employs a number of part-time pilots for its tours of the Alaskan back country, which originate from multiple airstrips located near the ports where cruise ships stop during their travels through the Inside Passage. Other than a small full-time administrative staff, everyone in the company works on a part-time basis, mostly during the May through September cruise ship season. The president of Crosswinds suspects that employee turnover may be specific to the geographic location of the pilots, so he asks the payroll manager to calculate employee turnover for the past year at each of the company's locations. The results are:

	Ketchikan	Skagway	Sitka	Wrangell
FTE resignations	1.0	4.5	0.8	0.5
Average FTEs	7.2	8.0	12.0	9.5
Turnover	14%	56%	7%	5%

The employee turnover calculation clearly shows that there is a major problem with the Skagway flight operation, which experienced 56% turnover in the past year. The president personally interviews all of the pilots who left the Skagway operation, and finds that they had trouble with the local flight scheduler. He promptly replaces the Skagway flight scheduler, and works on hiring back the departed employees.

There will always be some employee turnover due to issues that are beyond the control of a company, such as a spouse being hired in another city, caring for parents, and so forth. It can also be difficult to retain employees in a tight job market where they have skills that are in high demand. Consequently, there will be a certain amount of unavoidable employee turnover. Thus, the proper use of the employee turnover measurement is to know when turnover is exceeding a normal baseline level, which requires a considerable knowledge of the precise reasons why employees are leaving.

The employee turnover metric can be manipulated by shifting work to outside contractors who fall outside of the parameters of this measurement. Consequently, if a large amount of work is outsourced, this may not be a useful measurement.

Annualized Compensation per Employee

Some pay structures are quite complex, with employees being paid bonuses, stock, overtime, and other forms of compensation. It is quite useful to aggregate all forms of compensation on an individual employee basis, in order to fully understand pay levels. This information can be used to determine the amount of additional pay raises, as well as for comparing a company's pay levels to those in the industry. It is also useful when compiling annualized wages for a specific job title or position, and comparing that average compensation level to industry standards.

If you elect to compile annualized pay for one person, then the calculation is to add together the following amounts for the past 12 months:

+	Fixed base pay
+	Wages
+	Commissions
+	Overtime
+	Bonuses
+	Stock
+	Other pay
=	Total annualized compensation

If you are compiling this information for a group of employees, then compile the same information for the entire group for the past 12 months, and then divide it by the number of full-time equivalents to arrive at the average annual compensation for that group.

EXAMPLE

Colossal Furniture manufactures chairs for its oversized customers. The company's repair department has been overwhelmed with work recently, as the company finds that its customers are so large that they are crushing its chairs, which must be reinforced with metal support struts. Colossal's president compiles the following information about the annual compensation being paid to the repair department employees:

$$\frac{\$600,000 \text{ Wages} + \$250,000 \text{ Overtime} + \$50,000 \text{ Bonuses}}{10 \text{ FTEs}} = \$90,000/\text{FTE}$$

Clearly, the repair staff is being paid a princely amount, largely because of the overtime they are working to keep up with their repair queue. The president decides that it is time to redesign the company's chairs to handle a heavier load.

It is extremely useful to track annualized total compensation for each employee on a trend line, to see compensation changes over the course of a person's employment.

Salary Competitiveness Ratio

To keep employee turnover levels reasonably low, it makes sense to compare the company's pay rates to those of its competitors. If a company's pay levels are relatively low, it is more likely to see some drift of employees away to its competitors. In addition, low pay usually equates to a work force with less training and experience, which can have a negative effect on corporate productivity levels.

The calculation of the salary competitiveness ratio is to divide the salary offered by your company by the average salary offered by competitors. The formula is:

$$\frac{\text{Salary offered by your company}}{\text{Average salary offered in the industry}}$$

Industry pay data is usually published by each industry's trade association, so the inputs to the measurement should not be too difficult to collect. In other cases, where there are many competitors (such as the casinos in Las Vegas) it is relatively easy to obtain pay information from them.

EXAMPLE

The Munchable Donuts chain of restaurants is having trouble hiring store managers, which may be due to a pay disparity within the industry. The human resources staff consults local job postings from competitors to ascertain what they are paying, and concludes that the average store manager rate is $45,000. The company is currently offering its new hire store managers $42,000. This results in a salary competitiveness ratio of 93.3%, which is calculated as the $42,000 in-house rate, divided by the $45,000 industry average rate. It appears that Munchable might have better luck hiring store managers if it were to raise its annual salaries by at least $2,000.

There are several concerns with this ratio that one should be aware of. Consider the following issues:

- The salaries offered to employees do not constitute the sum total of their compensation. For example, an employer might have quite a loyal workforce despite rather low pay rates, because it has a rich benefits package and also commits to lifetime employment. Also, some companies offer much higher commission and bonus plans than others. Thus, the ratio does not address the full scope of the compensation packages being offered to employees.
- The ratio cannot be applied to specialized jobs for which industry information is not tracked. This is a concern even for the more common positions, such as sales associates, accountants, and materials handlers, because these jobs may contain special requirements that are not found elsewhere in the industry.

Given these concerns, it makes sense to calculate the ratio only on a highly targeted basis for very specific jobs, and only with a full knowledge of the complete compensation packages being offered elsewhere in the industry for those positions. A more effective human resources manager will probably target this analysis only at those positions within the company for which maintaining a low employee turnover level is considered to be critical.

Net Benefits Cost per Employee

Management tends to spend a great deal of time observing the wage and salary cost of company employees, but has a much lower awareness of the cost of net benefits per employee. This can be a major failing, especially when a company has adopted a disparate group of benefits whose total cost is difficult to discern. In many cases, the net cost of benefits may be much higher than expected, which can cut deeply into profits.

Measure the net benefit cost on a per-person or departmental basis, rather than as an average figure for all employees, since employees make differing use of benefits. For example, some employees may elect to take advantage of a company 401(k) plan that requires matching funds from the company, while others will not.

To calculate the net benefits cost per employee at the company level, follow these steps:

1. Summarize the cost of all benefits. Examples of the more common benefits are the cost of medical insurance, dental insurance, life insurance, and disability insurance, as well as pension matching funds. Less-common benefits are reimbursements for health club or country club memberships, and the leases on company cars.
2. Subtract employee deductions. If the company is deducting the cost of a portion of benefits from employee pay, compile this amount and subtract it from the total derived in the first step.
3. Calculate the average number of full-time equivalents during the measurement period, and divide this number into the net benefit cost derived in the first two steps.

Thus, the calculation of the net benefit cost per employee is:

$$\frac{\text{Insurance cost} + \text{Pension matching cost} + \text{Other benefits} - \text{Employee deductions}}{\text{Average number of full-time equivalents}}$$

To calculate the net benefit cost for an individual employee, run the same calculation using the benefit costs and deductions specific to that employee, and skip the third calculation step.

EXAMPLE

Alien Battles Corporation (ABC) creates digital space battles for science fiction movies. To stay ahead of its competitors, ABC offers a first-rate benefits package to its software developers. The president of ABC wants to know the net benefits cost per employee, which the accounting staff derives from the following information:

Benefit Item	Gross Cost	Employee Deductions	Net Cost
Medical insurance	$420,000	$(85,000)	$335,000
Dental insurance	35,000	(7,000)	28,000
Pension matching	85,000	--	85,000
Long-term disability	15,000	--	15,000
Short-term disability	48,000	--	48,000
Other	39,000	--	39,000
Totals	$642,000	$(92,000)	$550,000

ABC had an average of 40 full-time equivalent employees during the one-year measurement period. Thus, the net benefits cost per employee is $13,750, which is calculated as the net cost of $550,000 divided by 40 FTEs.

It is not always wise to use the information provided by this measurement to cut back on the total cost of benefits, especially when employees are particularly sensitive about benefit levels. However, a close examination of the various benefit components may allow management to reconfigure the benefit package to provide the largest amount of those benefits that are of the greatest value to employees, while paring back less necessary benefits.

Sales per Person

In some industries, there is a direct relationship between the efficiency and effectiveness of a company's employees and its resulting sales. This relationship is particularly true in industries where employees bill customers for their time. In such industries, the sales per person measurement is closely watched.

To calculate sales per person, divide the total sales for the preceding 12 months by the average number of full-time equivalents during that period. The calculation is:

$$\frac{\text{Revenues (trailing 12 months)}}{(\text{Beginning FTEs} + \text{Ending FTEs}) / 2}$$

185

EXAMPLE

Pulsed Laser Drilling Corporation (PLD) manufactures lasers that use a pulsed laser beam to drill through rock. Its products are used in such applications as drilling for oil and gas, water wells, and laying subsurface fiber optic cables. The company only employs full-time technicians who assemble and field service its complex laser products. Headcount tends to closely follow sales levels, since a great deal of the manufacturing process is by hand. During the past year, PLD had revenues of $18 million and 90 full-time equivalents. The calculation of its sales per person is:

$$\frac{\$18,000,000 \text{ Sales}}{90 \text{ Full-time equivalents}} = \$200,000 \text{ Sales per employee}$$

The sales per person measurement is not useful, and may even be misleading in the following situations:

- *Product based.* If a company derives its sales from standardized manufactured goods, there may not be a causal relationship between sales and headcount, especially when production activities are highly automated.
- *Step headcount.* It is possible that a company may be able to use a fixed number of employees to generate an increasing amount of sales, until it reaches a "step" point where the company must hire a number of additional employees to support the next incremental block of sales. This situation arises when sales are supported by a single facility that requires a certain minimum amount of staffing.

The sales per person measurement is a popular one, but it only focuses on top-line sales. A company may have an astoundingly high sales per person measurement, and still lose money. A more focused measurement is the profit per person measurement, which is covered next.

Profit per Person

In a service-intensive industry, there is a direct relationship between employees and the amount of profits generated. This is particularly true in such service areas as equipment field servicing, management consulting, and auditing. In these situations, it makes sense to track profits per employee, not only for the company as a whole, but also for those individual employees who are billable.

To calculate profit per employee, divide the company's operating profit by the average number of full-time equivalent employees. Do *not* use net after-tax profits for this measurement, since doing so would include such financing line items as interest expense and interest income, which have nothing to do with employee performance. Also, do not include the impact of income taxes, since this expense can be altered by tax strategy that has nothing to do with the operational efficiency of employees. The calculation is:

$$\frac{\text{Operating profit}}{(\text{Beginning FTEs} + \text{Ending FTEs}) / 2}$$

EXAMPLE

Maid Marian is a nationwide maid service that is run by friars within the Franciscan Order. The friars want to introduce a bonus system that encourages part-time maids to work additional hours, and needs to determine the existing profit per employee, so that it can determine how large a bonus pool to create.

During the past 12-month period, employees of Maid Marian worked a total of 832,000 hours, which is an FTE equivalent of 400 employees. This equivalent is calculated as 832,000 hours divided by the 2,080 hours worked by a full-employee in one year (52 weeks × 40 hours/week). During that period, the service generated an operating profit of $3 million, which is a profit per employee of:

$$\frac{\$3,000,000 \text{ Operating profit}}{400 \text{ Full-time equivalents}} = \$7,500 \text{ Profit per employee}$$

The friars want to create a bonus pool that is 20% of operating profits, which is a $600,000 pool. Based on the 400 FTEs in Maid Marian, this works out to a potential bonus per FTE per year of $1,500.

There are three caveats to the use of the profit per employee measurement, which are:

- *Industry-specific.* The profit per employee measurement is least useful in industries where there is a large investment in fixed assets and a proportionally smaller number of employees, such as heavy industry. In these situations, there is not such a direct linkage between the quality or quantity of employees, which makes the profit per employee measurement less relevant.
- *Minimal profits.* There is no point in measuring profit per employee when the operating profit is near zero, since it divulges no relevant information.
- *Manipulation.* The measurement is subject to manipulation by shifting work to suppliers. Doing so reduces headcount, which drives up the profit per employee.

Despite the caveats just noted, profit per person is an excellent measurement in many services industries.

Administrative Staff Ratio

Only a certain number of employees are directly involved in the generation of revenue for a business. This group must generate a sufficient amount of profit to pay for the administrative staff that supports them. It is entirely too common for a business to gradually accumulate more and more administrative staff for reasons that may appear plausible on an individual hiring-decision basis, but which gradually wear away at company profits. Thus, a key concern of management is to minimize the proportion of administrative staff to revenue-producing staff.

Defining a position as administrative or revenue-producing is not always clear, since someone may not directly engage in billable work, and yet supports the sales effort. One of the simpler alternatives is to designate entire departments as administrative or revenue-producing areas. For example, the corporate, accounting, and human resources departments are unquestionably administrative, while the sales and production departments are usually considered to be revenue-producing. A case could be made in either direction for the marketing, materials handling, and engineering departments.

The administrative staff ratio could be designed based on headcount, but this is misleading, given the differences in pay among various positions. For example, a low-cost accounting clerk qualifies as one administrative position, while a highly-paid consultant qualifies as one revenue-producing position; this is a one-to-one headcount ratio, but their corresponding pay rates are wildly different. Consequently, we recommend that the fully burdened costs of the administrative and revenue-producing employees be used in the administrative staff ratio. The calculation is:

$$\frac{\text{Fully burdened cost of administrative staff}}{\text{Fully burdened cost of revenue-generating staff}}$$

The chief concern with this measurement is its binary nature – either someone is designated as administrative or revenue-producing, with no intermediate designation. This can result in pressure to skew the definitions of these two areas in order to push more people into the revenue-generating classification and make the ratio look better than is really the case.

There is also a risk that managers will simply outsource administrative positions in order to remove the cost of these positions from the ratio. However, this concern can be remedied by adding the outsourcing cost to the fully-burdened cost of administrative staff.

EXAMPLE

The CEO of Pensive Corporation has noticed a marked decline in profits over the past two years, and initiates an investigation to determine the cause. A financial analyst notes the following change in the administrative staff ratio over the past three years:

	Year 1	Year 2	Year 3
Administrative staff cost	$492,000	$711,000	$726,000
Revenue-producing staff cost	$2,460,000	$2,810,000	$2,792,000
Administrative staff ratio	20%	25%	26%

The surge in administrative staff costs beginning in Year 2 can be traced directly to the company's expansion into government contracts, which require a large administrative staff to create responses to request for proposal (RFP) documents. The CEO must now decide if the incremental cost of this new business is resulting in such a large drop in profitability that the government contract business should be shuttered.

Ergonomic Injury Rate

The human resources staff may be responsible for a program of locating and correcting instances of ergonomic injuries in the workplace. For example, this may involve compiling workers' compensation claims for injuries caused by ineffective seating, computer keyboards, lighting, and so forth. If there is such a program, it can be useful to track the ergonomic injury rate before and after the implementation of ergonomic changes, such as the wholesale upgrading of the types of chairs used in a business. The change in the injury rate can be used as justification for the expense associated with the ergonomic changes made. The formula for the ergonomic injury rate is:

$$\frac{\text{Number of hours lost due to ergonomic injuries}}{\text{Total hours worked by all employees}}$$

A modification of the formula is to multiply the hours lost by the hourly compensation rates of the affected employees, and to then divide by the total corporate compensation expense. This approach restates ergonomic injuries into monetary terms. However, this alternative approach can also under-represent the impact of ergonomic injuries, since they are usually incurred by data entry and manual labor employees who are paid less than other employees.

EXAMPLE

The human resources manager of Tsunami Products (maker of high-flow shower heads) has noticed that a large proportion of employee sick time appears to be related to ergonomic injuries, particularly among the order entry staff that spends all day entering customer orders into the computer system. She implements changes to upgrade chairs, keyboards, and monitor viewing angles, resulting in the following before-and-after ergonomic injury rates within the order entry department:

(monthly hours worked)	Before Upgrades	After Upgrades
Number of hours lost due to ergonomic injuries	288	58
Total hours worked by all employees	2,400	2,880
Ergonomic injury rate	12%	2%

The measurements reveal that the changes made have had a profound impact on hours worked within the department.

One issue with using before-and-after measurements of the ergonomic injury rate is that the recovery period from such injuries can be quite lengthy. This means that the "after" measurement may need to be a number of months after ergonomic upgrades have been implemented, to ensure that everyone affected by ergonomic issues has had sufficient time to recover.

Outsourcing Cost Effectiveness

Managers may be tempted to outsource certain functions, on the grounds that the net labor cost of shifting to a low-cost region will result in incremental profits to the business. This is not always the case, since there are a number of additional costs associated with outsourcing, including the following:

- Management time to oversee the outsourced operations
- Legal costs to create and monitor contracts with outsourcing suppliers
- Travel costs to and from outsourcing locations to oversee operations
- Customers lost due to dissatisfaction with outsourced services
- Inefficiency of staff brought in by outsourcing suppliers
- Initial costs to terminate staff and transfer knowledge to outsourcing suppliers

When a company elects to engage in outsourcing, it can be useful to enumerate the costs of the new arrangement and then compare them to the costs that the company has eliminated by switching to outsourcing. The measurement is:

$$\frac{\text{Total cost of outsourcing arrangement}}{\text{Costs eliminated by outsourcing}}$$

There are additional factors involved in the outsourcing decision that are less easy to quantify. For example, outsourcing can allow a company to avoid investing cash in fixed assets, which can be critical for a rapidly-growing business. Conversely, outsourcing some functions may shift a core competency to a supplier. Also, a supplier in a dominant position may gain the ability to enforce outsized pricing increases on a company that has few other alternatives.

EXAMPLE

The management of Blitz Communications is considering outsourcing its entire accounting function to a supplier located in India. The attraction of this move is a 50% reduction in hourly labor costs, though the company will need an on-site supervisor, as well as a generous travel and living allowance for that person. Given the higher employee turnover rate in India, there is also likely to be a cost associated with more inefficient staff. An analyst models the projected outsourcing cost effectiveness of the move, and compiles the following information:

Cost of current department	$500,000
Cost of replacement staff	250,000
Management oversight needed	85,000
Travel and living allowance	60,000
Cost of inefficient staff	75,000

This information is aggregated into the following outsourcing cost effectiveness ratio:

$$\frac{\$250,000 \text{ Replacement staff} + \$85,000 \text{ Oversight} + \$60,000 \text{ Travel} + \$75,000 \text{ Inefficiency}}{\$500,000 \text{ Current cost}}$$

$$\$470,000 \div \$500,000 = 94\%$$

The analysis reveals that the initial promise of a 50% cost reduction is closer to a 6% cost reduction. Since there are likely to be additional costs that have not yet been quantified, there may be no savings from outsourcing at all. Based on this information, management might want to rethink its decision.

General Management Measurements

There are several additional measurements that can be used to monitor the costs incurred within the human resources department. Consider the following possibilities:

- Employee turnover within the department
- The percentage of human resources staff pay to median rates in the region
- The total cost of the human resources function as a percentage of sales
- The proportion of human resources staff to total employees

Most of the cost of this department is derived from headcount, so the general management measures should focus almost exclusively on this area. When deriving measurements, a key concern is whether to measure headcount or the total cost of employees. Since there can be a wide disparity in pay rates within the department, we suggest that a focus on the total cost of employees yields more relevant measures.

Summary

The measurements discussed in this chapter are at a high level, and so only provide a general clue that there are issues requiring further exploration. To be more effective, human resources measurements should be applied at the department level, in order to more specifically identify issues requiring correction. Further, it will probably be necessary to provide supporting reports that identify the exact issues causing negative measurement results. For example, the employee turnover measurement should be accompanied by a list of the reasons given by departing employees for quitting. Similarly, changes in the administrative staff ratio should be accompanied by a listing of exactly which positions have been added or deleted during the measurement period, and the justification for each change.

Chapter 16
Inventory Measurements

Introduction

Any business that sells tangible products to its customers must deal with inventory, either as the simple transfer of merchandise from a supplier to a customer, or as part of a more comprehensive production system. In this chapter, we address the general concepts of inventory turnover and obsolete inventory, along with several ancillary measurements that are designed to focus attention on whether the amount of inventory on hand is the correct amount, and what to do with any excess inventory.

> **Related Podcast Episode:** Episode 27 of the Accounting Best Practices Podcast discusses inventory measurements. The episode is available at: **accountingtools.com/podcasts** or **iTunes**

Overview of Inventory Measurements

Inventory is technically considered an asset – at least, it is categorized as such on a company's balance sheet. However, it can be considered a liability, since inventory is not easily liquidated, can become obsolete in short order, and can physically clog a facility to such an extent that it interferes with operations. Because of the liability aspects of inventory, all of the measurements in this chapter are intended to spotlight when a business has too much inventory – not when it has too little.

The traditional measurement of inventory is turnover, which is a comparison of the amount of inventory to sales, to see if the proportion is reasonable. We also subdivide this measurement into turnover for raw materials, work-in-process, and finished goods – each of which can be applicable under certain circumstances. When using inventory turnover measurements, keep in mind that the results will be largely based on the manufacturing system in place, as well as purchasing practices. For example, a practice of buying in bulk and using a "push" production system will inevitably lead to lower inventory turnover, while just-in-time purchasing and a "pull" production system will be associated with much higher turnover results.

We also discuss inventory accuracy, which is an enormously important concept. Inventory records must be as close to 100% accurate as possible, or else there will be major issues with the ability to meet scheduled production targets and fulfill customer orders in a timely manner.

Our last remaining major area addresses the concept of excess inventory. There should be measurements for detecting any inventory that is either clearly obsolete or which has aged past a certain number of days. These items will likely require disposition at a reduced price, so we also address the amount of returnable inventory and the rate at which its value is likely to decline over time. These concepts should be built into an ongoing process of identifying and selling off inventory at a rapid clip, so that no excess funds are stored in inventory that is unlikely to provide an adequate return on investment.

Average Inventory Calculation

Average inventory is used to estimate the amount of inventory that a business typically has on hand over a longer time period than just the last month. Since the inventory balance is calculated as of the end of the last business day of a month, it may vary considerably from the average amount over a longer time period, depending upon whether there was a sudden draw-down of inventory or perhaps a large supplier delivery at the end of the month.

Average inventory is also useful for comparison to revenues. Since revenues are typically presented in the income statement not only for the most recent month, but also for the year-to-date, it is useful to calculate the average inventory for the year-to-date, and then match the average inventory balance to year-to-date revenues, to see how much inventory investment was needed to support a given level of sales.

In the first case, where you are simply trying to avoid using a sudden spike or drop in the month-end inventory number, the average inventory calculation is to add together the beginning and ending inventory balances for a single month, and divide by two. The formula is:

$$(\text{Beginning inventory} + \text{Ending inventory}) \div 2$$

In the second case, where you want to obtain an average inventory figure that is representative of the period covered by year-to-date sales, add together the ending inventory balances for all of the months included in the year-to-date, and divide by the number of months in the year-to-date. For example, if it is now March 31 and you want to determine the average inventory to match against sales for the January through March period, then the calculation would be as noted in the following exhibit.

Average Inventory Calculation

January ending inventory	$185,000
February ending inventory	213,000
March ending inventory	142,000
Total	$540,000
Average inventory = Total ÷ 3	$180,000

A variation on the average inventory concept is to calculate the exact number of days of inventory on hand, based on the amount of time it has historically taken to sell the inventory. The calculation is:

$$365 \div (\text{Annualized cost of goods sold} \div \text{Inventory})$$

194

Thus, if a company has annualized cost of goods sold of $1,000,000 and an ending inventory balance of $200,000, its days of inventory on hand is calculated as:

$$365 \div (\$1,000,000 \div \$200,000) = 73 \text{ Days of inventory}$$

Though useful, the average inventory concept has some problems, which are as follows:

- *Month-end basis.* The calculation is based on the month-end inventory balance, which may not be representative of the average inventory balance on a daily basis. For example, a company may traditionally have a huge sales push at the end of each month in order to meet its sales forecasts, which may artificially drop month-end inventory levels to well below their usual daily amounts.
- *Seasonal sales.* Month-end results can be skewed if a company's sales are seasonal. This can cause abnormally low inventory balances at the end of the main selling season, as well as a major ramp-up in inventory balances just before the start of the main selling season.
- *Estimated balance.* Sometimes the month-end inventory balance is estimated, rather than being based on a physical inventory count. This means that a portion of the averaging calculation may itself be based on an estimate, which in turn makes the average inventory figure less valid.

Inventory Turnover Measurements

The turnover of inventory is the rate at which inventory is used over a measurement period. This is an important measurement, for many businesses are burdened by an excessively large investment in inventory, which can consume the bulk of available cash. When there is a low rate of inventory turnover, this implies that a business may have a flawed purchasing system that bought too many goods, or that stocks were increased in anticipation of sales that did not occur. In both cases, there is a high risk of inventory aging, in which case it becomes obsolete and has reduced resale value.

When there is a high rate of inventory turnover, this implies that the purchasing function is tightly managed. However, it may also mean that a business does not have the cash reserves to maintain normal inventory levels, and so is turning away prospective sales. The latter scenario is most likely when the amount of debt is high and there are minimal cash reserves.

In this section, we address the classic inventory measurement, which is inventory turnover, followed by the calculations for each component of inventory – raw materials, work-in-process, and finished goods.

Inventory Turnover Ratio

To calculate inventory turnover, divide the ending inventory figure into the annualized cost of sales. If the ending inventory figure is not a representative number, then use an average figure instead. The formula is:

$$\frac{\text{Annual cost of goods sold}}{\text{Inventory}}$$

The result of this calculation can be divided into 365 days to arrive at days of inventory on hand. Thus, a turnover rate of 4.0 becomes 91 days of inventory.

EXAMPLE

An analyst is reviewing the inventory situation of the Hegemony Toy Company. The business incurred $8,150,000 of cost of goods sold in the past year, and has ending inventory of $1,630,000. Total inventory turnover is calculated as:

$$\frac{\$8,150,000 \text{ Cost of goods sold}}{\$1,630,000 \text{ Inventory}}$$

$$= 5 \text{ Turns per year}$$

The five turns figure is then divided into 365 days to arrive at 73 days of inventory on hand.

Raw Materials Turnover

If a large part of a company's total inventory investment is in raw materials, it may be useful to focus attention specifically on this area with the raw materials turnover measurement. This measurement is of interest to the purchasing manager, who is responsible for maintaining the flow of goods into the production area. This measurement can also be used by the engineering manager, who can focus on designing products that use common parts already found in stock. Raw material turnover is of particular interest in just-in-time environments where the intent is to drive the investment in raw materials down to a level very close to zero.

To calculate raw materials turnover, divide the dollar value of raw materials consumed in the period by the average amount of raw materials on hand through the period, and then annualize the result. For example, if the measurement is for a one-month period, multiply the result by 12. The calculation is:

$$\frac{\text{Dollar value of raw materials consumed in period}}{\text{Average dollar value of raw materials inventory}} \times 12 = \text{Raw materials turnover}$$

There are a few situations in which raw materials turnover can be further refined. Consider the following possibilities:

- *Obsolete inventory.* A high proportion of obsolete raw materials may be keeping the turnover figure from being improved. If so, run a calculation of which items have not been used recently, and forward this list to the purchasing staff to see if the indicated items can be sold off. Then run the turnover measurement without the obsolete items.
- *Overnight delivery costs.* The turnover figure can be artificially reduced by paying extra to have raw materials delivered through an overnight delivery service. If this is happening, track the cost of incoming freight in conjunction with the raw materials turnover measurement.

EXAMPLE

Aberdeen Arquebus sells its old gun replicas in a highly seasonal business, where most purchases are made in the spring, in anticipation of the summer battle re-enactment season. Accordingly, the owner exerts pressure on the purchasing staff to minimize raw material levels, so that there are few raw materials left in stock after the selling season is complete. The following table shows the results of this effort by quarter, where production ramps up in the fourth and first quarters, followed by a rapid decline in the second quarter.

	Quarter 1	Quarter 2	Quarter 3	Quarter 4
Raw materials consumed	$380,000	$210,000	$85,000	$420,000
Raw materials inventory	$254,000	$93,000	$28,000	$335,000
Raw materials turnover	6x	9x	12x	5x

Note: The results of each calculation are multiplied by four to annualize results.

Work-in-Process Turnover

An excessive amount of work-in-process inventory is a strong indicator of an inefficient production process. When production is not well-organized, clumps of inventory will pile up throughout the production area. Conversely, a just-in-time system can operate with very small amounts of work-in-process inventory.

To measure work-in-process turnover, divide the annual cost of goods sold by the average cost of work-in-process inventory. The calculation is:

$$\frac{\text{Annualized cost of goods sold}}{\text{Average work-in-process inventory}}$$

This is the most difficult inventory turnover figure to compile, for there is usually no formal system for tracking specific units of inventory through the production process, as well as the state of completion of each unit. If so, compiling this measurement is nearly impossible. However, if there is a formal tracking system in place, then the average work-in-process figure may be available through a standard report.

Another issue with work-in-process inventory is its extreme variability. The amount in process may vary to a noticeable extent on a daily or even hourly basis, so the use of an average inventory level is advisable.

EXAMPLE

Creekside Industrial is in the throes of a manufacturing system changeover, from a manufacturing resources planning (MRP II) system to a just-in-time system. The production manager wants to be sure that the company is realizing the full benefits of the transition, and so authorizes the compilation of before-and-after work-in-process turnover measurements. The results are:

(results are annualized)	MRP II Turnover	Just-in-Time Turnover
Cost of goods sold	$16,500,000	$15,900,000
Average work-in-process inventory	$1,375,000	$795,000
	12x	20x

The measurement comparison reveals that Creekside has experienced a notable drop in its work-in-process investment as a result of the switch to a just-in-time system.

Finished Goods Turnover

There are situations where a company may have quite a large investment in finished goods inventory in comparison to its sales level. This situation most commonly arises for one of the following reasons:

- *Fulfillment policy.* Senior management wants to differentiate the company from its competitors by offering a fast fulfillment rate for all customer orders, which can only be achieved with a large amount of finished goods on hand.
- *Seasonality.* Sales are highly seasonal, so the seller increases its finished goods during the months prior to the selling season, in order to meet demand.
- *Obsolescence.* Some portion of the finished goods inventory is obsolete, and so is selling at a very low rate.

To calculate finished goods turnover, divide the dollar value of finished goods consumed in the period by the average amount of finished goods on hand through the period, and then annualize the result. For example, if the measurement is for a one-month period, multiply the result by 12. The calculation is:

$$\frac{\text{Dollar value of finished goods consumed in period}}{\text{Average dollar value of finished goods inventory}} \times 12 \quad = \text{Finished goods turnover}$$

One issue with finished goods turnover is how costing information is compiled. The cost of finished goods is comprised of the costs of direct materials, direct labor, and overhead. These amounts can vary if there are changes in the standard costing methodology that a company employs. Also, these costs can be fraudulently altered in order to increase the amount of ending inventory, thereby reducing the cost of goods sold and increasing profits. Thus, the costing methodology can have an impact on finished goods turnover.

EXAMPLE

The senior managers of Billabong Machining want to ensure the highest level of customer satisfaction by promising order fulfillment on 99% of all orders placed within one day of order receipt. Given the large array of widgets that Billabong offers for sale, this pledge requires the company to maintain an inordinately large investment in finished goods. The following table reveals the finished goods turnover rate before and after the fulfillment policy was begun.

(results are annualized)	Before Fulfillment Policy	After Fulfillment Policy
Finished goods consumed	$4,800,000	$5,100,000
Finished goods inventory	$400,000	$1,275,000
	12x	4x

Given the massive decline in turnover, the management team might want to rethink its decision to fulfill customer orders so quickly, especially since sales have not increased much as a result of the decision.

Inventory Accuracy Percentage

A business relies upon the accuracy of its inventory records to maintain its production and customer fulfillment systems. For these records to be truly accurate, they must contain accurate information in the following areas:

- Quantity on hand
- Location of inventory
- Unit of measure
- Part number

If any one of these items within an inventory record is wrong, then the entire set of information can be considered sufficiently incorrect to render the entire record useless. For example, the inventory quantity may be completely accurate, but if the location code is wrong, the materials handling staff cannot find the item. Or, if the part number is wrong, a component cannot be used. Consequently, the inventory accuracy formula encompasses all four elements.

To calculate inventory accuracy, divide the number of *completely* accurate inventory test items sampled by the total number of all inventory items sampled. An accurate inventory test item is considered to be one for which the actual quantity, location, unit of measure, and part number matches the information stated in the inventory record. If even one of these items is found to be incorrect, then the entire item tested should be flagged as incorrect. The formula for inventory accuracy is:

$$\frac{\text{Number of completely accurate inventory test items}}{\text{Total number of inventory items sampled}}$$

EXAMPLE

An internal auditor for Radiosonde Corporation conducts an inventory accuracy review in the company's storage area. He compiles the following incorrect information for a sample test of eight items:

	Audited Description	Audited Location	Audited Quantity	Audited Unit of Measure
Alpha unit	No	No		
Beta unit	No			
Charlie unit		No		
Delta unit	No	No		
Echo unit		No		
Foxtrot unit	No			No
Golf unit				No
Hotel unit				No

The result of the test is inventory accuracy of 0%. The test score astounds the inventory manager, who has been focusing solely on quantity accuracy. Even though the quantity counts did indeed prove to be accurate, the inventory records were well below expectations for the other data items.

Excess Inventory Measurements

If a company maintains any inventory at all, it is quite likely that some portion of this investment is obsolete. A business needs to have an ongoing inventory evaluation system that highlights obsolete items, as well as a well-defined system for disposing of these items as quickly as possible, and at the highest price. In this section, we address several variations on obsolete inventory measurement, as well as how to focus attention on the opportunity cost of not disposing of inventory in a timely manner.

Obsolete Inventory Percentage

When a company has a significant investment in inventory, one of the more essential accompanying metrics is the obsolete inventory percentage. This measurement is needed to derive that portion of the inventory that is no longer usable. The percentage should be tracked on a trend line and compared to the results of similar businesses, to see if a company is experiencing an unusually large proportion of inventory problems. Actions taken that relate to this percentage can include:

- Changes in the reserve for obsolete inventory, if the percentage is varying from the long-term trend.
- Changes in the amount of activity to disposition obsolete inventory in a manner as advantageous to the company as possible.
- Actions taken to reduce the underlying causes of obsolescence, such as buying in smaller quantities, switching to a production system that is based on customer orders, and better management of engineering change orders.

To derive the obsolete inventory percentage, summarize the book value of all inventory items which have been designated as not being needed, and divide it by the book value of the entire inventory. The formula is:

$$\frac{\text{Book value of inventory items with no recent usage}}{\text{Total inventory book value}}$$

The main problem with this percentage is figuring out which inventory to include in the numerator. Whatever method is chosen should be used in a consistent manner, so that trends in the percentage can be more reliably tracked over time.

EXAMPLE

The warehouse manager of Mole Industries wants to investigate the extent of obsolete inventory in his warehouse, so that he can remove items and consolidate the remaining inventory. He prints a parts usage report from the company's manufacturing resources planning system that only shows the cost of those items that are in stock and which have not been used for at least two years. The total cost listed on this report is $182,000, which is 19% of the total book value of the entire inventory. The warehouse manager brings this high percentage to the attention of the purchasing manager, who immediately contacts suppliers to see if they will take back the obsolete items in exchange for a restocking fee.

Percent of Inventory Greater than XX Days

A variation on the obsolete inventory percentage is to track the amount of any inventory that is older than a certain number of days. If an inventory item exceeds the threshold, it could be targeted for return to the supplier in exchange for a restocking fee. This approach is particularly useful when a company has instituted just-in-time deliveries, but still has excess inventory on hand from before implementation of the new system.

The precise number of days used for the threshold in this measurement can vary, based on several factors. Consider the following:

- *Warehouse-specific*. If tighter inventory controls are being implemented at just one location, set a minimal threshold for that facility, in order to target the largest possible amount of inventory for disposition.
- *SKU-specific*. If a particular stock-keeping unit (SKU) is being targeted for reduction, set a minimal threshold just for that item. This is particularly common for any SKUs for which a company has a large amount of funds tied up in inventory.
- *Class specific*. The measurement can be restricted to just raw materials, in order to focus on tighter purchasing practices. Alternatively, it can be restricted to just finished goods, in order to focus on production scheduling and sales forecasting issues.
- *Early warning*. Analysis of obsolete inventory may have shown that any inventory over a certain number of days old is more likely to eventually be designated as obsolete. Thus, the threshold can be set for a certain number of days prior to when inventory is usually declared obsolete, which gives the company early warning to draw down these stocks.

The steps required to calculate the percent of inventory over a certain number of days are:

1. Set the threshold number of days and the inventory type to be measured.
2. For the block of inventory to be measured, determine the dollar amount of all inventory items exceeding the threshold number of days.
3. Divide the aggregate total from the second step by the total dollar amount of inventory. Note that this should be the ending inventory balance (not an average balance), since the inventory figure derived in the second step is as of the ending inventory date.

The calculation of the percent of inventory greater than XX days is:

$$\frac{\sum (\text{Inventory dollars greater than XX days old})}{\text{Total inventory valuation}}$$

This measurement can be misleading in two situations, which are:

- *Seasonal production build*. A company may build inventory levels throughout the year, in anticipation of a short selling season. If so, the amount of all types of inventory may appear inordinately old with this measurement. In this situation, consider only using the measurement immediately after the selling season, to identify the extent to which inventory items did not sell.

- *Production schedule.* Certain raw materials may only be used in specific products, for which production runs are only scheduled at relatively long intervals. If the measurement is generated just prior to such a production run, it could reveal what may appear to be an inordinate amount of raw materials on hand. This issue can be spotted by comparing the production schedule to any items appearing in an initial version of the measurement.

EXAMPLE

Rapunzel Hair Products sells a hair spray that has been proven to lose much of its hold characteristics after six months in storage; at that time, any remaining stocks cannot be sold, and so are thrown in the dumpster. Accordingly, Rapunzel's sales manager requests that an inventory report be generated that aggregates the percentage of this inventory that is more than 90 days old, so that coupons can be issued in a timely manner that will spur additional sales of the hair spray. For example, as of the end of the last month, the ten products that use the hair spray formulation, and which were more than 90 days old, had an aggregate book value of $80,000. Since the total hair spray inventory value was $1,000,000, the percent of inventory greater than 90 days old was 8%.

Returnable Inventory Valuation

Only a portion of all excess inventory can be returned to suppliers. Other items are too old or damaged to be returned, or suppliers refuse to take them back, even for a restocking fee. Management should be aware of the total dollar amount of returnable inventory, since the amount of cash that can be realized could be of use to the company. This measurement usually takes the form of a report, which itemizes in declining dollar value the amount of inventory that can be returned, based on the expected disposal price, net of any restocking charges.

A key concern with the returnable inventory valuation is not to include in the report any items for which there is a reasonable short-term prospect of usage. Otherwise, the company will incur a restocking charge to return items to a supplier, followed shortly thereafter by the repurchase of the same items at their full retail price.

One concern is whether to include in the valuation report any items for which suppliers only offer a credit, rather than a cash repayment. If the company does not expect to make any further purchases from a supplier that only offers a credit, then the credit is essentially useless. In this case, it is better to exclude such items from the report.

Opportunity Cost of Excess Inventory

Most companies have pockets of excess inventory on hand. This inventory may be obsolete, or there may simply be more on hand than the company can reasonably expect to use or sell in the short term. In these situations, the purchasing department should be working on ways to disposition the goods in exchange for the largest possible amount of cash. The disposition value of inventory almost always declines over time, so there is an opportunity cost associated with not actively pursuing inventory dispositions. To measure the opportunity cost of excess inventory, follow these steps:

1. Compile the units of inventory that must be disposed of.
2. Estimate the disposal price that the company can obtain for these units if it were to do so today.
3. Estimate the rate at which the disposal price will drop on a monthly basis.
4. Estimate the direct cost of holding the inventory on a monthly basis.
5. Multiply the disposal units by their estimated disposal prices, and multiply the result by the monthly rate of price decline. Add the incremental cost of holding the inventory.

The calculation of the opportunity cost of excess inventory is:

$$((\text{Disposal units} \times \text{Disposal price}) \times \text{Price decline \%}) + \text{Inventory holding cost}$$

$$= \text{Opportunity cost}$$

When deriving this opportunity cost, be careful not to include fixed costs in the inventory holding cost, such as the cost of warehouse utilities. The only relevant inventory holding costs are those that will be eliminated if inventory is sold off – thus, only completely variable holding costs should be considered.

An issue that will likely arise when this measurement is presented to management is the amount of loss the company will record on its books as a result of an inventory disposition. The correct response is that the company should be recording an updated obsolete inventory reserve each month, irrespective of whether the inventory is disposed of. Thus, the only decision remaining for management is whether to hold onto old inventory or sell it now and convert it to cash at whatever prices the company can obtain.

While there are a number of estimates involved in this measurement, it is still one of the best ways to get the attention of management regarding the cost of holding onto inventory for longer than is necessary.

EXAMPLE

Green Lawn Care sells battery-powered lawn mowers, for which the selling season is quite short. In the current season, the sales department estimates that the company will have 5,000 excess lawn mowers. The company can expect to sell these units for $200 right now (August), and can expect this price to decline by 5% in each successive month. There is also a holding cost of $2 per unit, per month, since the company is renting storage space for the units from an independent warehouse. Based on this information, the opportunity cost of excess inventory is:

((5,000 Disposal units × $200 Disposal price) × 5% Price decline) + $10,000 Holding cost

= $60,000 Opportunity cost

In short, the company stands to lose $60,000 for each month in which it does not dispose of the excess lawn mower inventory.

Summary

It may appear that all inventory measurements are designed to draw attention to an excessive investment in inventory. This is largely true, but can also represent a problem, for *some* investment in inventory is usually needed. If inventory levels are drawn down to near zero, the logistics and production functions of a business must be precisely tuned to operate correctly at such a minimal level. If not, the business will likely experience continually-stalled processes that interfere with its ability to produce and sell goods to the satisfaction of its customers.

The intent of this chapter was to establish a tight focus on just those measurements pertaining specifically to the inventory asset. In reality, inventory crosses over with several functional areas – product design, purchasing, and production. Consequently, you may need to review these other areas to find additional measurements that have a tangential impact on the inventory asset.

Chapter 17
Payroll Measurements

Introduction

The payroll function is a cost center, so its focus is on handling large numbers of transactions at the lowest possible cost, and with few processing errors. In this chapter, we describe a number of measurements designed to focus attention at a high level on transaction errors, as well as the cost of payroll services provided.

> **Related Podcast Episode:** Episode 26 of the Accounting Best Practices Podcast discusses payroll measurements. The episode is available at: **accountingtools.com/podcasts** or **iTunes**

Overview of Payroll Measurements

The ultimate goal of the payroll function is to eliminate all manual labor by the payroll staff in the collection of hours worked information, as well as in the calculation and distribution of payments to employees. Ideally, data entry for time worked should be performed by employees, rather than the payroll staff, while payroll software should handle all calculation and payment activities. With these goals in mind, the first few measurements in this chapter are targeted at errors in the payroll system, which are then used by the payroll staff to drill down into the payroll data to understand why an error occurred. We also note a measurement for the cost of payroll activities that are outsourced. When these measurements are actively used, the result should be a payroll department with minimal transaction errors, which can process employee pay at minimal cost.

Payroll Transaction Error Rate

A massive amount of raw data must be organized by the payroll department and translated into a payroll, with the volume of data being highly dependent upon the number of employees who are paid on an hourly basis. If there is an error in this data stream, it takes a considerable amount of time by an experienced payroll person to track down and correct it. If there are many such errors, the payroll staff will be perpetually buried by the sheer volume of corrections. Consequently, it makes sense to track not only the proportion of payroll errors, but also the *types* of errors.

To calculate the payroll transaction error rate, divide all errors detected by the total number of payroll entries made. Use in the denominator the total amount of all entries made, such as hours worked, deductions, memo entries, and goal entries, since errors can occur in all of these areas.

EXAMPLE

Milagro Corporation employs a large staff of hourly production workers to assemble its signature home espresso machines. Milagro's payroll department is being overwhelmed by a large number of payroll transaction errors. The payroll manager summarizes the payroll errors from the past month into the following table:

Transaction Type	Total Entries	Total Errors	Error Rate
Hours entry	1,440	180	12.5%
Salary change entry	36	1	2.8%
Deductions entry	150	4	2.7%
Address change	14	--	0.0%
Direct deposit	60	6	10.0%
Exemptions entry	24	2	8.3%
Totals	1,724	193	11.2%

The information in the table reveals that there is a significant error rate in its hours entry, both on a proportional basis and in terms of the gross number of errors. The payroll manager realizes that fixing the underlying problem will nearly obliterate her transactional errors, and so targets this area for correction.

Of particular concern to the payroll manager is the proportion of *recurring* payroll errors, rather than the stray errors that arise in small numbers on an occasional basis. Recurring errors should be the focus of an intense amount of corrective action. By making such corrections, the department can eliminate entire layers of transaction errors.

Form W-2c to Form W-2 Ratio

When a payroll department makes mistakes in its calculation and recording of employee pay, the information rolls into the annual wage and tax withholding information contained in the Form W-2, which a company issues to its employees and the government. If an employee spots an error in a Form W-2, the company must issue a corrected version on the Form W-2c. It is important to track the proportion of Forms W-2c to the total number of Forms W-2 issued, since it is an indicator of the transactional errors being made by the payroll system.

The calculation of the Form W-2c to Form W-2 ratio is a simple one:

$$\frac{\text{Total Forms W-2c issued}}{\text{Total Forms W-2 issued}}$$

This measurement can be calculated well after the initial issuance of all Forms W-2, in order to give sufficient time for all errors to be located and Forms W-2c to be issued.

EXAMPLE

Milford Sound issues a Form W-2 to each of its 412 employees following the end of the calendar year. During the following few weeks, 38 employees point out that the pay totals listed on their forms are incorrect. Milford issues 38 Forms W-2c to replace the incorrect Forms W-2. The resulting ratio of Forms W-2c to Forms W-2 is calculated as:

$$\frac{38 \text{ Forms W-2c issued}}{412 \text{ Forms W-2 issued}} = 9.2\% \text{ Ratio of W-2c to W-2}$$

This ratio does not represent a sufficient amount of information for corrective action to be taken, so it should be accompanied by a detailed report that itemizes the underlying transaction errors.

Proportion of Manual Checks

Manual payroll checks are usually cut because there was an error in the normal payroll process that resulted in an under-payment to an employee. When there are a significant number of manual checks, it can be an indicator of persistent data collection or pay calculation problems somewhere within the payroll system.

The presence of manual checks can be measured as a simple total of these checks cut, or it can be compared to the total number of payments (both direct deposit and checks) issued to employees. In many cases, the payroll manager will want to investigate *every* manual check, irrespective of the relative proportion of these payments issued, in order to delve into the reasons for payroll errors.

If using this measurement, be aware that a manual payroll check could also be issued to an employee as an advance, which is not indicative of an error. This exception can be eliminated from the payroll system either by imposing a no-advances policy or by issuing the payments through the accounts payable system, rather than the payroll system.

Payroll Entries to Headcount Ratio

In some companies there may be a broad array of payroll deductions, goal entries such as targets for annual pension deductions, and memo entries regarding the amount of vacation or sick time remaining. If these entries are entered manually as part of every payroll, then the payroll department is facing not only a major efficiency problem, but also a high risk of data entry errors. These problems will likely result in a major degradation of the efficiency of the payroll department. Consequently, the payroll manager should be keenly aware of the number of payroll entries being made, particularly in proportion to the number of employees.

The calculation of the number of payroll entries to headcount is:

$$\frac{\text{Total deductions} + \text{Total goal entries} + \text{Total memo entries}}{\text{Average number of full-time equivalents}}$$

In a reasonably automated payroll department, many deductions are automatically recurring, while goal entries may only be entered once a year. Consequently, the level of automation drives the need for this measurement.

EXAMPLE

The extremely detail-oriented payroll manager of Milford Sound has retired. Her replacement knows that the department has been burdened with an immense amount of data entry work for years, primarily because the former payroll manager wanted to carefully track all possible information about employees. The replacement manager compiles the following information about the various payroll entries being made in each of Milford's biweekly payrolls:

Type of Payroll Entry	Description	Number of Entries
Deduction	Medical insurance	240
Deduction	Dental insurance	224
Deduction	Long-term disability	183
Deduction	Short-term disability	172
Deduction	Cafeteria plan – child care	36
Deduction	Cafeteria plan – medical	92
Memo	Vacation time remaining	270
Memo	Sick time remaining	270
	Total entries	1,487

$$\frac{1{,}487 \text{ Payroll entries}}{270 \text{ FTEs}} = 5.5 \text{ Entries to headcount ratio}$$

The preceding information reveals that the payroll department is making an average of 5 ½ payroll entries per person, per payroll. The new payroll manager takes immediate steps to consolidate and automate the entries.

There are several action items that may arise from the use of this measurement, including:

- The automation of as many payroll entries as possible
- Using recurring payroll entries that automatically populate the next payroll
- Consolidating deductions (such as one deduction for the entire package of employee benefits)
- Having the company pay for *all* of a benefit, so there is no employee-paid portion

Outsourced Payroll Cost per Employee

It is extremely common for a company to outsource its payroll processing to a supplier, since doing so eliminates a great deal of payroll calculation, payment, and tax remittance work. However, once outsourced, management tends not to closely track the cost of this activity. The cost of outsourcing commonly balloons over time, since suppliers typically bid low to obtain a company's business, and then escalate or add to the fees. These fees can involve special charges for garnishments, direct deposit, sealing checks inside envelopes, tracking vacation as a memo item, and so forth.

When calculating the outsourced transaction fees per employee, the simplest approach is to add up the supplier's invoices for the measurement period and divide by the number of employees paid during that period. Supplier invoices tend to contain a mixture of per-person charges and fixed fees; for the purposes of this measurement, it does not matter if a cost is variable or fixed. Instead, obtain the gross supplier cost and divide it by the headcount paid. Thus, the calculation is:

$$\frac{\text{Total payroll cost billed by supplier during the measurement period}}{\text{Total number of employees paid}}$$

EXAMPLE

Kelvin Corporation produces a variety of thermometers. The payroll director feels his temperature rise when he reads the latest supplier invoice for processing the company's payroll. He runs a comparison of the outsourced payroll cost for the most recent month and for the same period one year ago, which results in this summary table:

	February 20X1	February 20X2
Monthly payroll fee	$1,900	$3,045
Employees paid	380	420
Cost per employee	$5.00/person	$7.25/person

The payroll director then compares the supplier billings from the two periods and discovers the following three issues:

- The supplier implemented a 6% price increase, which accounts for $0.30 of the increase.
- The company authorized overnight delivery by the supplier of check payments to 14 company locations twice a month, which accounts for $0.80 of the increase.
- The human resources department authorized activation of the supplier's on-line human resources package, which enables employees to update their own records on-line. This purchase accounts for $1.00 of the increase.

Several minor items account for the remaining $0.15 of the cost increase. Based on this information, the payroll director has the cost of the human resources package charged to the human resources department, and arranges to have the payroll supplier use the company's own overnight delivery billing code to pay for the check deliveries.

This measurement will yield valuable insights into cost escalations over time. Though it may not persuade you to shift payroll processing in-house, it may at least initiate some management discussion of how to minimize supplier fees.

Summary

Of the purely payroll-related measurements described in this chapter, the most important is the payroll transaction error rate, especially when the payroll staff delves into the specific transactions that caused the errors. If they investigate and correct the causes of these errors, it is possible to substantially improve the efficiency of the payroll department. However, these measurements only provide general indicators of the underlying problems – a *great* deal of additional investigation is required to arrive at a truly efficient payroll department.

Chapter 18
Pricing Measurements

Introduction

The prices at which products and services are sold are somewhat resistant to evaluation, in terms of whether the correct prices are being used. We do not present a perfect measurement for evaluating prices, but offer instead a set of measurements and concepts that can be used to evaluate how the market may react to pricing changes, internal factors that can impact price setting, and several variances that can be used to evaluate the results of existing pricing policies.

Overview of Pricing Measurements

When setting prices, the management team must be cognizant of the extent to which customer order volumes will change as the result of a new price. This concept is known as the price elasticity of demand, which is caused by a variety of factors. A small pricing change could engender a startling alteration in customer order volume, or be greeted with indifference. A related concept is cross price elasticity of demand, which is the change in the demand for one product when the price of a different product changes. Both concepts should be considered when setting prices.

Price setting should be based on what the market will bear. However, a business should also be aware of which products and services generate the most profit, and design their marketing campaigns to maximize the sales of these items. Another result may be that price increases can be attempted for less-profitable items. The throughput per minute concept is the best measure for evaluating the profitability of products.

Once prices have been set, a company may find that it is difficult to force customers to accept the prices. This is particularly common when services are being offered at an hourly billing rate. The proportion of discounted prices concept is used to quantify the extent to which customers are requiring discounts before they will place orders. This measurement can result in adjustments to the standard prices offered, to reduce the number and volume of discounts taken.

We conclude the chapter with two classic variance analyses. One is the selling price variance, which compares actual prices to budgeted prices. The second variance is the sales volume variance, which compares the actual number of units sold to the budgeted number expected to be sold. Both measurements are used when there is a baseline budget against which actual sales are being compared. If there is no budget, there is no way to calculate these variances.

In summary, the establishment of prices is an imperfect science for which measurements provide a certain limited value. Understanding price elasticity, throughput, and discounts taken can assist with the evaluation of prices, but there is no ideal way to establish the perfect price.

Price Elasticity of Demand

Price elasticity is the degree to which changes in price impact the unit sales of a product or service. The demand for a product is considered to be inelastic if changes in price have minimal impact on unit sales volume. Conversely, the demand for a product is considered to be elastic if changes in price have a large impact on unit sales volume.

A product is more likely to have inelastic demand if customers buy it for reasons other than price. This typically involves high-end luxury goods, or the "latest and greatest" products that are impacted by style considerations, where there are no obvious substitutes for the product. Thus, altering the price of a custom-made watch may not appreciably alter the amount of unit sales volume, since roughly the same number of potential customers are interested in buying it, irrespective of the price (within limits).

A product is more likely to have elastic demand when it is a commodity offered by many suppliers. In this situation, there is no way to differentiate the product, so customers only buy it based on price. Thus, if prices were to be raised on a product that has elastic demand, unit volume would likely plummet as customers go elsewhere to find a better deal. Examples of products having elastic demand are gasoline and many of its byproducts, as well as corn, wheat, and cement. The key considerations in whether a product will have elastic or inelastic demand are:

- *Uniqueness*. If there is no ready substitute for a product, it will be more price inelastic. This is particularly true where intensive marketing is used to make the product appear indispensable in the minds of consumers.
- *Percent of income*. If something involves a significant proportion of the income of the consumer, the consumer is more likely to look for substitute products, which makes a product more price elastic.
- *Necessity*. If something must be purchased (such as a drug for a specific medical condition), then the consumer will buy it, irrespective of price.
- *Duration*. Over time, consumers will alter their behavior to avoid excessively expensive goods. This means that the price for a product may be inelastic in the short term, and increasingly elastic over the long term. For example, the owner of a fuel-inefficient vehicle will be forced to pay for higher gasoline prices in the short term, but may switch to a more fuel-efficient vehicle over the long term in order to buy less fuel.
- *Payer*. People who can have their purchases reimbursed by someone else (such as the company they work for) are more likely to exhibit price inelastic behavior. For example, an employee is more likely to stay at an expensive hotel if his or her company is paying for it.

The elasticity or inelasticity of demand is a consideration in the pricing of products. Clearly, inelastic demand offers a great deal of room in price setting, whereas elastic demand means that the appropriate price is very well defined by the market. However, products having inelastic demand tend to have smaller markets, whereas products with elastic demand can involve much larger sales volume. Thus, a company pursuing a strategy of only selling products with inelastic demand is also limiting its potential sales growth.

From a practical perspective, companies are most likely to set prices based on what competitors are charging for their products, modified by the perceived value of certain product features. Price elasticity can also be used to fine-tune prices, but it is still more of a theoretical concept than one that has practical applicability.

The calculation for the price elasticity of demand is the percent change in unit demand as a result of a one percent change in price. The formula is:

$$\frac{\text{Percent change in unit demand}}{\text{Percent change in price}}$$

A product is said to be price inelastic if this ratio is less than 1:1, and price elastic if the ratio is greater than 1:1. Revenue should be maximized when a business can set the price to have an elasticity of exactly 1:1.

EXAMPLE

Horton Corporation wants to test the price elasticity of demand for two of its products. It alters the price of its blue widget by 3%, which generates a reduction in unit volume of 2%. This indicates some inelasticity of demand, since the company can raise prices while experiencing a smaller offsetting reduction in sales.

Horton then tests the price elasticity of its purple widget by altering its price by 2%. This results in a reduction in unit volume of 4%. This indicates significant elasticity of demand, since unit sales drop twice as fast as the increase in price. In this case, the company clearly has little ability to raise prices.

Cross Price Elasticity of Demand

Cross price elasticity of demand is the percentage change in the demand for one product when the price of a different product changes. The formula is:

$$\frac{\text{Percentage change in demand of one product}}{\text{Percentage change in price of a different product}}$$

If there is no relationship between the two products, then this ratio will be zero. However, if a product is a valid substitute for the product whose price has changed, there will be a positive ratio – that is, a price increase in one product will yield an increase in demand for another product. Conversely, if two products are typically purchased together (known as complementary products), then a price change will result in a negative ratio; thus, a price increase in one product will yield a decrease in demand for the other product. The following exhibit contains examples of different ratio results for the cross price elasticity of demand.

Examples of Cross Price Elasticity Ratio Results

Positive ratio	When the admission price at a movie theater increases, the demand for downloaded movies increases, because downloaded movies are a substitute for a movie theater.
Negative ratio	When the admission price at a movie theater increases, the demand at the nearby parking garage also declines, because fewer people are parking there to go to the movie theater. These are complementary products.
Zero ratio	When the admission price at a movie theater increases, the demand at a nearby furniture store is unchanged, because the two are unrelated.

A company can use the concept of cross price elasticity of demand in its pricing strategies. For example, the food served in a movie theater has a strong complementary relationship with the number of theater tickets sold, so it may make sense to drop ticket prices in order to attract more movie viewers, which in turn generates more food sales. Thus, the net effect of lowering ticket prices may be more total profit for the theater owner.

A business can also use heavy branding of its product line to mitigate the substitution effect. Thus, by spending money on advertising, a business can make customers want to purchase its products so much that a price increase will not send them out to buy substitute products (at least not within a certain price range).

Throughput per Minute

Prices should rarely be based on the underlying costs incurred by a business, since doing so could severely misprice a product in relation to the price that the market will bear. However, there is an internal consideration that can impact the price charged; this is the amount of throughput generated per minute at a company's bottleneck operation. The bottleneck is anything in a business that restricts the ability of the entity to increase its sales and profitability. The classic bottleneck is a machining operation in the production area, but it could also be too few salespeople, a raw materials shortage, and so forth. When there is a bottleneck, its use must be maximized by only processing through it those products that generate the largest amount of throughput. Throughput is sales minus all variable costs directly related to the sales. Thus, throughput per minute must be maximized in order to generate the highest possible profit.

The concept of throughput per minute has a direct impact on prices charged, since a company that wants to maximize profits should sell at the highest sustainable prices that will maximize throughput per minute through the bottleneck operation.

EXAMPLE

Horton Industrial Designs manufactures four types of widgets, each of which has a different price point and which require differing amounts of bottleneck time. The relevant information is:

	Throughput	Bottleneck Time (minutes)	Throughput per Minute
Aluminum widget	$15.00	3.5	$4.29
Iron widget	4.00	2.0	2.00
Magnesium widget	9.00	1.5	6.00
Titanium widget	27.00	8.0	3.38

The information in the table reveals that the company should sell as many magnesium widgets as possible, since doing so maximizes the throughput per minute. Also, management should consider whether it is possible to increase the price of the iron widget, which has one-third the throughput per minute.

The example shows which products have lower throughput per minute than others, so it is a comparative measure. The measurement does not reveal the optimum price that should be charged, but rather which products generate the most throughput per minute, and which therefore should be sold in the greatest volume. This leads to the following possible actions:

- Increased marketing expenditures to support those products generating the most throughput per minute.
- A possible reduction in marketing expenditures for products having low throughput per minute, on the grounds that increased sales of these items will crowd out the production of items that generate more throughput per minute.
- The possibility of raising a product's price in order to increase its throughput per minute.

Proportion of Discounted Prices

A company may set a standard list price for a product or service, but then allows the sales staff to grant discounts from the standard price at their discretion. This situation is particularly common under the following circumstances:

- *Volume purchases.* If a buyer is willing to buy in large volume, then a volume discount is granted.
- *Lead buyer.* A prominent buyer is willing to buy a new product or service in exchange for a discount. The seller is willing to grant the discount in order to use the buyer's name in its marketing of the new product rollout.
- *Soft prices.* The standard price may be considered too high in some geographic regions, forcing the use of discounts in order to complete sales.

Management should be particularly concerned when it sees the proportion of discounted prices increasing over time, since it implies that the sales staff cannot make the list price "stick" in the current market environment. In this case, a reduction in the standard price may be warranted.

There are two variations on how the proportion of discounted prices can be calculated. One option is to divide the total number of discounted deals by the total number of customer orders. However, this approach does not factor in the size of the discounts given. The alternative approach is to divide the total dollar amount of discounts granted by the total dollar volume of customer orders. However, this latter approach can be skewed by a small number of very large discounts. The alternative formulas are:

Option One:

Total number of discounted deals
Total number of customer orders

Option Two:

Total dollar amount of discounts granted
Total dollar volume of customer orders

EXAMPLE

Newton & Matthews is an international safety consulting firm. The company is headquartered in New York City (NYC), where hourly rates are set. The NYC pricing structure is $500 per hour for partners and $250 per hour for associates. These rates are accepted in the NYC area, but the regional offices are reporting that few customers will accept the rates. The accounting staff reviews contracts being signed by branch offices, and notes the following proportions of discounted prices reported by a selection of offices during the last quarter:

	Dollar Amount of Discounts Granted	Total Dollar Volume of Customer Orders	Proportion of Discounted Prices
Boston	$1,050,000	$21,000,000	5%
Charleston	1,200,000	8,000,000	15%
Des Moines	2,000,000	4,000,000	**50%**
Oklahoma City	3,375,000	7,500,000	**45%**
Seattle	2,520,000	14,000,000	18%

It is apparent that the central region of the country is having a particularly difficult time enforcing the company-wide pricing structure. As a result, the senior management team authorizes the use of regional pricing that is adjusted based on how local prices compare to NYC prices.

Selling Price Variance

The selling price variance is the difference between the actual and expected revenue that is caused by a change in the price of a product or service. The formula is:

(Actual price - Budgeted price) × Actual unit sales

An unfavorable variance means that the actual price was lower than the budgeted price.

The budgeted price for each unit of product is developed by the sales and marketing managers, and is based on their estimation of future demand for these products and services, which in turn is affected by general economic conditions and the actions of competitors. If the actual price is lower than the budgeted price, the result may actually be favorable to the company, as long as the price decline spurs demand to such an extent that the company generates an incremental profit as a result of the price decline.

EXAMPLE

The marketing manager of Hodgson Industrial Design estimates that the company can sell a green widget for $80 per unit during the upcoming year. This estimate is based on the historical demand for green widgets.

During the first half of the new year, the price of the green widget comes under extreme pressure as a new supplier in Ireland floods the market with a lower-priced green widget. Hodgson must drop its price to $70 in order to compete, and sells 20,000 units during that period. Its selling price variance during the first half of the year is:

($70 Actual price - $80 Budgeted price) × 20,000 units = -$200,000 Selling price variance

---

There are a number of possible causes of a selling price variance. For example:

- *Discounts*. The company has granted various discounts to customers to induce them to buy products.
- *Marketing allowances*. The company is allowing customers to deduct marketing allowances from their payments to reimburse them for marketing activities involving the company's products.
- *Price points*. The price points at which the company is selling are different from the price points stated in its standards.
- *Product options*. Customers are buying different product options than expected, resulting in an average price that differs from the price points stated in the company's standards.

Sales Volume Variance

The sales volume variance is the difference between the actual and expected number of units sold, multiplied by the budgeted price per unit. The formula is:

(Actual units sold - Budgeted units sold) × Budgeted price per unit

An unfavorable variance means that the actual number of units sold was lower than the budgeted number sold.

The budgeted number of units sold is derived by the sales and marketing managers, and is based on their estimation of how the company's product market share, features, price points, expected marketing activities, distribution channels, and sales in new regions will impact future sales. If the product's selling price is lower than the budgeted amount, this may spur sales to such an extent that the sales volume variance is favorable, even though the selling price variance is unfavorable.

EXAMPLE

The marketing manager of Hodgson Industrial Design estimates that the company can sell 25,000 blue widgets for $65 per unit during the upcoming year. This estimate is based on the historical demand for blue widgets, as supported by new advertising campaigns in the first and third quarters of the year.

During the new year, Hodgson does not have a first quarter advertising campaign, since it is changing advertising agencies at that time. This results in sales of just 21,000 blue widgets during the year. Its sales volume variance is:

(21,000 Units sold - 25,000 Budgeted units) × $65 Budgeted price per unit
= $260,000 Unfavorable sales volume variance

There are a number of possible causes of a sales volume variance. For example:

- *Cannibalization.* The company has released another product that competes with the product in question. Thus, sales of one product cannibalize sales of the other product.
- *Competition.* Competitors have released new products that are more attractive to customers.
- *Price.* The company has altered the product price, which in turn drives a change in unit sales volume.
- *Trade restrictions.* A foreign country has altered its barriers to competition.

Summary

There is no perfect pricing measurement that identifies the best price at which a company should sell a product or service. Proper pricing can be identified within a general range, using the measurements described in this chapter. However, pricing is also highly dependent upon the pricing strategy used by a business. For example, if the freemium strategy is used, where a basic service is provided for free, then none of the preceding measurements will be of much use. Conversely, a premium pricing strategy under which prices are set extremely high might not yield the largest amount of gross sales. In short, a business must first determine its pricing strategy, and then decide how it is going to measure the efficacy of the resulting prices within the boundaries set by the strategy.

Chapter 19
Production Measurements

Introduction

In a manufacturing business, the production area typically absorbs the bulk of all expenditures, and so is worth examining in the greatest detail. In this chapter, we depart somewhat from the usual monetary measurements, and instead focus on ways to improve the operational characteristics of production. This includes measurements of the department as a whole, of specific equipment, and of the ability to produce goods without error. We conclude with several of the more traditional expense measurements.

Overview of Production Measurements

The production area achieves the highest level of performance when viewed as an assemblage of systems that work together. To that end, we begin with department-level performance measures that focus on order cycle time, manufacturing efficiency, degree of unbalance, and similar metrics. By using these measurements, management can sharpen its focus on those production areas that, when enhanced, can contribute to department performance to the greatest extent.

Though the production system as a whole is of the most importance, it is still necessary to attend to individual equipment measurements. To do so, we use the most comprehensive measure, that of equipment effectiveness, as well as setup time, unscheduled downtime, run time, and similar measures that provide clues about the ability of equipment to adhere to the mandated production schedule.

We then shift to another aspect of production, which is the ability to produce goods without error. Two measurements are presented that focus attention on production yield without scrap or rework, so that the cost of materials is minimized.

Finally, we turn to expenditure levels, using comparisons of different aspects of overhead and direct costs to highlight situations where indirect costs are trending upward, and so may require attention.

Taken as a whole, the measures presented here can form the basis for a well-run and responsive production department that can spot developing problem areas and correct them in short order.

Department-Level Performance

The most important production measures are usually those that monitor the performance of the entire system of production, rather than the performance of an individual machine. The reason for this high level of performance is that goods are not produced by a single machine or work station, but rather by an assemblage of people and equipment, working together. In this section, we have several aggregate-level measurements worth considering. These measures deal with the duration of a customer order, the overall efficiency of operations, productivity, unbalance between work stations, and the pace of production.

Order Cycle Time

A key competitive point in many business strategies is how quickly customer orders can be fulfilled. An unusually short cycle time for an order can lock in customers who value quick delivery. However, cycle time may not be an issue in cases where the company strategy is to offer a very low price in exchange for a longer wait to receive goods.

To calculate order cycle time, subtract the date of receipt of an order from the ship date of the order. This calculation does not factor in any orders that are late for delivery and have not yet been shipped, so also include in the calculation the estimated ship date for these late orders. The resulting formula is:

(Ship date or if late, best estimate of ship date) – order date

This measurement should be presented in two parts, as an aggregated order cycle time for all orders, and also as a detailed report that shows the measurement for each underlying order. This type of presentation allows management to drill down into the supporting information to determine which orders are causing problems, and correct whatever the related issues may be.

A variation on the order cycle time concept is to run it for each individual customer on a trend line, to see if any of the more important customers are suffering from below-standard fulfillment rates. The same approach can be used for product families, to see if certain types of products are more difficult to produce.

EXAMPLE

Sharper Designs is having trouble fulfilling some of its orders for an advanced form of ceramic knife that has achieved cult status among executive chefs. The trouble appears to be cracking in some of the blades, which can only be found through detailed inspection of every knife. Each of the knives scrapped must be replaced from current production, which throws off the shipping schedule.

The production manager calculates an aggregate order cycle time of 4.0 days to fill an order, but then subdivides the information by product family to derive much more troubling results, as noted in the following table:

Product Family	Order Cycle Time	Gross Margin
Steel knives	0.8 days	15%
Tungsten knives	1.2 days	24%
Titanium knives	1.1 days	18%
Ceramic knives	42.5 days	75%

The table shows a massive fulfillment problem for the ceramic knife product family. This is particularly troubling, seeing that the high prices charged for these knives could yield excellent profits for the company – if only the knives could be shipped. This information is the basis for a full-scale assault by management on the production processes used to manufacture ceramic knives.

Manufacturing Efficiency

The manufacturing process can be highly inefficient in terms of the time required to produce goods. There are many areas in which work-in-process may be held up in a work queue that can massively increase time requirements. It can be useful to compare the total time required to produce goods to the actual time during which goods are being transformed, to gain an understanding of the amount of wasted time in the process. This wasted time represents an opportunity to cut deeply into the time required to produce goods and get them into the hands of customers more quickly, which can represent a major competitive advantage.

To calculate manufacturing efficiency, aggregate the total amount of time during which products are being transformed, and divide it into the total time period during which a job is in the production area. The formula is:

$$\frac{\text{Total job time}}{\text{Total transformation time}}$$

The main problem with the manufacturing efficiency measurement is that it *only* leads to a reduction in the total time required to manufacture goods. There may be no corresponding improvement in profits. For example, if there is a finished goods inventory buffer already in place between the production process and customers, customers may experience no change in the time required to fill orders, since their orders are already being filled from stock. Also, there may be no increase in throughput, since time reduction efforts could target areas other than the bottleneck operation that controls throughput. Consequently, this measurement should be targeted at those situations in which the result can actually yield a monetary gain.

EXAMPLE

Giro Cabinetry currently fills all orders for its generic apartment cabinets from stock, which requires a large investment in finished goods. The president wants to reduce this investment by shrinking the time required for jobs to pass through the company's production process. He must first understand the level of manufacturing efficiency of the production operation, so he commissions a study that yields the following results:

(hours)	Transformation Time in Work Center	Total time in Work Center
Band saw	0.5	6.0
Drilling	1.0	10.0
Assembly	2.5	8.0
Finishing	3.0	40.0
Totals	7.0	64.0

If the president wants to improve the efficiency of the manufacturing operation, the area in which the most time can be cut is the finishing department. The most efficient group appears to be the assembly area, where any improvement efforts would yield the least results.

Productivity Cause and Effect Ratio

There are many instances where the production manager wants to test whether a change in activity or expenditure will have a positive cause-and-effect relationship with an output from the production system. If so, the relationship can be tested by comparing the incremental change in activity or expenditure to the incremental change in output. This is less of a performance ratio, and more of a tool for testing whether various changes should be made to the production process. The formula is:

$$\frac{\text{Incremental change in output}}{\text{Incremental change in activity or expenditure}}$$

This is a notably vague measurement, but needs to be in order to accommodate the many uses to which it can be put. Here are samples of possible applications:

- *Scrap reduction.* Invest in new equipment for which production tolerances can be more easily set, thereby reducing scrap levels. The cause is the cost of the equipment, and the effect is the reduced cost of scrap.
- *Electricity reduction.* Invest in solar panels to power production equipment. The cause is the price of the solar panels, and the effect is the reduction in electricity costs.
- *Units of production increase.* Add staff to the bottleneck operation in order to prolong the run time of this work center. The cause is the cost of the extra staff, and the effect is an increase in the number of units produced.

This measurement only works when there is a clear causal relationship between the supposed cause and the effect. It is also not especially useful where there are a cluster of causes that lead to one effect; in this case, improvement in one cause may be offset by declines in other causes, leading to no discernible change in the effect.

EXAMPLE

The bottleneck operation of Dude Skis is the lamination machine, which laminates graphics on top of skis. The machine is already being run 24×7. The production manager discovers that the machine is actually *not* running during company holidays. He learns that machine operators would be willing to run the machine during these periods for an aggregate cost of $200 per hour. For each of these additional hours of production, the company can produce an additional $1,000 of throughput. This results in an excellent productivity cause-and-effect ratio of 5:1.

Degree of Unbalance

In a lean manufacturing environment, machines are commonly clustered together to most efficiently produce certain types of goods. Within each of these work cells is likely to be a bottleneck operation that cannot produce as fast as the surrounding equipment. If the capacity of this bottleneck is well below that of the nearby machines, there is considered to be a high degree of unbalance in the work cell, which affects its overall performance. When there is a high degree of unbalance, the industrial engineering staff can review operations to see if the bottleneck operation can be improved, resulting in a higher output level.

To calculate the degree of unbalance in a work cell, divide the maximum capacity level of the bottleneck operation by the maximum capacity level of the next most restrictive operation in the work cell. The formula is:

$$\frac{\text{Maximum actual capacity of bottleneck operation}}{\text{Maximum actual capacity of next most restrictive operation}}$$

The formula reveals two key points about this measurement:

- Use actual capacity, rather than theoretical capacity. Actual capacity takes into account normal downtime for maintenance and other expected stoppages, while theoretical capacity reflects perfect running conditions with no stoppages. Theoretical capacity is rarely attainable.
- Only measure the difference in capacity between the bottleneck and the next most restrictive operation, since adjusting this difference will lead to an improvement in the overall output of the work cell. Using the average capacity of the entire work cell does not pinpoint the extent to which output can be improved.

This measurement operates best in work cells that are heavily utilized, so that improvements in the degree of unbalance are most likely to yield actual increases in the rate of output. If a work cell is operating well below its capacity level, then the industrial engineering staff might want to spend its time working on more critical areas of the production facility.

EXAMPLE

The Billabong Machining Company operates a work cell that produces a large number of pink widgets for the fashion trade. The clear bottleneck in this work cell is the paint application machine, which can produce no more than 100 units per hour. The other operations in the work cell have the following capacity levels:

	Maximum Actual Capacity per Hour
Stamping	360
Lathe	425
Deburring	200

The next most restrictive operation is deburring, which can produce twice the number of units as the paint application machine, resulting in a 50% degree of unbalance. The industrial engineering staff could acquire an additional paint application machine to equalize the maximum capacity of these two operations at 200 pink widgets per hour.

Operational Takt Time

A company is typically faced with a roughly predictable number of units that it can expect customers to purchase within a given period of time. If so, the production team must ensure that the manufacturing facility maintains an average pace of unit production that ensures the number of items to be sold can be created. This concept is called operational takt time, which includes all downtime expected during the measurement period; downtime may include such factors as stoppages for maintenance, equipment breakdowns, holidays and so forth.

To measure operational takt time, calculate the average amount of time that a production facility is actually in operation each day, and divide by the number of units that must be built each day in order to meet demand. The formula is:

$$\frac{\text{Average amount of time in operation per day}}{\text{Number of units that must be built each day}}$$

The measurement can be surprisingly useful for determining the amount of output that an operation must complete within a given period of time. If the number of units actually produced falls below the operational takt time, then management can take steps to increase production, such as by authorizing a third shift or by outsourcing work. Takt time is typically posted in a work cell or factory, so that employees can see how closely they are adhering to production requirements.

The operational takt time concept can also be adjusted for conditions expected to exist in the near future. For example, if a key work cell is scheduled to be down for maintenance for a certain period of time, this can be incorporated into the numerator of the measurement, resulting in a different requirement for the pace of production.

EXAMPLE

Crumb Cake Café usually receives a massive number of orders in the days leading up to Mother's Day, to the extent that approximately 80,000 cakes must be baked within a four-day period and then frozen for delivery by mail to customers. This means the company must produce 20,000 cakes in four days. During this period, the company typically operates two shifts, which involve a total of 960 minutes of production time per day. There is a 10-minute downtime during the shift changeover, so the number of minutes in operation per day is actually 950 minutes. The operational takt time for the facility is:

$$\frac{950 \text{ minutes in operation per day}}{20,000 \text{ cakes per day}} = 0.0475 \text{ minutes/cake}$$

Historically, the facility has only been able to produce at a rate of 0.06 minutes/cake, so there is a projected shortfall of 0.0125 minutes/cake. The production manager decides to pay overtime and have the two shifts work 12 hours each for one day, in order to catch up on the required operational takt time.

Equipment Measurements

It may be necessary to measure individual machines, though this is not recommended unless they are so heavily utilized that the performance of a specific machine will detract from the overall output of the production department. If it is necessary to do so, then the following five measurements can be used to monitor equipment effectiveness, setup times, unscheduled downtime, maintenance and repair time, and average run times.

Equipment Effectiveness

A production operation may include several machines that are operated at near-capacity levels in order to meet production targets. For these machines, the highest-possible number of units must be manufactured that meet product specifications. An excellent measure of this capability is equipment effectiveness, which combines three different aspects of machine usage and output, as follows:

- *Output quality.* The units produced must meet targeted specifications. If not, the units must be reworked or scrapped.
- *Availability.* The machine should be available for use as much as possible, which calls for proper staffing and accurate preventive maintenance.
- *Efficiency.* The machine must operate as close to its rated number of units of output as possible.

These concepts are combined into the following equipment effectiveness measurement:

Percent of units accepted × Percent of time available for use × Percent of maximum run rate

It is nearly impossible to attain 100% equipment effectiveness for any period of time, since so many factors can impair effectiveness. The following examples are issues that can interfere with effectiveness:

- A machine setup is incorrect, resulting in unacceptable units produced
- A machine operator calls in sick, so that no one can run the machine
- A machine is getting old, and so requires much more maintenance downtime, which in turn reduces the percent of time available for use

Management can review the various components of machine effectiveness and decide which steps to take to improve the overall effectiveness of a machine at the least cost. For example, there may be a tradeoff of running at a reduced speed in order to reduce the number of maintenance intervals. Alternatively, there could be a tradeoff between paying the cost of a more skilled machine operator in exchange for the machine running at a higher speed.

EXAMPLE

The production manager of Armadillo Industries, maker of body armor, has concluded that the graphite lamination machine used to bond layers of graphite is a high-usage area that is operating near its maximum capacity. He finds that the acceptance rate of the units produced from this operation is 80%, the percentage of time available for use is 92%, and the percentage of the maximum run rate is 98%. The resulting equipment effectiveness is:

80% Percent of units accepted × 92% Percent of time available for use × 98% Percent of maximum run rate

= 72% Equipment effectiveness

Based on the components of the measurement, it appears that the best area in which to pursue improvement is the quality of the units produced. For example, if the 80% acceptance rate could be improved to 90%, this would result in a revised equipment effectiveness rating of 81%.

Setup Time

When equipment requires a lengthy setup time prior to manufacturing a part, there is a natural inclination to favor long production runs, so that the cost of the setup is spread over many units. This is a problem in a just-in-time environment, where production runs may be for as little as one unit. Setup time is also an issue when the use of equipment is being maximized due to high demand, and every second counts. In both cases, it makes sense to focus intently on setup time, to see if the setup process can be reduced.

To calculate setup time, measure the time period from the termination of the last production run to the beginning of the next production run for a machine. This time interval covers every aspect of the setup process, including bringing tools, adjusting equipment, and testing output to see if it falls within specifications. The formula is:

$$\text{Start time for next job} - \text{Stop time for last job}$$

Setup time can be difficult to measure manually, especially when the production staff is being asked to self-report on its own performance. A better alternative, though a potentially expensive one, is to install monitoring equipment that automatically reports setup times.

EXAMPLE

The production manager of Ambivalence Corporation is concerned about the setup time required for the potions line. When a batch of blue toadstools has been brewed, the vat must be scrubbed and bleached before the next batch can be started. The result is a lengthy setup process where the average setup time is roughly one hour. A consultant is brought in, who suggests rotating out the old vat on a railing system and swapping in a replacement vat, so that the old vat can be cleaned off-line. The resulting setup time declines to 30 seconds. Based on this result, the company is now considering just-in-time potion manufacturing.

Unscheduled Downtime Percentage

When the demand for a company's products is high, the production area must run at a high level of utilization in order to meet demand. Under these circumstances, every minute of downtime can result in a delayed delivery and unsatisfied customers. Accordingly, the production scheduling staff blocks out specific time periods in the production schedule when machines are to be maintained – and no additional time. If unscheduled downtime occurs, the production schedule must be reconfigured to work around the problem, causing delays and bottlenecks in the production area. This issue can be highlighted by the unscheduled downtime percentage.

To calculate unscheduled downtime, divide the total minutes of unscheduled downtime for a machine by the total number of minutes in the measurement period. The formula is:

$$\frac{\text{Total minutes of unscheduled downtime}}{\text{Total minutes in the measurement period}}$$

This measurement should not be used in aggregate for all of the machines in the production area, for some of this equipment is already underutilized, and additional downtime is not of much importance. Also, requiring the recordation of downtime can be quite a chore for the production staff. Instead, only measure unscheduled downtime for the equipment that is regularly operating at a high level of utilization, and which can impact the production flow if it is not available for use at all times. Measuring just these items correctly places attention on areas that should be closely monitored by the maintenance staff.

EXAMPLE

The Atlas Machining Company is experiencing heavy demand for its widgets just prior to the popular Wabash Widget Festival. The production manager is particularly concerned about three work centers that have historically been brought down for unscheduled maintenance. In the past week, the unscheduled maintenance for these work centers was as follows:

	Unscheduled Downtime (minutes)	Total Time in Period (minutes)	Unscheduled Downtime Percentage
Wire wrapping	1,500	10,080	15%
Extrusion	2,120	10,080	21%
Thread rolling	1,915	10,080	19%

Given the downtime issues at these work centers, the production manager elects to have some scheduled work outsourced to a third party.

Maintenance and Repair Ratio

Part of the capital budgeting decision is whether to replace equipment now or wait until later, and incur a larger maintenance and repair cost in the meantime. This decision is particularly important in the production area, where most of a company's fixed asset base is located. One way to track this issue is to compare the maintenance and repair cost of a production fixed asset to its run time. The formula is:

$$\frac{\text{Maintenance and repair cost}}{\text{Equipment run time}}$$

Note that the expense and the equipment run time are both measured for the current reporting period only. The ratio is then compiled on a trend line, and will probably show an increasing cost per hour of run time over the life of the equipment. If the trend line reveals a sudden spike in the ratio, this is a strong indicator of the end of the practical life of an asset, at which point it should be replaced.

Though this ratio is a good indicator of the increasing cost of old equipment, it does not necessarily point to the exact date on which equipment should be replaced. It is entirely possible that the replacement cost of a machine is so high that even an elevated maintenance and repair cost does not justify swapping it for a new machine.

230

EXAMPLE

Blitz Communications owns an injection molding machine that is used to produce plastic casings for the company's line of office phones. The machine is twenty years old, and is requiring more maintenance expenditures as the company continues to use it. The production manager asks for a review of the maintenance and repair costs of the machine for each of the past five years, which is as follows:

	Maintenance and Repair Cost	Run Time (hours)	Maintenance and Repair Ratio
Year 1	$16,500	2,000	$8.25/hour
Year 2	17,000	1,900	8.95/hour
Year 3	23,000	1,850	12.43/hour
Year 4	45,000	1,600	28.13/hour
Year 5	47,000	1,625	28.92/hour

The ratio reveals a spike in the cost per hour in Year 4, which has since increased. It appears to be time to replace the injection molding machine.

Average Run Time

When a company produces large numbers of units in a single production run, the most efficient scenario is when equipment can run for extremely long periods of time without interruption. In these cases, it makes sense to track the average run time of a machine. A machine stoppage is assumed to be bad – perhaps due to a raw materials shortage, power failure, or machine breakdown. When the average run time declines, these underlying issues are examined and corrected in order to increase the run time.

To calculate average run time, divide the sum of all run times by the number of production runs. The formula is:

$$\frac{\text{Aggregate production run duration}}{\text{Number of production runs}}$$

This measurement is not to be used for just-in-time production environments where batch sizes are very small. It is only useful when equipment is being run at maximum capacity, so do not use it in cases where capacity levels are low and equipment is therefore not used at all from time to time.

EXAMPLE

The Excalibur Shaving Company does immensely long production runs for its razor blades, which are necessary in order to meet demand for refills on the company's shaving systems. The production manager has noticed that the length of these production runs has declined of late, due to problems with blade edges being out of spec. He accumulates the following information about production run lengths:

Run Number	Run Duration (hours)
1	132
2	129
3	111
4	98
5	82
6	78

The average run time is 105 hours, which compares unfavorably to the historical run rate of 160 hours. Of more importance to the production manager is the obvious declining trend in the duration of production runs. This may be due to a pending failure in the equipment. Accordingly, he schedules a complete overhaul of the equipment.

Yield Measurements

A key element of the profitability of a manufacturing operation is its ability to produce goods without error. Otherwise, the operation may incur extremely high costs related to wasted raw materials, machine usage, and rework. The following two measurements focus on yield, which is the ability to produce the expected number of units.

First-Pass Yield

A potentially massive amount of additional work is required in the production area when goods cannot be manufactured correctly on the first pass. These costs include the repurchase of raw materials to create replacement goods, as well as rework for those items that can be recovered. Management can focus on the measurement of first-pass yield on the most troublesome work stations on a continuing basis, so that issues are continually highlighted and corrected.

To measure first-pass yield, divide the number of units successfully completed by a manufacturing process by the total number of units initiated. The formula is:

$$\frac{\text{Number of units successfully completed}}{\text{Number of units initiated}}$$

EXAMPLE

The owner of Smithy Ironworks is annoyed that so many of the iron garden curios produced by the company are found to have flaws, and must be melted down for recasting. The owner closely follows the first-pass yield, which highlights the following problems with the company's casting process:

Number of units initiated	10,000
- Mold damage	-237
- Incorrect furnace temperature	-150
- Defective iron ore	-80
- Improper finishing	-270
First-pass yield	9,263

The first-pass yield is 92.6%. Based on the volume of errors, the owner elects to focus on improper finishing issues in more detail.

Material Yield Variance

The material yield variance is the difference between the actual amount of material used and the standard amount expected to be used, multiplied by the standard cost of the materials. The formula is:

$$\text{(Actual unit usage - Standard unit usage)} \times \text{Standard cost per unit}$$

An unfavorable variance means that the unit usage was greater than anticipated.

The standard unit usage is developed by the engineering staff, and is based on expected scrap rates in a production process, the quality of raw materials, losses during equipment setup, and related factors.

EXAMPLE

The engineering staff of Hodgson Industrial Design estimates that eight ounces of rubber will be required to produce a green widget. During the most recent month, the production process used 315,000 ounces of rubber to create 35,000 green widgets, which is nine ounces per product. Each ounce of rubber has a standard cost of $0.50. Its material yield variance for the month is:

$$\text{(315,000 Actual unit usage - 280,000 Standard unit usage)} \times \$0.50 \text{ Standard cost/unit}$$

$$= \$17,500 \text{ Material yield variance}$$

There are a number of possible causes of a material yield variance. For example:

- *Scrap.* Unusual amounts of scrap may be generated by changes in machine setups, or because changes in acceptable tolerance levels are altering the amount of scrap produced. A change in the pattern of quality inspections can also alter the amount of scrap.
- *Material quality.* If the material quality level changes, this can alter the amount of quality rejections. If an entirely different material is substituted, this can also alter the amount of rejections.
- *Spoilage.* The amount of spoilage may change in concert with alterations in inventory handling and storage.

Expense Proportions

The previous sections of this chapter were primarily concerned with ways to enhance specific aspects of the production area. In this section, we turn to the examination of expenses for the entire production department, with a particular emphasis on changes in the relative proportions of production expenses over time.

Indirect Labor to Direct Labor Ratio

The modern production environment requires a substantial amount of indirect labor support for such activities as production planning, quality control, and management. The amount of indirect labor should be tightly controlled, to ensure that the minimum expenditure is made in exchange for an adequate level of production oversight. We can estimate the correct amount of indirect labor by comparing it to the expenditure for direct labor. The proportion of expenditures between these two categories of labor should remain relatively static over time.

To calculate the ratio of indirect labor to direct labor, compile the total labor cost of indirect labor and divide by the total labor cost of direct labor. The costs of benefits and payroll taxes are not included. The formula is:

$$\frac{\text{Indirect labor compensation}}{\text{Direct labor compensation}}$$

The relationship between indirect and direct labor does not move in lockstep, for indirect labor tends to be incurred as a step cost. That is, an indirect labor position will be hired when unit volume reaches a certain point, such as when a new shift is added. When such a position is added, the proportion of indirect labor will increase and then remain at a new and higher level.

The ratio can also change if there are differences in the pay increases awarded to employees. For example, the direct labor group might be paid a guaranteed wage increase under the terms of a union agreement, while the indirect labor staff may have its wages frozen. These types of disparities can create variations in the ratio over time that are not related to the amount of staffing.

EXAMPLE

The production manager of Barbary Coast Rifles closely monitors the ratio of indirect to direct labor, because he likes to keep overhead as low as possible. Despite his best efforts, however, a shift supervisor must be added for the third shift, which the company just started in order to meet recent increases in customer orders. This change occurs in the third quarter, which causes a spike in the ratio, as shown in the following table. There is also a 3% pay raise for the indirect labor staff in the fourth quarter, and a union-negotiated 5% raise for the direct labor staff in the same quarter.

	Quarter 1	Quarter 2	Quarter 3	Quarter 4
Indirect labor compensation	$240,000	$240,000	$293,000	$302,000
Direct labor compensation	$960,000	$960,000	$1,010,000	$1,061,000
Ratio	25%	25%	29%	28%

Overhead to Direct Cost of Goods Ratio

The overhead portion of the cost of goods sold can be extraordinarily high, and encompasses much more than the indirect labor noted in the last measurement. There can also be such expenses as depreciation, factory rent, utilities, insurance, and production supplies. It can be useful to compare the cost of this overhead to the total direct cost of goods sold on a trend line, to see how the cost of overhead is changing over time. This can be used as a general control over overhead.

To calculate the ratio, divide the cost of all factory overhead by the direct cost of goods sold. The direct cost is comprised of direct materials and direct labor. It is also acceptable to include the cost of commissions in the direct cost of goods, if commissions vary directly with sales volume. The formula is:

$$\frac{\text{Factory overhead}}{\text{Direct materials} + \text{Direct labor} + \text{Commissions}}$$

The direct cost of goods sold tends to vary more with sales volume than factory overhead. These characteristics mean that sharp swings in sales can result in outsized changes in the ratio, as the numerator reacts slowly to the changes while the denominator shifts in concert with sales levels.

EXAMPLE

Entwhistle Electric produces compact batteries for a variety of mobile applications. The equipment used to manufacture the batteries is highly automated, requiring major overhead expenses for depreciation, utilities, and maintenance staff. There are also significant direct materials costs for the batteries, with minimal direct labor. The company is implementing a new sales channel that will sell internationally with large commission percentages for the sales staff in this channel. The before and after ratio results for the company are as follows:

	Before International Sales Channel	After International Channel Installed
Factory overhead	$1,200,000	$1,350,000
Direct cost elements:		
Direct materials	$650,000	$737,000
Direct labor	150,000	170,000
Commissions	0	400,000
Overhead to direct cost of goods	1.5:1	1.0:1

The table reveals that the direct cost component of the company's cost of goods sold has risen markedly as a result of allowing commissions for the new sales channel.

General Management Measurements

The production manager must be careful not to incentivize employees based on other measurements that will cause them to take actions that do not benefit the department. In particular, do not use the following measurements:

- *Total output.* There should be no incentive to produce more than the production plan requires, since this will result in an excess investment in inventory, and which may eventually result in obsolete inventory that must be written off.
- *Overtime reduction.* If there is a bottleneck operation in the production area, it must be operated at maximum capacity at all times, irrespective of any attendant labor costs. This means that overtime *in this area* is entirely allowable, and should not be discouraged.
- *Equipment utilization.* When equipment has been used to fulfill the production schedule or the requirements of a kanban notification, the equipment should then be shut down, irrespective of what this might do to its utilization percentage. If there is an undue focus on maintaining high rates of equipment utilization throughout a facility, there will inevitably be too much work-in-process cluttering up the shop floor.

Summary

This chapter has delved into the measurements associated with not only the entire production area as an operating unit, but also measurements for individual machines and production yield. However, it has not addressed constraint and throughput measurements. These issues are critical to the effective operation of a production department; since they are also needed to evaluate other parts of a business, constraint and throughput measures have been listed in a separate chapter. Please refer to the Constraint and Throughput Measurements chapter to review this additional topic. When constraint and throughput measurements are combined with the metrics stated in this chapter, management will have a complete set of tools for maximizing the flow of production through high-usage production areas, with the goal of enhancing profits.

Chapter 20
Product Design Measurements

Introduction

It is all too common for a business to pour money into its product design efforts without understanding how those funds are used, or whether the organization is realizing a reasonable return on its investment. In this chapter, we address the best ways to measure product development, as well as the financial outcome of new product introductions.

Overview of Product Design Measurements

The measurement of the product design function centers on the efficiency of the design teams and the financial outcomes of their efforts. We begin with an analysis of how well product designers can use existing design platforms and components, which can drastically reduce the time required to develop products. We also note the design cycle time, which covers the time period from design inception to product release (and which therefore covers considerably more than the time period under the control of a design team). There is also a discussion of the accuracy of a key work product, the bill of materials, which is used to order parts and assemble parts for production jobs. A not-insignificant additional topic is turnover among innovation personnel.

We then turn to the financial outcomes of the investment in product design. A key emphasis is on the cost of products, so we review the percentage of target cost attained. This figure is of some importance, since it refers to the cost designed *into* a product, and which can only be subsequently altered with difficulty. We also note the percentage of sales coming from new products, which can be of particular use in industries where product life cycles are extremely short. The cost and profit figures are then combined into a return on research and development measurement. However, the calculation we use for this return on investment is more comprehensive than a simple gross margin analysis, since we also include other types of income that may be derived from research funding. We finish with a discussion of the warranty claims percentage, which can be indicative of the quality of a product design.

Product Development

In this section, we focus on the efficiency of product design, with particular emphasis on the economical usage of design platforms and existing components, as well as the time required to develop products and the accuracy of the accompanying bill of materials. We also note the need to keep track of the reasons for employee turnover in areas relating to innovation.

Number of Design Platforms

The most efficient way to develop a range of products is to use a common design platform as the basis for as many products as possible. Each design platform has a common set of parts, can be produced by a production line that is specifically constructed for it, and is supported by a group of experienced design engineers. This leads to the following advantages for each product developed using an existing design platform:

- A smaller incremental investment in inventory, since many of the component parts are already in stock.
- Less time to ramp up production, since the manufacturing capability already exists.
- Less risk of warranty claims, since the underlying platform has already been tested by users.
- Less time to design new products, since designs may only be slight tweaks of existing products.

Clearly, measuring the number of design platforms can be a key consideration for a company that wants to rationalize a wildly proliferated set of products. A variation on the measurement is to track the number of products using each design platform.

EXAMPLE

A new CEO has just been hired to run Grizzly Golf Carts, which is known for its robust designs catering to overweight golfers. The CEO comes from a lean manufacturing background where vehicle designs are based on the minimum number of design platforms. He finds that Grizzly offers 30 models based on 15 different design platforms. He immediately slashes 10 of the products, because they not only have poor sales, but also operate on unique design platforms. Of the remaining 20 models, he orders the staggered redesign of 14 models, so that they are based on one of the five remaining design platforms. At the end of this process, the CEO expects to have 20 models that are based on five platforms, for an average of four models per platform.

Reused Components Percentage

A company can reduce the complexity of its operations by using the same components in multiple products. Doing so yields the following benefits:

- Fewer items to maintain in the inventory records
- Can purchase the smaller number of items in bulk, resulting in volume purchase discounts
- Fewer suppliers to deal with
- Less likely to have obsolete inventory items, since parts can be repurposed if a product is eliminated
- More historically-based knowledge of component failure rates

In short, there are many reasons to push the design staff in the direction of creating new products that reuse existing components.

To calculate the reused components percentage, aggregate the number of existing parts in the bill of materials of a new product and divide by the total number of parts in the bill. Ideally, the existing parts listed in the numerator are only those that have been specifically approved in advance for re-use in new products. The formula is:

$$\frac{\text{Number of existing parts in bill of materials of new product}}{\text{Total number of parts in the bill of materials}}$$

This measurement only works if the engineering department has issued a comprehensive bill of materials.

If too much emphasis is based on this measurement, there may be a tendency for the design staff to not experiment with new materials or suppliers. To mitigate this concern, consider assigning some of the staff to an ongoing review of replacement components that can be adopted throughout the company's various product lines.

EXAMPLE

The Black Cat Ladder Company has a strong incentive to reuse existing parts for new ladder designs, since some components have been certified to not collapse – a key element of a ladder. Consequently, when the design manager envisioned a No Slip ladder, the reused components percentage was mandated to be at least 85%, with new components only being allowed for the grid pads used on the ladder steps to reduce slippage. As a result, 34 parts out of 38 were reused, which is an 89% reused components percentage.

Design Cycle Time

In some industries, a distinct competitive advantage can be gained by designing new products within the shortest possible period of time. By doing so, a business can launch products ahead of competitors and gain market share.

To calculate design cycle time, subtract the design start date from the product launch date for each product. Note that this time period encompasses not only the work of the product design staff, but also the time required to procure components, manufacture goods, distribute goods in preparation for sale, and launch a marketing campaign. Thus, the responsibility for design cycle time rests with many departments, not just the product design team. The calculation is:

$$\text{Product launch date} - \text{Design start date}$$

If the design cycle time is aggregated across all products, a number of minor product updates could artificially give the appearance of an extremely rapid cycle time. To avoid this skewed result, differentiate between minor updates and major new products, and measure their cycle times separately.

A possible issue with an excessive focus on design cycle time is that products may be released to the market before they have been fully tested, possibly resulting in excessive warranty claims or even product recalls. Thus, it can be useful to review the trend line for warranty costs in conjunction with design cycle time.

EXAMPLE

The president of Grubstake Brothers is concerned that the Japanese competition is developing new backhoes at a much faster pace than Grubstake, resulting in lost sales. He initiates sweeping product development changes, with the following results in design cycle time:

Year	Average Design Cycle Time
20X1	304 days
20X2	291 days
20X3	268 days

Thus, over the three-year measurement period, the company has succeeded in shrinking the average cycle time by 12%.

Bill of Material Accuracy

When the engineering staff completes a product, it must also generate a bill of materials, which is a listing of every component used to manufacture a product. The bill of materials is used by the purchasing staff to acquire parts, and by the warehouse staff to pick parts from stock for a production job. Every bill must be extremely accurate, or else parts will be ordered incorrectly, and kitted jobs will not contain the parts needed by the production staff.

Bill of material accuracy is calculated for each individual bill of materials. For each one, conduct an audit to verify that the correct part numbers, quantities, and units of measure are included. Then divide each accurate line item by the total number of line items in the bill. The formula is:

$$\frac{\text{Number of accurate line items in bill of materials}}{\text{Total number of line items in bill of materials}}$$

This measurement should be conducted whenever there is an engineering change order associated with a product, since these changes will typically result in an adjustment to the contents of the associated bill of materials.

EXAMPLE

The design team of Billabong Machining Company just completed a new agricultural widget. As part of the design process, a junior member of the team is assigned the task of creating a bill of materials. An audit of his bill of materials results in the following analysis:

Item Description	Quantity	Unit of Measure	Audit Result
Metal casing	1	Each	Correct
¼" ball bearing	3	Each	Correct
½" lug nut	4	Each	Incorrect
Back plate	1	Each	Correct
Cyan paint	3	Ounce	Incorrect
Plug assembly	1	Each	Correct
Label	2	Each	Incorrect

The analysis reveals that the junior team member will remain junior until he can attain a higher level of precision in his documentation of the bill of materials, since bill of material accuracy is only 57%.

Innovation Personnel Turnover Rate

A business should be making significant and sustained investments in its innovation personnel (typically in the engineering function), since these people are the primary drivers of its growth and competitiveness. Ideally, this group should have an extremely low turnover rate, so that the business is not losing its investment in them. Measuring turnover for these people should take into account the following factors:

- *Incompetence.* Some innovation personnel are simply not able to innovate, and so should be let go as expeditiously as possible, so that they can be replaced by new hires with more potential. This means that there can certainly be a minimum level of expected turnover.
- *Reasons.* Some reasons for turnover are benign, such as a spouse taking a job on the other side of the planet, while others could be an indicator of a problem, such as being hired away by a competitor for a higher salary. Consequently, any measurement should include a summary of the exit interview conducted with each person who has left.

EXAMPLE

Glow Atomic operates the world's most advanced experimental fusion reactor, using a new spherical tokamak design. Its design staff is comprised of 40 physics PhDs from the world's best universities. Given the extremely advanced nature of its work, Glow's CEO is concerned whenever one of the design team leaves the company. Accordingly, he receives a rolling 12-month report of all departures from the firm, which includes commentary on the underlying reasons. The latest report is as follows:

Name	Departure Date	Commentary
Becquerel, Pierre	February 15, 20X1	Received inheritance and retired
Cherenkov, Abraham	June 21, 20X1	Hired by General Fusion for twice the salary
Schwinger, Albert	October 2, 20X2	Fired for being unable to work with colleagues

---

Financial Outcomes

The preceding measurements were targeted at the efficiency with which products are designed, as well as the accuracy of related information. In this section, we turn to the monetary outcome of product design, which encompasses product cost, sales from new products, the return on investment, and the cost of warranty claims.

Percentage of Target Cost Attained

One of the best ways to assure that a product will generate a reasonable profit is to design it to meet a specific cost target. If that target is met, and customers will accept the product at a certain price point, then a reasonable margin can be earned on a consistent basis. Consequently, if a company has a design program in place that emphasizes cost goals, the engineering manager should routinely track the percentage of target cost attained for each product.

To calculate the percentage of target cost attained, divide the actual cost at which a product is being manufactured by its original cost target. The formula is:

$$\frac{\text{Actual production cost per unit}}{\text{Targeted production cost per unit}}$$

There are several issues to consider when using this measurement. They are:

- *Unit volumes.* The cost of a product typically declines as its unit volume increases, due to volume purchase discounts and the inherent efficiencies of high-volume production. Thus, the percentage will look more favorable if the underlying costs are based on more units being produced.
- *Product features.* The actual cost of a product can be forced down to the target cost in almost all cases, if the number of product features or the quality of the product is reduced. Such reductions may not make the originally-anticipated price point tenable.

Given the preceding issues, it may make more sense to compare the actual product margin to the planned margin for an entire reporting period. Doing so incorporates the actual volumes of units being produced, as well as the price points being accepted by customers.

EXAMPLE

Billabong Machining Company has had a recurring problem with the costs at which its titanium widgets have been produced for the consumer market. To mitigate the problem, the engineering manager institutes a cost management program, under which the newest widget model is targeted at a $12 cost per unit, and a price point of $20. The design project is expected to take four months with four month-end milestone reviews to examine the ongoing ability of the design team to create a widget that meets the $12 cost target. The outcomes of the four milestone reviews are as follows:

	Milestone Cost Target	Milestone Cost Achieved	Percent Variance
January review	$18.50	$18.00	+3%
February review	15.75	16.00	-2%
March review	13.25	13.75	-4%
April review	12.00	13.00	-8%

The table reveals that the design team started out ahead of the milestone cost target, but then steadily fell further behind in later milestone reviews, ultimately resulting in a product cost that is 8% higher than expected.

Percentage of New-Product Sales

One way to force the engineering staff to continually develop new products is to set a target for what proportion of sales will come from new products, typically on a rolling basis that looks back anywhere from one to three years. Doing so forces the engineering staff to look for larger product opportunities that can have a notable impact on sales.

To measure the percentage of new-product sales, divide all sales related to new stock-keeping units by total net sales for the measurement period. We use the creation of a new stock-keeping unit as the most likely threshold for a product being considered sufficiently new that it is given a separate identification. The formula is:

$$\frac{\text{Sales from new stock-keeping units}}{\text{Total net sales}}$$

This measurement is most commonly used in markets where there is such intense competition that the only way to maintain sales is to continually release a stream of new products. If the marketplace is instead a staid one, it may not be necessary to place such a focus on new product sales.

EXAMPLE

Dude Skis manufactures wide skis most applicable to powder skiing. The buyers of these skis are a fickle lot, basing their decisions mostly on the graphics laminated to the tops of the skis. Consequently, Dude must continually issue new models with different graphics in order to appeal to its buyers. The company targets having 75% of its sales come from new models each year. In the most recent year, $3,400,000 of its total sales of $4,850,000 were from the sale of new ski designs. This represents a proportion of 70% of new models, which is below the corporate target. Accordingly, the company hires an additional graphics designer to develop more ski graphics.

Return on Research and Development

One of the most puzzling aspects of funding allocation is how much money to invest in research and development. Typically, the same amount spent historically is spent again in the current period, or else funding is based on a percentage of sales, or perhaps on the amounts being spent by competitors. An alternative approach is to calculate the return on funds spent on research and development. This approach is concerned with the effectiveness of funds spent, rather than with the gross amount of cash plowed into research and development. To calculate the return on research and development, follow these steps:

1. Aggregate the net profit from licensing deals generated by research and development.
2. Aggregate the net profit from the sale of all products generated by research and development.
3. Aggregate the net profit from all lawsuits related to intellectual property derived from research and development.
4. Add together the preceding items and divide by the research and development expense (which should include the cost of filing for and maintaining patents).

The formula is:

$$\frac{\text{Licensing net profit} + \text{New product net profit} + \text{Lawsuit net profit}}{\text{All research and development expenses}}$$

The expenditures for research and development that led to the various forms of income noted in the numerator of this calculation may have occurred several years in the past. Consequently, this measurement should span a long period of time. For example, consider a trend line analysis, on which each data point represents one year of activity.

EXAMPLE

High Noon Armaments has spent $5,000,000 per year on research and development for the past five years, and the president is interested in the type of return the company has achieved from this investment. In the most recent year, the company has earned $750,000 from licensing the use of a new form of flashless gunpowder, as well as $250,000 from a lawsuit settlement, and $1,500,000 from the ongoing sale of a newly-developed sniper rifle to the military. Thus, the return on research and development for the current year is:

$$\frac{\$750,000 \text{ Profit} + \$1,500,000 \text{ New product profit} + \$250,000 \text{ Lawsuit profit}}{\$5,000,000 \text{ Research and development investment}}$$

$$= 50\% \text{ Return on research and development}$$

Warranty Claims Percentage

A customer may choose to return a product for a variety of reasons, many of which can be traced to other parts of a business than the design of a product. Nonetheless, product design is the core reason for a product return, for the design stage impacts the following:

- The robustness of the product, which impacts its ability to survive transport to the customer location, as well as its subsequent usage.
- The look and feel of the product, which impacts the perceptions of customers regarding the perceived value of goods received.
- The safety of the product, which could fail at an inopportune moment and cause much greater losses for a company than a simple warranty claim.

For these reasons, we have inserted the warranty claims percentage in this chapter. To calculate the percentage, divide the total number of product claims received by the total number of units sold. An alternative measurement is to divide the replacement cost of warranty claims by the aggregate price of the units sold. The latter approach does a better job of quantifying the cost of warranty claims for the seller. The two formulas are:

Option One:

$$\frac{\text{Number of warranty claims received}}{\text{Number of units sold}}$$

Option Two:

$$\frac{\text{Replacement cost of warranty claims}}{\text{Aggregate sales of units sold}}$$

Depending on the length of a product's warranty period, there may be a significant time lag between the incurrence of a warranty claim and the original product sale. If so, consider using as the measurement period the length of the standard company warranty. Thus, if the warranty period is six months, the measurement period should be six months on a rolling basis.

EXAMPLE

Green Lawn Care produces electric lawn mowers. The company has been plagued by failed batteries on several of its lawn mower products. In the most recent quarter, the company paid $120,000 for replacement batteries on sales of $2,000,000. The related warranty claims percentage is:

$$\frac{\$120,000 \text{ Replacement cost}}{\$2,000,000 \text{ Sales of units}} = 6\%$$

Summary

The number of measurements in this chapter indicates the considerable extent to which the results of a product development effort can be quantified. Product design teams can be judged based on the efficiency of their work, the amount of time taken, and the use of existing components, as well as their profitability. Consequently, we recommend that a complete suite of these measurements be applied to each project team, as well as to the product design department as a whole. By doing so, managers can gain an understanding of how the investment in new products is paying off.

Chapter 21
Purchasing Measurements

Introduction

The amount of cash spent on purchased materials can be the single largest expenditure area of a company, even exceeding the cost of payroll. If so, particular attention should be paid to how well a business is managing these costs. In this chapter, we address how the purchasing department controls costs with purchase orders, procurement cards, and a spend management program, while also noting a variety of ways to track the performance of individual suppliers, and how well the purchasing staff can dispose of excess inventory.

Overview of Purchasing Measurements

Purchasing measurements are designed to control costs. This cannot be done when measurements are made at an aggregate level, since there is not a sufficient amount of actionable information. Instead, virtually every purchasing measurement should be produced at the individual transaction or supplier level. The purchasing staff then uses this information to track down specific instances where costs can be more tightly controlled. However, when creating detailed reports for the following measurements, incorporate a cutoff materiality level, below which no measurements are provided. Doing so focuses the attention of the report recipient on the most actionable information.

   The traditional method of controlling the cost of purchased goods has been to issue a carefully-researched purchase order to each supplier. However, the cost of generating a purchase order is impractical for low-value purchases, so a useful metric is to track the proportions of purchases made both above and below a designated threshold level with purchase orders. Similarly, the most cost-effective method of purchasing below this threshold level is the procurement card. A card usage percentage can be tracked that reveals the level of acceptance of procurement cards among employees and suppliers.

   A well-run purchasing department typically has a spend management system in place, where purchases for certain commodities are concentrated with a small number of suppliers in order to take advantage of volume purchase discounts. This activity can be viewed with a measurement that tracks the proportion of total spend managed. A variation is to track the proportion of spend already being directed toward preferred suppliers.

   The purchasing staff can assist the receiving and production departments by certifying suppliers to bypass the receiving department and send their deliveries directly to the production line. The associated measurement for the proportion of certified suppliers yields general information about the number of qualified suppliers with which the company is dealing, as well as the effort being put into the certification program.

The purchasing manager needs a way to evaluate the performance of suppliers. There are several measurements available for doing so, including the ability of suppliers to fulfill orders in a timely manner, the proportion of received goods that are defective, and whether suppliers tend to bill the company more than was authorized by underlying purchase orders. All of this information can be used to develop report cards for suppliers, which may eventually lead to their replacement.

We also make note of the classic economic order quantity, which is used to determine the most cost-effective purchasing quantity, based on inventory carrying costs and order costs. This calculation is not always used in more progressive purchasing environments, where the absolute minimum order quantity is requested in order to minimize total inventory levels.

Finally, we measure the ability of the purchasing staff to disposition inventory that has been identified as not being usable by the company's production processes, or unlikely to be sold as merchandise. This is an area frequently ignored, since it does not directly impact sales, but which can result in inventory obsolescence write-offs if not addressed on a regular basis.

In total, the measurements described in this chapter are designed to fulfill a valuable monitoring function that can yield notable cost reductions, not only in the cost of the purchasing function, but also in the cost of purchased goods.

Proportion of Purchase Orders above Threshold

Purchase orders have traditionally been considered a key part of the purchasing process, for they embody a formal authorization to purchase goods. Purchase orders are also used in the three-way matching process by the accounting staff to ensure that supplier invoices have been properly authorized for payment. However, it is quite time-consuming to research and issue purchase orders, which makes them wildly expensive for lower-cost orders. Accordingly, most organizations dispense with purchase orders for smaller orders, electing to use procurement cards instead. Consequently, a measure of when purchase orders should be applied is to set a threshold above which purchase orders should be used, and track the usage level above and below this threshold.

To measure the proportion of purchase orders above the ordering threshold, create a report in the accounts payable system that aggregates all purchases made, sorted by the dollar size of each purchase, and noting which ones had an associated authorizing purchase order. Then aggregate the proportion of authorizing purchase orders above and below the designated threshold at which purchase orders are supposed to be used. The formula is:

$$\frac{\text{Number of authorizing purchase orders issued above threshold}}{\text{Total number of purchases made above threshold}}$$

EXAMPLE

Sharper Designs, maker of ceramic knives for professional chefs, has long had a policy of requiring a purchase order for all purchases made. The result has been a massive purchasing staff that dutifully researches each order, puts larger purchases out to bid, and issues detailed purchase orders. In an effort to save money, the CEO requires the purchasing manager to cut his staff in half. To do so, procurement cards are to be used for all purchases under $5,000. After three months, the purchasing manager measures the results of the program by measuring the issuance of purchase orders both above and below the $5,000 threshold. The results are:

	Above Threshold	Below Threshold
Number of purchase orders issued	640	82
Total number of purchases made	670	5,400
Proportion of purchase orders issued	96%	2%

The measure shows good initial compliance with the new program. The organization is generally taking the purchase order threshold into consideration when the decision is made to use a purchase order or a procurement card.

Procurement Card Usage Percentage

A procurement card is a company-sponsored credit card that can be used to make many types of purchases. The use of procurement cards drastically reduces the amount of time required by the purchasing department to create purchase orders, and so should be strongly encouraged for smaller purchases. To track the company's performance in using procurement cards, divide the total number of these transactions below the procurement card threshold by the total number of purchasing transactions below the card threshold. The card usage threshold typically starts fairly low, at perhaps $250, and then tends to ratchet upward as an organization becomes more accustomed to this form of purchasing.

EXAMPLE

The purchasing manager at Milford Sound has been pleased with the reduced purchasing time spent by her staff since procurement cards were introduced a year ago, but suspects that additional time can be saved. Her particular focus is on shifting 100% of purchases under $500 to these cards. She conducts an analysis of card usage by department, and arrives at the following information:

	Purchases with Procurement Cards	Total Purchases Under $500 Limit	Card Usage Percentage
Accounting	40	43	93%
Engineering	208	212	98%
Maintenance	72	520	14%
Sales and marketing	190	202	94%

The information reveals that the best source of additional time reduction is purchases made by the maintenance department, where the person in charge of the procurement card is clearly not using it very much.

As illustrated in the example, the measure will typically reveal that a specific card user is not employing the card to its full effect. Once corrected, there tend to be only a few residual transactions for which procurement cards are not used.

Proportion of Spend Managed

An active procurement program should aggregate all purchasing information by type of commodity purchased, and gradually work through these commodities, concentrating purchases with a smaller number of suppliers to gain volume discounts. As the spending for each commodity is reviewed and improved upon, the company should create a monitoring infrastructure to verify that the improvements made will continue, thereby ensuring continuing reduced costs. To monitor the amount of this active spend management, the purchasing manager should receive a measurement for the proportion of spend managed. The calculation is to divide the total spend on commodities under active management by the total amount of company spend.

It is entirely possible that some portions of company spend are so minor or difficult to manage that the company will never achieve 100% spend management. At some point below the 100% level, the purchasing manager will likely find that assigning more staff to spend management is not a cost-effective proposition, and will cease further efforts in this area.

EXAMPLE

The purchasing manager of Armadillo Industries initiated a spend management program several months ago, and wants to start tracking his progress toward a higher level of active spend management. The company is in the business of manufacturing body armor, protective shielding, and high-pressure containers (such as submarine hulls). This complex business contains many commodity types, so the manager has been focusing on the top commodities on which the company spends money. His analysis of spend being actively managed so far is as follows:

NAICS Code	Commodity Area	(000s) Spend	Percent of Total Spend	Cumulative Spend Percentage
332111	Iron and steel forging	$90,000	18.0%	18.0%
331523	Nonferrous metal die-casting	12,000	2.4%	20.4%
332114	Custom roll forming	42,000	8.4%	29.2%
332119	Metal stamping	4,500	0.9%	30.1%
332313	Plate work manufacturing	7,800	1.6%	31.7%
332912	Fluid power values	3,900	0.8%	32.5%
332613	Spring manufacturing	1,800	0.4%	**32.9%**

The table reveals clear progress toward a high level of active spend management, with nearly a third of all spend now being closely monitored.

Proportion of Spend with Preferred Suppliers

The use of preferred suppliers is the best way not only to obtain volume purchase discounts, but also to buy from those suppliers proven to have the best product quality, delivery times, and other services and terms considered important to the buyer. There are several ways to measure the amount of total spend being directed toward preferred suppliers. Consider the following alternatives:

- Do so in aggregate, as a single percentage. This is most useful when reporting high-level performance information to management.
- Do so by commodity type. This approach shows where commodities are actively being managed, since close observation of a commodity tends to lead to considerable supplier concentration.
- Do so by business unit. This approach shows the commitment to purchasing management, and can lead to the revamping of purchasing departments where the use of preferred suppliers is negligible.

EXAMPLE

The vice president of procurement at Electronic Inference Corporation is pushing for the redirection of spend to a small group of preferred suppliers. He elects to aggregate preferred supplier information at the business unit level, which results in the following information:

(000s)	Spend with Preferred Suppliers	Total Spend	Proportion of Spend with Preferred Suppliers
Atomic computing division	$17,890	$21,200	84%
Calculators division	5,230	38,100	14%
Memory chip fabrication division	81,000	96,500	84%
National security computing division	58,280	60,800	96%
Totals	$162,400	$216,600	75%

The vice president finds that, despite an overall excellent 75% spend rate with preferred suppliers, the calculators division is far behind the other business units, which presents a large opportunity for further improvement.

Proportion of Certified Suppliers

In a production environment, a large non-value-added step is the receiving department, where incoming deliveries intended for the production area are first identified, inspected, and logged into the computer system. If there are any hitches in this area, there can be significant delays in the amount of time required for materials to reach the production department. Because of this built-in delay, the production staff will build up an inventory buffer to protect the production process from any shortages in incoming materials. The delay represented by the receiving department can be eliminated by certifying suppliers to deliver their goods directly to the production area. Further benefits are a reduction of staffing in the receiving area, and no need for a protective inventory buffer in front of the production area. Clearly, there is a substantial payoff in maintaining a large proportion of suppliers who have been thoroughly examined and certified to bypass the receiving department.

To calculate the proportion of certified suppliers, first determine the number of suppliers that service the production area (all other suppliers are ignored for the purposes of this calculation). Then aggregate from this subset the total number of suppliers that have been certified within the past 12 months, and divide by the total number of suppliers servicing the production area. The formula is:

$$\frac{\text{Number of production suppliers certified within the last 12 months}}{\text{Total of all production suppliers}}$$

The measurement focuses on recent certifications, on the grounds that the company will likely want to re-certify all suppliers on a regular basis. A variation on the concept is to ignore minor suppliers that rarely send in any deliveries, since it will not be worth the time of the company's certification staff to subject these suppliers to a certification examination.

EXAMPLE

Mole Industries has a convoluted receiving process that adds an extra day to the process of obtaining goods from suppliers. In an effort to eliminate this delay, the purchasing manager and engineering manager jointly undertake a project to certify suppliers to make direct deliveries to the production line for Mole's Ditch Digging machines. There are 43 suppliers involved with this production line. After three months of certification activity, the analysis team has concluded that 18 suppliers can be certified, and that the remaining suppliers have such unreliable processes that they must be replaced. Thus, the company has a 42% certified supplier rate for the designated area, until such time as it can upgrade its supplier base.

Supplier Performance Measurements

The purchasing department is responsible for the performance of suppliers, especially those that supply the company's production department. If a supplier performs poorly, it is up to the purchasing staff to inform the supplier of the problem and to rectify the situation – either by replacing the supplier or upgrading its performance. In this section, we describe three measurements that can be used to grade the performance of suppliers.

Supplier Fulfillment Rate

When a company is operating in a just-in-time production environment, it is absolutely critical that items ordered from suppliers arrive on time. If not, the company is forced to either stop its production lines or build inventory buffers to protect against late supplier deliveries. In this situation, one of the key performance metrics is the supplier fulfillment rate. This is the aggregate amount of order line items that are received on time, divided by the total number of order line items placed. The formula is:

$$\frac{\text{Sum of all order line items received by due date}}{\text{Number of all order line items placed}}$$

It is too simplistic to conduct this measurement at the level of purchase orders placed and fulfilled, since there may be many line items on one purchase order, and only a single line item on another.

When evaluating the results of the measurement, keep in mind whether the purchasing staff has set unrealistic delivery goals for suppliers that are well inside of their stated delivery capabilities. In these cases, the company should not have placed the orders at all, or at least should not use the measurement as the basis for a poor performance evaluation for a supplier that may have actually shipped in accordance with its normal lead times.

EXAMPLE

The production manager of Quest Adventure Gear is planning to shift the company's production of backpacker stoves to a just-in-time process flow. To do so, it is critically important that all suppliers involved with the parts for the stoves deliver their assigned components to Quest by the designated dates and times. The purchasing manager is assigned the task of measuring the performance of three suppliers. The measurement results are noted in the following table:

	Fuel Pumps Ltd.	Titanium Corp.	Windscreens Intl.
Sum of order lines filled	327	490	310
Total order line items	330	520	605
Supplier fulfillment rate	99.1%	94.2%	51.2%

The table reveals that the company has a potentially serious fulfillment problem with Windscreens International, which only appears capable of delivering wind screens for the stoves by the specified date and time for about half of all order line items placed. The purchasing manager decides to look for a replacement supplier.

Supplier Defect Rate

Another element of supplier performance is whether they can deliver goods that are free of defects. The concept of defectiveness means that the delivered goods meet the specifications set by the buyer. Thus, if the buyer sets unusually tight tolerances for a component, and the supplier delivers goods that are considered acceptable for general usage but which do not fit the buyer's tolerance limits, then those goods are considered to be defective. Defective components are an especially pernicious problem in a just-in-time manufacturing environment, for there may be no buffer stock on hand to prevent production from stopping if a part proves to be defective.

To measure the defect rate, divide the total number of rejected components by the total number of components received from a supplier during the measurement period. The formula is:

$$\frac{\text{Total number of rejected units}}{\text{Total number of units received}}$$

Defect rates are one of the more important ways in which to evaluate a supplier, so consider breaking down the measurement in several ways, such as by individual part, by supplier facility, by defect type, and by the trucking firm used to deliver the goods – in short, in any way that can yield insights into the reasons for defects or damage.

Another issue to be aware of is increases or decreases in the defect rate that are caused by changes in the company's threshold tolerance limits. If these limits are relaxed, then the defect rate will improve, and vice versa – and without any change in supplier performance. Thus, it is useful to lock down the tolerance limits over multiple reporting periods, if the supplier defect rate is being measured on a trend line.

Otherwise, there will be unusual spikes and declines in the reported defect rate that have nothing to do with the supplier.

EXAMPLE

Billabong Machining Co. manufactures high-tolerance widgets for the military market. These combat-ready widgets must be exactly ¼" thick. In recent months, the receiving department has rejected a substantial number of deliveries from the company's steel plate supplier, because the delivered plates have been as much as 1/8" thinner than specified in the authorizing master purchase order. This has resulted in several late widget deliveries to the military, and a threatened cancellation of the company's sole source contract with the military. Accordingly, Billabong's purchasing manager prepares the following defect rate table, which clearly shows how the problem has increased over the past three months:

	January	February	March
Rejected plate deliveries	5	10	15
Total plate deliveries	55	50	60
Supplier defect rate	9%	20%	25%

The purchasing manager uses this table as the basis for a difficult discussion with the steel plate supplier, to either upgrade its performance or be dropped as a preferred supplier.

Supplier Billed Price Variance

A high-quality supplier will negotiate the price of goods and services with the buyer up-front, and will not attempt to alter this price in subsequent billings under the related purchase order. In this case, the billed price and purchase order price should always match. A more ethically challenged supplier, or one with severe disconnects between its billing and sales departments may issue invoices that bear little relationship to the prices stated in the original purchase order. In the latter case, the buyer may incur such excessive overbillings that the profitability of the business is threatened, or at least seriously eroded. Consequently, management should know which suppliers continually have price variances in their billings.

To calculate the supplier billed price variance, aggregate the amount of excess billings over the amounts stated on purchase orders, divided by the extended prices stated on the purchase orders. The formula is:

$$\frac{\text{Total of excess billings}}{\text{Total of extended prices stated on purchase orders}}$$

This measurement is designed to be calculated for each individual supplier, so it typically takes the form of a report that is sorted in declining order of billed price variance. To save space, the report only lists those variances above a predetermined materiality threshold.

There are cases where a billed price variance is justified. For example, a purchase order may allow the supplier to ship slightly more than the requested amount, in which case the extended price charged by the supplier will be higher than what is noted on the purchase order. This situation usually arises when items are purchased in very large quantities on an ongoing basis, so that slight overages in the units delivered are a standard practice.

EXAMPLE

The purchasing manager of Luminescence Corporation is being paid a bonus if she can restrict the amount the company pays to its LED suppliers for the components used in Luminescence light bulbs. In investigating the company's materials costs, she notes that several suppliers are charging more than the contractual amounts for components. She compiles the following information:

Supplier Name	Extended Price Paid	Purchase Order Price	Billed Price $ Variance	Billed Price % Variance
Dome Ports Ltd.	$52,600	$50,000	$2,600	5.2%
Flange Brothers	40,800	35,000	5,800	16.6%
Glow LED Modules Inc.	21,700	20,000	1,700	8.5%
Totals	$115,100	$105,000	$10,100	9.6%

Based on these results, the purchasing manager meets with the controller and demands tighter three-way matching of supplier invoices, so that these overages will be flagged in the future.

Economic Order Quantity

The economic order quantity is a formula used to derive that number of units of inventory to order that represents the lowest possible total cost to the buyer. It essentially creates a least-cost balance between the cost of ordering inventory and the cost of holding inventory. The economic order quantity is derived from the following formula:

$$EOQ = \sqrt{\frac{2(\text{Annual usage in units})(\text{Order cost})}{(\text{Annual carrying cost per unit})}}$$

The inputs to the model are noted within the formula.

EXAMPLE

Smithy Smelter uses 100,000 pounds of aluminum ingots per year, and the cost to place each order is $15. The carrying cost for one pound of aluminum ingots is $5 per year. The economic order quantity, based on this information, is the square root of:

$$(2 \times 100{,}000 \text{ Pounds of ingots} \times \$15 \text{ Order cost}) \div \$5 \text{ Carrying cost}$$

$$= 775 \text{ Units economic order quantity}$$

It is useful to test variations on the ordering cost and annual carrying cost to see how they impact the economic order quantity. It is possible that driving down the annual carrying cost of inventory can significantly alter the economic order quantity. A key factor in this analysis is determining which carrying costs actually vary with inventory volumes, and which are unrelated fixed costs. If they are unrelated, do not include them in the denominator of this calculation.

The economic order quantity is not used in a "pull" manufacturing system, where components are ordered from suppliers only as needed and in the quantities needed; thus, a pull system tends to order fewer components at a time than would be indicated by the economic order quantity formula.

Proportion of Targeted Inventory Dispositioned

Despite the best efforts of the purchasing and production planning staffs, some inventory will never be used. There may be no demand for goods or raw materials, or perhaps product redesigns leave some unused components in limbo. Whatever the reason may be, a large amount of inventory may be targeted for dispositioning by means other than sale to customers. If so, the purchasing department is typically tasked with the dispositioning effort, where the items are sold off to third parties for the best possible price, or returned to suppliers in exchange for a restocking fee.

It is useful to track the proportion of targeted inventory dispositioned on a monthly basis, since the value of old inventory declines rapidly over time. Ideally, the majority of all targeted items should be sold off within a few months of their initial identification, while these items still retain some value. To measure the dispositioning effort, divide the amount of cash and credits obtained through dispositioning by the aggregate estimated disposition value of all targeted inventory items. The formula is:

$$\frac{\text{Cash receipts from dispositioning} + \text{Supplier credits from dispositioning}}{\text{Total estimated dispositioned value of targeted inventory items}}$$

A potential problem with this measurement is that the actual amounts received from dispositioning activities may vary from what was originally estimated. For example, it may be estimated that a widget can be sold to a third party for $100, while it turns out that the widget must be scrapped. Thus, even if every targeted item is dispositioned within a single reporting period, it is possible that the proportion of the receipts from dispositioned items to their estimated values may not be 100%.

EXAMPLE

Smithy Iron Works has just acquired a small competitor, and intends to earn back a large part of the $5,000,000 purchase price by disposing of excess inventory held by the competitor at the highest possible price. An initial evaluation reveals that it may be possible to eliminate inventory having a disposal value of $1,000,000. After two months of brisk activity, the purchasing manager reports that he and his staff have generated $250,000 in cash from dispositioned inventory, as well as $350,000 in supplier credits. This results in a proportion of targeted inventory dispositioned of 60%.

General Management Measurements

The purchasing department has traditionally been buried under an enormous pile of paperwork, especially when purchasing polices require large numbers of purchases to be put out for competitive bidding, and where there are ongoing negotiations with suppliers over the terms of prospective orders. To streamline purchasing, the general measurements used for the department should change. Consider the following measurements:

- *Total department expense as a percentage of total spend.* This places an increased focus on the cost efficiency of the department.
- *Employee turnover within the department.* Purchasing agents are skilled employees, so a strong effort to retain them should be encouraged.
- *Process training hours per employee.* Advanced purchasing techniques that focus on spend management and a reduction in purchase orders involves a considerable knowledge of the purchasing process. Tracking the hours of training per employee per year places a particular focus on the importance of staff training.

Summary

Nearly all of the measurements in this chapter are designed to support a streamlined and efficient purchasing department. One measurement that has *not* been included is the classic performance measurement for the department – the purchase price variance. This variance is the difference between the standard price at which a component should be purchased and the actual price. When the purchasing manager wants to produce a positive purchase price variance, the simplest way to do so is to purchase in bulk, so that prices per unit are at their lowest. The trouble with this approach is that it goes against all modern manufacturing principles – to minimize inventory balances on hand, so there is a reduced investment in working capital, less storage space required, less risk of damage to materials, and so forth. Consequently, we strongly recommend eliminating this measurement in favor of a mix (or all) of the measurements stated in this chapter.

Chapter 22
Payables Measurements

Introduction

The payables manager should calculate measurements to determine how well the department is performing. These are usually ratios, in which case they only provide a high-level view of potential issues, which must then be investigated by drilling deeper into the data to determine underlying causes. In this chapter, we delve into a number of less-common measurements that can be used to detect excessive supplier billings, transaction error rates, cost per person, the success of paperless efforts, and similar issues.

Overview of Payables Measurements

The management of accounts payable has traditionally focused on the cost of the department, usually in terms of its gross cost divided by the number of invoices processed. We deal with this measurement in a more refined way with several variations on the comparison of full-time equivalents to measures of departmental activity. A factor contributing to the cost of the department is its efficiency, for which key triggering items are transaction errors, the use of paperless transactions, and the elimination of manual checks. We can measure these topics with the transaction error rate, percent of paperless invoices, percent of paperless payments, and manual payments tracking measurements.

The days payables outstanding measurement is a major payables measurement; it was already covered in the Liquidity Measurements chapter.

Transaction Error Rate

It is critical to avoid transaction errors, since the cost of correcting them is several multiples of the cost of initially completing them correctly. Consequently, one of the better measurements is to monitor the transaction error rate. The error rate should be monitored in conjunction with the total number of transactions processed by each person, to see if error rates are higher for newer or less-trained employees. The measurement can be further refined by focusing on those transaction errors that require the most time to repair.

To formulate the transaction error rate, add up all transaction-related errors in a reporting period and divide them by the total number of transactions completed within the same reporting period. This calculation should match transactional errors to the pool of the same types of transactions completed, which will result in a separate error rate for each general type of transaction.

EXAMPLE

The senior payables clerk of the Divine Gelato Company wants to reduce the amount of staff time spent correcting transactional errors. She has derived the following information for the last reporting period:

Processes	Number of Errors	Total Number of Transactions	Transaction Error Rate
Supplier ACH payments	28	3,010	0.9%
Supplier address changes	175	1,390	12.6%
Supplier invoice data entry	200	1,720	11.6%

Based on the error rates of the types of transactions measured, it is evident that the clerk should concentrate her attention on the address changes and invoice data entry. Of these two processes, the one requiring the most effort to repair is invoice data entry, so she elects to begin work in this area.

Full-Time Equivalent Measurements

There are several measurements available in which we can compare the headcount in the payables area to various activity levels or costs. The outcome can then be compared to the same measurement for "best in class" companies, to see if the payables function has an appropriate amount of headcount or is paying its employees a reasonable wage. Before discussing these measurements, we must define the concept of the full-time equivalent.

The acronym "FTE" is a contraction of the term "full-time equivalent," and refers to the hours worked by an employee on a full-time basis. On an annual basis, an FTE is considered to be 2,080 hours, which is calculated as:

8	Hours per day
5	× Work days per week
52	× 52 Weeks per year
2,080	= Hours per year

When a business employs a significant number of part-time staff, it can be useful to convert their hours worked into FTEs, to see how many full-time staff they equate to.

EXAMPLE

There are 168 working hours in January, and the Big Data Corporation staff works 7,056 hours during the month. When 168 hours are divided into 7,056 hours, the result is 42 FTEs.

There are 8 working hours in the day on Monday, and the Cupertino Beanery staff works 136 hours during that day. When 8 working hours are divided into 136 hours, the result is 17 FTEs.

There are 2,080 working hours in the year, and the Hubble Corporation staff works 22,880 hours during that year. When 2,080 working hours are divided into 22,880 hours, the result is 11 FTEs.

The 2,080 figure can be called into question, since it does not include any deductions for holidays, vacation time, sick time, and so forth. Alternative measures of FTE that incorporate these additional assumptions can place the number of hours for one FTE as low as 1,680 hours per year.

FTEs per $1 Million of Revenue

One way to examine payables headcount is to compare it to the amount of revenue being generated by a business. This could be defined as FTEs per $1 million or $1 billion of revenue. For example, a business has $500 million of revenue, and a payables staff of 15 FTEs. This organization has one payables FTE for every $33.3 million of revenue.

This measurement can be of use when compared to the results of competitors in the same industry, since the competitors will presumably have similar sales environments and suppliers. The measure is of less use when compared to results in other industries, since revenues in some industries can be supported with substantially lower or higher payables volumes.

Staff Cost per FTE

The total labor cost of the payables department can be divided by the number of payables FTEs to arrive at the average staff cost per FTE. For example, a payables department has total labor costs of $2,000,000 and 50 FTEs, which translates into a $40,000 staff cost per FTE.

This measurement can be compared to labor rates in the same industry or geographic region to see if the company is paying an appropriate amount per person. However, there are several factors that can skew labor costs. For example, a company may be located in an unusually high-cost region, such as a major city, where the cost of living is higher. Also, the corporate benefit plan may be unusually rich or poor, which can impact the total cost assigned to labor. Further, a relatively new and inexperienced staff may be paid less, but this does not factor in their reduced level of effectiveness.

Line Items per FTE

One of the better activity measures is to compare the number of FTEs to the number of line items processed in supplier invoices. This approach accounts for the differing amounts of detail included in each invoice received. This calculation only works if the computer system can report on the total number of invoice line items processed in each measurement period. For example, a payables department has entered 120,000 invoice line items in the past month, and the department employs 15 FTEs. This equates to 8,000 line items per FTE.

This measure is more comparable across industry lines, and so can be used to match a company's results to those of a "best in class" organization located elsewhere.

This approach may not work if only invoice totals are entered into the payables system, rather than individual line items. If so, alter the measurement to track invoices entered per FTE.

Paperless Measurements

If there is an efficiency drive to eliminate paperwork from the payables function, it can make sense to track two paperless measurements, which are the percent of paperless invoices and the percent of paperless payments. They are both described in this section.

Percent of Paperless Invoices

If the company uses an electronic data interchange system or an on-line portal into which suppliers can enter their invoices, invoices will be sent directly to the payables software without any data entry. This is to be encouraged, since it reduces payables staff time. For example, a company processes a total of 6,000 invoices in a month, of which 500 were entered through paperless systems. This constitutes an 8.3% paperless invoice percentage.

It is entirely likely that this percentage will reach a certain point and then stall, with no further improvement. The trouble is that some suppliers will continue to send paper invoices, despite all encouragement to the contrary. Only when a company is large enough to really influence the actions of its suppliers can it assume that a high paperless invoice percentage can be achieved.

Percent of Paperless Payments

The payables manager can reduce the cost of check payments by switching to ACH (Automated Clearing House) electronic payments instead. Doing so requires that the company obtain bank account information for its suppliers. If they do not provide this information, it will not be possible to issue ACH payments. Suppliers may not provide this information when the relationship is not expected to be long-term, or is only occasional. Consequently, the percent of paperless payments is likely to be close to 100% for the core group of suppliers, and much lower for all other suppliers.

For example, a company has 800 suppliers, of which 160 are considered the core group. The payables manager convinces 152 of this sub-group to accept ACH payments, while only 300 of the remaining suppliers are amenable to the idea. This results in a 95% success rate for the core group, and a 47% rate for the remaining suppliers.

Additional Payables Measurements

There are several additional measurements for the payables area that can have a noticeable impact on the function's operations. The following measurements are intended to be reviewed daily and to trigger immediate corrective action by the payables staff:

- *Remaining three-way matches.* If a business uses alternative verification and payment methods, there should be relatively few remaining supplier invoices that are still being reviewed with the cumbersome three-way matching process. Three-way matching involves comparing a supplier invoice to the authorizing purchase order and a proof of receipt. Consider creating a report that itemizes every invoice for which three-way matching was used, with the intent of finding alternative ways to review these invoices.
- *Invoices not mailed to accounts payable.* Whenever an invoice arrives that was mailed to someone other than the accounts payable department, include the supplier name on a contact list. The payables staff should contact these suppliers to request that the contact name be shifted to the payables department. Doing so eliminates a possible bottleneck where invoice recipients might not immediately forward invoices to the accounting staff.
- *Supplier late fees.* Any late payment fee charged by a supplier should be recorded in a separate general ledger account. The information in this account is reviewed regularly to determine what circumstances caused the late fee. The result may be procedural or other changes to keep the issue from occurring again in the future.
- *Manual payments.* Track every manual payment made (including payments by check, ACH, or wire transfer), determine the reasons why manual payments were mandated, and see if they can be converted to the regular payment system in the future.

Note that none of these additional measurements involve ratio analysis. Instead, they mostly require that the payables staff investigate individual transactions in detail, with the objective of locating transactions that either resulted in errors or which required an inordinate amount of effort to complete. The result of these investigations should be a continual improvement in the efficiency of the payables function.

Summary

It is not necessary to maintain a comprehensive set of measurements for the payables function. The payables manager is more likely to adopt a few measurements for the duration of a specific project, such as the rollout of ACH payments, and then stop bothering with the measurements as soon as the project has been completed. These measurements are needed as a feedback loop to determine the success of the project. However, it can be useful to calculate a complete set of measurements once a year, to see if there has been any backsliding in areas that had been considered high-performance when they were originally addressed.

If there is one payables measurement worth monitoring on an ongoing basis, it is the transaction error rate. This is more of a report than a measurement, and is designed to detect and correct errors that creep into the payables system. Consider it an early warning report for issues that can then be corrected before they expand into more wide-ranging problems.

No matter which measurements are used, consider tracking them on a trend line. Doing so gives immediate visual feedback regarding declines in performance, which can trigger an investigation to locate underlying causes.

Chapter 23
Sales and Marketing Measurements

Introduction

The sales and marketing functions of a company can absorb a notable proportion of its total expenditures, and so are worthy of multiple measurements to ensure that funds are expended wisely. In this chapter, we pay particular attention to measurements that track the efficiency and effectiveness of the sales department. Measurements for the marketing area are noted separately; there are far fewer measurements for marketing, since this area is particularly resistant to evaluation.

Overview of Sales and Marketing Measurements

The traditional focus in the sales area is on the ability of a salesperson to generate sales dollars. However, since this is a top-line item in the income statement that does not necessarily relate to profitability, we instead suggest that the focus be placed on the effectiveness of sales activities, which is essentially a comparison of the cost of the department to the profits generated. Several measures are provided that deal with different aspects of sales effectiveness.

Depending on the type of sales efforts being used, it may also be worthwhile to examine the amount of solicitations being made to existing customers, since they tend to buy more goods and services than first-time customers. Ancillary measurements are sales per customer, the order placement rate, and the quote to close ratio.

An extremely important measurement is the sales backlog ratio, which is a strong indicator of the ability of a business to maintain its current sales level. This is an excellent predictive measure for the amount of sales that will be recognized in the near future.

We then turn to the concept of throughput, which is sales minus all totally variable expenses. This is a much better measurement of the quality of selling activity than the usual focus on gross sales, because throughput is a much stronger indicator of profitability. If the sales staff remains tightly focused on the underlying throughput of what they are trying to sell, there is a strong probability that low-margin sales will not be pursued. The throughput measurements presented are throughput quoted, the ratio of throughput awarded to quoted, and the ratio of throughput booked to billed.

Though the marketing area tends to be quite resistant to detailed measurement, we have aggregated several possibilities into the Marketing Measurements section that can be used to gain some knowledge of the value of customers and media activities, website sales, and the effectiveness of direct mail campaigns.

Of particular interest in this chapter is the number of measurements that can be applied at the level of the individual employee, rather than for an entire department. In particular, the incremental salesperson effectiveness, sales effectiveness, order placement rate, sales per customer, and quote to close ratios can all be used to judge the abilities of individual salespeople.

Sales Productivity

Sales productivity is the ability of the sales staff to generate profitable sales. A profitable sale is considered to be one that has a high throughput, where throughput is sales minus all totally variable expenses. We do not measure the sales generated by the sales staff, since there may be little throughput associated with those sales.

To calculate sales productivity, divide the total estimated throughput booked by the sales staff by the total sales department expense incurred. The formula is:

$$\frac{\text{Total sales booked} - \text{All variable expenses associated with sales booked}}{\text{Total sales department expenses}}$$

EXAMPLE

The president of Armadillo Security Armor is concerned that the sales department is not being overly productive in booking new sales. He has the company controller accumulate the following information:

	January	February	March
Bookings	$4,200,000	$4,315,000	$4,520,000
Related variable expenses	$1,470,000	$1,726,000	$2,034,000
Throughput percentage	65%	60%	55%
Sales expenses	$250,000	$260,000	$265,000
Sales productivity	10.9x	10.0x	9.4x

The analysis reveals that the sales staff is increasing sales, but giving away margin in order to do so. The result is an ongoing decline in the department's sales productivity. It would be better to book fewer sales at higher margins, thereby generating more profit for the company.

Sales productivity should be judged over multiple periods, since some sales can take several reporting periods to finalize, and so might yield a measurement that spikes and slumps from month to month. Also, the measurement correlates with the experience level of the sales staff, so expect it to decline immediately after new sales employees are hired.

Incremental Salesperson Effectiveness

A sales territory or product line typically supports a certain number of salespeople. Beyond that optimal sales level, the profitability of each incremental salesperson added to the sales department will decline. There are a number of reasons for this peak level of effectiveness, including:

- The first salesperson in a territory has snapped up all of the higher-volume customers
- All remaining potential customers are further away from the company location, and so require more travel time for each incremental sale
- All remaining customers already buy from competitors, and so must be pried away with more prolonged sales efforts
- It takes a long time to train additional salespeople
- New sales regions have different product requirements or cultural norms that require a different type of sales effort

Whatever the reason may be, the sales manager needs a tool for determining at what point it may not be useful to hire additional sales staff. That tool is the incremental salesperson effectiveness measurement. This measures the sales generated by each incremental salesperson added, divided by the total variable cost of that salesperson. The formula is:

$$\frac{\text{Incremental sales dollars}}{\text{Salesperson compensation} + \text{benefits} + \text{travel} + \text{other variable costs}}$$

One problem with this measurement is that the numerator does not indicate the amount of profits generated, only the amount of sales. A new salesperson might decide to only sell the lowest-priced items in order to generate massive unit volume, without necessarily generating much profit. This issue can be remedied by instead using the incremental amount of throughput generated in the numerator (see the Throughput Measurements section). This revised formula is:

$$\frac{\text{Incremental throughput dollars}}{\text{Salesperson compensation} + \text{benefits} + \text{travel} + \text{other variable costs}}$$

This measurement assumes that all salespeople are equally effective in their selling ability, which is clearly not the case. However, the measurement is still useful for tracking the effectiveness of a large number of salespeople, since effectiveness tends to be clustered about an average point for this group.

EXAMPLE

Tsunami Products has developed a new shower head with a patented pulse feature that creates a result similar to a massage. The product is initially sold through a group of salespeople who sell it in bulk to large home construction companies. Tsunami's sales manager then decides to hire additional sales staff to sell to smaller home builders, followed by another tranche of sales staff that sell to home supply stores. Each group of salespeople hired is less effective, because each targeted group of customers is progressively less profitable. The result of these efforts is shown in the following table.

	Incremental Throughput	Variable Cost of Sales Staff	Incremental Salesperson Effectiveness
Large home construction companies	$17,000,000	$4,000,000	4.3x
Small home construction companies	12,000,000	6,000,000	2.0x
Home supply stores	3,000,000	2,900,000	1.0x

The table clearly shows a declining trend in salesperson effectiveness as the company adds on a new sales channel. The sales manager should estimate the incremental salesperson effectiveness for any additional channels chosen, to ensure that the company will still earn a profit.

Sales Effectiveness

The preceding sales productivity measurement is useful for tracking the total amount of throughput generated, but does not track the amount of time required at the company's bottleneck operation to generate that throughput. If sales are made that require lots of processing time at the bottleneck, then a company will soon find itself unable to process additional orders. The sales effectiveness measurement is designed to monitor bottleneck usage in new orders. The measurement is used as feedback for the sales staff, which can be encouraged to have customers order those goods generating the largest amount of throughput per minute of bottleneck processing time.

To calculate sales effectiveness, divide the total throughput for all orders booked in a period by the total minutes of processing time required for these orders at the bottleneck operation. The formula is:

$$\frac{\text{Total sales booked} - \text{All variable expenses associated with sales booked}}{\text{Total minutes of bottleneck processing time required}}$$

EXAMPLE

Horton Corporation manufactures widgets. The CFO wants to focus more sales attention on the company's new olive widget, introduced in February, which generates $25.00 of throughput per minute of bottleneck processing time. This rate is significantly higher than the average throughput per minute of Horton's other widget products. The following table notes the effect of the new product on sales effectiveness, with a notable increase in the metric occurring in the final month.

	January	February	March
Throughput booked	$910,000	$868,500	$1,014,300
Bottleneck minutes	50,000	45,000	49,000
Average throughput/minute	$18.20	$19.30	$20.70

* Note that the amount *booked* in each month does not necessarily equate to the number of minutes of bottleneck processing time available in that month.

Sales and Marketing as Percentage of Sales

The selling and marketing effort in which a business engages is a hit-or-miss proposition, where the company must feel its way through a variety of possible marketing options and selling efforts to determine which mix of activities generates the highest sales and profitability. These activities are represented in the income statement by a number of costs that are largely fixed, and for which corresponding sales levels will not be clarified for several additional reporting periods. Thus, there is a disconnect between sales and marketing expenses and sales. Nonetheless, it is still useful to track these expenses as a percentage of sales on a trend line. Eventually, as management figures out the optimum way to market and sell the company's goods and services, the percentage should settle down at a certain percentage of sales.

To calculate sales and marketing as a percentage of sales, aggregate all selling and marketing department expenses, and divide by net sales. Since there can be a timing difference between these expenditures and related sales, consider running the measurement on a trailing quarterly basis. The formula is:

$$\frac{\text{Sales department expense} + \text{Marketing department expense}}{\text{Net sales}}$$

There is no perfect percentage that a company should pursue. In some industries, sales can be obtained with little effort, such as by maintaining an Internet store. In other industries, it can require considerable marketing and prolonged selling activities to procure a sale, such as in a competitive bidding situation for a large infrastructure project.

Another issue is that the measurement does not include the throughput generated by a sale, which would be a better measure of the ultimate profitability of sales and marketing efforts.

271

EXAMPLE

Milagro Corporation is a startup company that is figuring out the best way to sell its home espresso machines. Sales are tracked by the cost of marketing and selling in three different sales channels, which are direct sales through the company's Internet store, sales through department stores, and mailed catalogs. Sales and marketing as a percentage of sales appears in the following table for each of these sales channels:

	Internet Store	Department Stores	Mailed Catalogs
Sales and marketing expense	$108,000	$540,000	$210,000
Net sales	$500,000	$4,500,000	$500,000
Sales and marketing %	22%	12%	42%

The analysis does not include the throughput generated from each sales channel. However, it appears likely that the high cost of preparing and mailing catalogs makes this sales channel unprofitable. It is relatively easy to sell to department stores, but we cannot tell from the analysis whether Milagro is reducing its prices to obtain orders from the department stores.

Existing Customer Solicitation Ratio

When a business starts out, all sales calls are cold calls, which have a very low success rate. Over time, the company will build a base of recurring customers, from which the related sales will be substantially higher. The sales manager should track the ratio of solicitations made to existing customers, which should be indicative of a more efficient sales effort for a given volume of sales. Ideally, once a business is fully mature, the existing customer solicitation ratio should be very high, which indicates the highest level of efficiency in generating new sales.

To calculate the ratio, ascertain the total number of sales contacts made to existing customers in the current period, and divide by the total number of all sales contacts made. The formula is:

$$\frac{\text{Total sales calls to existing customers}}{\text{Total sales calls made}}$$

A 100% result for this ratio is not necessarily good, for it indicates that there are either no new customers to be gained, or that the sales manager is not being overly aggressive in pursuing new sales leads. Nonetheless, an increasing trend in the ratio over time is to be encouraged.

EXAMPLE

Hammer Industries is a start-up company that sells lightweight tools to construction companies that must haul gear into remote construction sites by helicopter. At its inception, the sales manager researches the potential market, and finds that the potential customer base is comprised of 500 companies. The sales department begins cold calling, and achieves notable success over the next four years in establishing relationships with this core group. The result is shown in the following table:

	20X1	20X2	20X3	20X4
Sales calls to existing customers	15	160	270	380
Total sales calls made	300	340	380	450
Existing customer solicitation ratio	5%	47%	71%	84%

The ratio trend line reveals that Hammer is beginning to run out of customers. Accordingly, the sales manager calls a meeting with the executive team to discuss how the company can expand its market to appeal to a larger group of potential customers.

Order Placement Rate

The core ability of a salesperson is to close a sales transaction. This means convincing a customer to buy goods or services, rather than dithering over a prospective purchase and delaying closing the deal. The ability to close a deal can be measured with the order placement rate. The sales manager should use this measurement on an ongoing basis to determine the closing capabilities of his or her sales staff. The outcome of the measurement may be additional sales training, or the termination of those salespeople who have not proven to be sufficiently capable.

To calculate the order placement rate, divide the total number of initial customer contacts into the total number of customers from this group that placed orders. The measurement can be further refined by excluding repeat orders from existing customers, and can also be broken down at the level of the business unit, region, or salesperson. The formula is:

$$\frac{\text{Number of customers placing an order}}{\text{Number of initial customer contacts}}$$

The order placement rate is best employed in high-volume environments where there are many customer interactions. It is least useful when multiple salespeople may be involved in a customer contact, so that assigning a successful sale to a specific salesperson is more difficult.

EXAMPLE

The sales manager of Colossal Furniture wants to determine the ability of his sales staff to sell the company's oversized furniture to the people entering its stores. The stores use automated counters to track the number of people entering each store, and order forms are used to track the number of orders placed by stores. He compiles the information by store, which yields the following information for the preceding month:

Store	Orders Placed	Initial Customer Contacts	Order Placement Rate
Ann Arbor	142	189	75%
Boston	319	560	57%
Chicago	241	636	38%
Denver	417	952	44%

The table reveals that the Ann Arbor store has an excellent order placement rate. The sales manager decides to investigate the sales staff at this location, to see if any best practices or training methods can be copied from there to the other stores.

Sales per Customer

A business can increase its sales either by adding new customers or by increasing the volume of sales to existing customers. Since it is quite expensive to obtain new customers, the sales and marketing staff should focus its attention on customers who have already made purchases from the company. For example, it may be possible to sell warranty services, additional products, or services on top of what a customer may have originally ordered.

To calculate sales per customer, aggregate net sales for the reporting period, and divide by the number of customers billed during the month. Given the need to count the number of customers, this calculation may not be possible in a retail environment where many sales are paid for in cash, since there is no tracking mechanism for aggregating sales by customer. The formula is:

$$\frac{\text{Net sales for the reporting period}}{\text{Number of customers billed}}$$

One issue with the outcome of this ratio is that a focus on acquiring entirely new customers will likely force the ratio to decline. The reason is that new customers tend to buy less than more established customers, who have a longer-term relationship with the company and so are more familiar with its products.

EXAMPLE

The sales manager of Pianoforte International is perusing information about the cost of acquiring a new customer, which is $5,000. Since the company's average sale is for a $20,000 concert-grade piano, the cost of customer acquisition is the next-largest cost after the cost of goods sold. Based on this information, the sales manager decides to concentrate the efforts of her staff on selling large numbers of pianos to the music departments of colleges and universities. The results of this effort are noted in the following table:

	Before New Sales Strategy (20X1)	After New Sales Strategy (20X2)
Net sales	$29,000,000	$40,000,000
Number of customers billed	1,450	800
Sales per customer	$20,000	$50,000

The table reveals that the sales staff tightly focused its efforts in 20X2 on a much smaller group of larger customers, resulting in higher sales per customer, and far more total sales. The only downside is that the company deliberately reduced the number of customers with which it interacts.

Quote to Close Ratio

In an environment where the sales process requires the issuance of a formal quote on a competitive basis, the quote to close ratio is valuable for determining the ability of the sales staff to convince a customer to accept a quote. A high ratio can indicate a combination of excellent quote writing ability, product quality, and product demonstration skill. Conversely, if few quotes are leading to customer orders, then the same factors must be investigated to see where the problem lies.

EXAMPLE

The sales manager of Milford Sound believes that the company's recent revamping of its quote-writing unit has improved sales. Accordingly, he asks the company's financial analyst to prepare a quote to close ratio for each of the last four quarters. The following results indicate that quoting effectiveness has indeed risen.

	1st Quarter	2nd Quarter	3rd Quarter	4th Quarter
Sales booked	$12,000,000	$12,500,000	$14,000,000	$17,000,000
Sales quoted	$54,500,000	$62,500,000	$56,000,000	$58,600,000
Quote to close ratio	22%	20%	25%	29%

An issue to be aware of is that the quote to close ratio only measures sales booked, not throughput booked. Thus, it is possible that an increase in the ratio could be caused by lower price points that give away profits.

Sales Backlog Ratio

The sales backlog ratio provides an indicator of the ability of a business to maintain its current level of sales. When noted on a trend line, the measurement clearly indicates changes that will likely translate into future variations in sales volume. For example, if the ratio exhibits an ongoing trend of declines, this is a strong indicator that a business is rapidly working through its backlog, and may soon begin to report sales reductions. The opposite trend of an increasing sales backlog does not necessarily translate into improved future sales, if a company has a bottleneck that prevents it from accelerating the rate at which it converts customer orders into sales.

To calculate the sales backlog ratio, divide the total dollar value of booked customer orders by the net sales figure for the past quarter. Only quarterly sales are used, rather than sales for the past year, in order to more properly reflect a company's short-term revenue-generating capability. The formula is:

$$\frac{\text{Total order backlog}}{\text{Quarterly sales}}$$

A different way of deriving the same information is to calculate for the number of days sales that can be derived from the existing order backlog. This figure is derived by dividing the average sales per day into the total backlog. The formula is:

$$\frac{\text{Total order backlog}}{\text{Quarterly sales} \div 90 \text{ days}}$$

The customer order information needed for this ratio cannot be entirely derived from a company's financial statements. Instead, it must be derived from internal reports that aggregate customer order information.

The ratio is of less use in the following situations:

- A retail environment, where there is no backlog
- A seasonal business, where the intent of the business model is to build order volume until the prime selling season, and then fulfill all orders
- A just-in-time "pull" model, where the intent is to fulfill orders as soon after receipt as possible

EXAMPLE

Henderson Mills reports the following sales and backlog information:

	April	May	June
Rolling 3-month sales	$9,000,000	$9,500,000	$9,600,000
Month-end backlog	5,000,000	4,000,000	3,500,000
Sales backlog ratio	0.55:1	0.42:1	0.36:1

The table indicates that Henderson is increasing its sales by chewing through its order backlog, which the company has been unable to replace. The result is likely to be the complete elimination of the order backlog in the near future, after which sales can be expected to plummet, unless steps are taken to book more customer orders.

Throughput Measurements

Thus far, we have offered a number of sales-related measurements that are fairly traditional in nature. In this section, we instead offer several sales measurements that are focused on throughput – which is sales minus all variable expenses. A company that generates a large amount of throughput can more easily cover its fixed costs, and so is more likely to generate outsized profits. There are three sales measurements related to throughput, which focus on the amount of throughput quoted, the proportion of these quoted sales awarded to the company, and the proportion of these awarded sales actually billed to customers. Thus, the measures are intended to track the volume of throughput quoted, the success of this quoting activity, and the ability of the company to fulfill its contracts. Some of the preceding measurements also incorporated throughput concepts; see the sales productivity and sales effectiveness measures.

Throughput Quoted

When formal quotes must be issued to customers in order to obtain a sale, the classic measurement is the total dollar amount of sales quoted in a period. This measurement gives management an impression of the overall activity level of the group that issues quotes. Unfortunately, it does not inform management of the throughput that will result from these quotes. After all, the quoting group could deliberately lower the price on a quote in order to increase the probability of securing a customer order, even though doing so may eliminate any possibility of generating enough throughput to earn a profit. To avoid this issue, consider replacing the total amount of sales quoted in a period with the total amount of throughput quoted. Doing so focuses the attention of the sales staff on generating bottom-line profits, rather than top-line sales.

To measure throughput quoted, subtract from each quoted price all variable costs expected to be incurred if a sale is made, and aggregate the result for all quotes issued in the measurement period. The formula is:

$$\sum (\text{Quoted sales} - \text{Expected variable costs})$$

EXAMPLE

Mulligan Imports is an importer of exotic foreign golf clubs, which it sells in bulk to the pro shops in golf clubs around the country via a formal quoting process. Mulligan's only variable cost is the cost of each club that it imports; all other costs relate to the sales and marketing of its inventory. The company is suffering from paltry profit levels, so the president reviews the throughput generated by each type of driver, to see if there are any differences that can be exploited. The result is the following table:

	Unit Price	Unit Throughput	Units Quoted	Total Quoted Throughput
Gold Coast Driver	$150	$20	14,000	$280,000
Mahogany Swing	210	55	750	41,250
Soviet Driver	180	70	210	14,700
Timbuktu Thumper	310	140	150	21,000
		Totals	15,110	$356,950

It appears that the sales staff is consistently quoting large quantities of the Gold Coast Driver, which has the lowest throughput of any of the drivers. The president decides to alter the commission plan of the sales staff to incentivize them to include more of the other drivers in quotes. Even if overall sales plummet, the throughput associated with these other drivers is so high that the company should still earn a larger profit.

Ratio of Throughput Awarded to Quoted

In the preceding measurement for throughput quoted, the outcome of using the measurement is likely to be a shift in quotes to focus on higher-throughput products. However, this shift may not be accepted by customers, who may not appreciate the change in product offerings or higher price points being quoted. If so, fewer quotes may be awarded to the company. To see if this is the case, measure the ratio of throughput quoted to awarded. The calculation is to aggregate the throughput contained within all awarded quotes, and divide by the aggregate throughput contained within all quotes issued in the period. The formula is:

$$\frac{\text{Aggregate throughput in quotes awarded}}{\text{Aggregate throughput in quotes issued}}$$

If there is a significant delay in the time required for customers to respond to quotes, it is entirely likely that the quotes awarded will be in a different reporting period than the period in which the quotes were issued. If so, expand the measurement period somewhat, such as by using a rolling three-month period.

EXAMPLE

To continue with the preceding example, the president of Mulligan Imports has forced his sales staff to issue bids to pro shops for drivers that have higher throughput rates than had previously been the case. The result is shown in the following table:

	Total Awarded Throughput	Total Quoted Throughput	Ratio of Throughput Quoted to Awarded
Gold Coast Driver	$65,000	$65,000	100%
Mahogany Swing	93,000	120,000	78%
Soviet Driver	160,000	200,000	80%
Timbuktu Thumper	82,000	215,000	38%
	$400,000	$600,000	67%

The result of this change in quoting practices is an increase in throughput of $43,000. Much of this increase can be traced to the Mahogany Swing and Soviet Driver products, which the president decides to support with an increased marketing expenditure.

Ratio of Throughput Booked to Billed

If a business wants its sales to remain steady, the amount of throughput in its backlog should roughly equate to the amount of throughput billed. If management is interested in growing sales, then the amount of throughput booked should also increase – otherwise, the backlog will eventually be eroded, and the company will suffer a catastrophic decline in its sales. Conversely, the amount of throughput booked should not continue to build, since this means that the company's bottleneck operation is controlling the amount of output, and the company is at risk of losing sales when it mandates longer lead times for its customers.

To calculate the ratio of throughput booked to billed, aggregate the total amount of throughput booked as of the end of the reporting period, and divide by the amount of throughput billed in the period. A ratio of approximately 1:1 indicates a steady-state and supportable sales situation, while an increase in the ratio reveals that the company's bottleneck is restricting sales. A decrease in the ratio indicates that the company is not replenishing its backlog, and is likely to suffer a major sales decline in the near future. The formula is:

$$\frac{\text{Total throughput booked as of the measurement date}}{\text{Total throughput billed in the period}}$$

EXAMPLE

To continue with the Mulligan Imports example, the company must import all of its products from overseas, which means that its bottleneck is the production operations of its suppliers. The president tracks the ratio of throughput booked to billed for each of the driver brands sold by the company, and notes the following disturbing trend for the Timbuktu Thumper:

	Throughput Booked	Throughput Billed	Ratio of Throughput Booked to Billed
May	$82,000	$41,000	50%
June	93,000	28,000	30%
July	107,000	21,000	20%

The table reveals that the supplier in Timbuktu is clearly unable to fulfill Mulligan's orders for the Thumper driver on a timely basis. It turns out that the supplier is dealing with an insurgency from Mauritania which keeps stealing drivers from its delivery trucks and selling them on the black market in nearby Niger. Consequently, the president concludes that the source of supply is too unreliable to continue offering the Thumper product.

Marketing Measurements

The marketing function is one of the more difficult areas in a company to measure, since there may be only a vague link between marketing expenditures and sales generated. Nonetheless, there are some niches in the marketing area for which performance can be measured, which we note in this section.

Advertising Value Equivalency

An ongoing conundrum for the marketing manager is how to split her budgeted funds and staff time between advertising and media coverage. Media coverage requires a much-reduced expenditure in comparison to advertising, but takes up far more staff time. It is possible to derive a common basis of measurement for these two marketing activities by converting the amount of printed media coverage to what it would have cost to purchase the space as advertisements. This is called advertising value equivalency.

To calculate equivalency, measure the physical dimensions of the space taken up by media coverage, and multiply the square inches of space by what it would have cost the company to purchase ad space in a similar quantity in an equivalent publication. The formula is:

Square inches of printed coverage × Equivalent ad rate

The same approach can be taken if the media coverage is of the audio or video variety; just measure the time interval covered, and multiply by the equivalent cost.

While advertising value equivalency at least provides some measure of the value of media coverage, it is only an approximation of value, for the following reasons:

- The value of a media piece can vary based on its content, where a highly positive article is worth much more than one that is neutral or negative.
- What if a media story is negative, and the marketing staff spends a large part of its time to keep the story from running? In this case, what is the value of having zero negative media coverage?
- Positive media coverage may be worth substantially more than advertising coverage, since consumers are more likely to trust information generated by an independent third party.
- Media coverage may only mention a company in passing, as part of a larger article. If so, how is the equivalency to be measured?
- A massive article about a company may have no advertising equivalent, since it may not be possible to derive a volume discount for the equivalent amount of advertising space.

EXAMPLE

The marketing manager of Quest Adventure Gear usually spends $20,000 per month on advertising, with little effort going toward positive media coverage. She is interested in the possibility, however, and remembers how a small profile about the company by a national news service generated a significant bump in sales. She estimates that the one-minute audio clip on the news service's radio program would have cost $8,000 as an advertisement, and so assigns this value to the media coverage.

Sales to Unique Visitors Ratio

When a business sells goods through a website, the profitability of the site will be highly dependent upon a number of factors, such as site design, price points, and promotions. Ultimately, the mix of these (and other) issues will yield a certain amount of sales in proportion to the number of unique visitors viewing the site. The ability of an organization to sell through such a site can be measured by comparing sales generated to the number of unique visitors to the site.

To measure the sales to unique visitors ratio, divide net sales by the number of unique visitors to the site during the measurement period. The unique visitors figure is available through a number of site tracking services. The formula is:

$$\frac{\text{Sales traceable to web site}}{\text{Number of unique visitors to web site}}$$

As has been noted elsewhere in this chapter, performance should be tied to throughput, rather than sales, so the measurement can be modified as follows to incorporate throughput into the numerator:

$$\frac{\text{Throughput traceable to web site}}{\text{Number of unique visitors to web site}}$$

It is not advisable to use the total number of sales transactions in the numerator, since this can have quite a distant relationship with profitability. Many small transactions could look impressive, but unless they generate throughput, there will be little contribution to profitability.

EXAMPLE

Prickly Corp. sells cactus plants through its website. Prickly recently paid an outside website developer to overhaul the site. In the most recent month, the number of unique visitors to the site was roughly the same as in previous months, but the resulting throughput was substantially different, as noted in the following table:

	Throughput Generated	Number of Unique Visitors	Throughput to Unique Visitors Ratio
Before site redesign	$36,000	150,000	$0.24/unique
After site redesign	92,000	152,000	$0.61/unique

Based on the success of the redesign, the owners of Prickly decide to hire the same website designer for a revision of the company's other website that sells thorn bushes.

Direct Mail Effectiveness

Some organizations send out targeted mailings to customers, usually advertising reduced pricing on specific products or services. If there is an identification number (such as a coupon code) attached to these offers, it should be possible to trace the sales generated by a direct mail campaign back to the cost of that campaign. The cost of a direct mailing can be substantial, since it includes the costs of mailer design, printing, mailing lists, and postage. This comparison can tell the marketing manager if a particular mailing campaign was effective, or should be revised to boost profitability.

To calculate direct mail effectiveness, divide the sales generated by a direct mail campaign by the variable cost of that campaign. The formula is:

$$\frac{\text{Incremental sales traceable to direct mail campaign}}{\text{Variable cost of the direct mail campaign}}$$

The flaw in this measurement is that sales dollars are assumed to be the key product of a direct mail campaign, when in fact the more desirable outcome is a large amount of throughput (see the earlier Throughput Measurements section). Accordingly, the measurement can be revised to use throughput in the numerator, as follows:

$$\frac{\text{Incremental throughput traceable to direct mail campaign}}{\text{Variable cost of the direct mail campaign}}$$

EXAMPLE

The Hegemony Toy Company's marketing director has developed a mailing piece that is sent to the company's mailing list of military toy collectors. The mailing piece comes in three versions, with one selling Roman-era soldiers, another highlighting Colonial-era soldiers, and yet another selling a set of Crusader knights. Based on subsequent sales information, she compiles the following direct mail effectiveness measurement for the mailers:

	Incremental Throughput	Incremental Mailer Cost	Direct Mail Effectiveness
Roman mailer	$120,000	$110,000	1.1x
Colonial mailer	42,000	105,000	0.4x
Crusader mailer	270,000	115,000	2.4x
Totals	$432,000	$330,000	1.3x

The incremental mailer cost is similar for all three direct mail campaigns, so the paltry returns from the Colonial mailer inevitably result in a major loss. However, the Crusader campaign is a major success, to such an extent that its profitability easily offsets the loss incurred on the Colonial mailer. Nonetheless, the marketing manager may need to consider selling the Colonial-era toy soldiers through a different sales channel.

Market Share

A general measure of the effectiveness of a company's sales and marketing efforts is market share, which is the proportion of sales in a market niche accumulated by a specific company. This measure is only available if someone is estimating the total size of the market; for example, a trade association may guesstimate the market size based on surveys of its members. Market share is a particularly important measurement if the size of a market is changing dramatically. For example, a company may be experiencing what it believes to be excellent sales growth, but which may actually represent a shrinking market share. Conversely, flat sales in a declining market may reflect excellent performance.

To measure market share, divide the company's net sales by the total reported size of the market. The formula is:

$$\frac{\text{Net sales}}{\text{Reported market size in sales dollars}}$$

This measurement should be treated with caution, for the following reasons:

- *Accuracy.* The market size may be wildly inaccurate, especially if market participants are self-reporting information to a trade association, and have a reason to overstate or understate their sales.
- *Profitability.* A company only wants market share if there is some associated profitability. Certain niches of any market may be seriously unprofitable, and so should be avoided, even if doing so represents lost market share.
- *Applicability of sales.* A company's sales may be associated with multiple markets, so do not apply the entire sales of the business to a specific market share calculation. Instead, the company may have a smaller share of several markets.

EXAMPLE

The Black Cat Ladder Company has seen ascending sales ever since the start of the last building construction boom. However, all other ladder manufacturers appear to have been doing fine as well, so the president commissions a market share study to ascertain the true position of the company. The results are noted in the following table.

(000s)	20X1	20X2	20X3
Black Cat sales	$20,000	$24,000	$28,000
Market size	$200,000	$300,000	$467,000
Market share	10%	8%	6%

The analysis reveals that Black Cat has actually been falling seriously behind its competitors for the last few years, despite what appeared to be robust growth.

We must extend a cautionary note about the ongoing pursuit of market share. An ever-increasing share of the market is not necessarily correlated with increasing profits, since some niches within the market are very price sensitive. However, profits *will* increase in markets where there are significant economies of scale (where unit costs decline as unit volumes increase). Consequently, one must consider the structure of the market before making market share the essential performance metric of a business.

Customer Lifetime Value

When deciding whether to engage in relationship-based sales, it helps to calculate the lifetime value of a customer. Lifetime value is the present value of the profits that will be generated from a customer over the life of the relationship. It is calculated as follows:

1. Forecast the timing and amounts of payments that a customer will make to the company over the estimated life of the relationship.

284

2. Forecast the timing and amount of payments related to referrals made by the customer that bring in new customers.
3. Forecast the cost and timing of the goods and services sold to the customer and the referred customers.
4. Forecast the unique relationship-related costs that will be expended to service the customer.
5. Convert these payments into their present values, using the cost of capital of the business as the discount rate.

The net amount of the present values of these revenues and expenses represents the estimated lifetime value of a customer. The concept can be useful when deciding upon the marketing activities to be used to obtain new customers, as well as the expenditures to be made to retain existing ones. For example, when customers are unlikely to make repeat visits and the sale amount per visit is relatively low, then marketing expenditures on a per-customer basis must also be low. Conversely, when a customer is likely to return many times to make significant purchases, it can make sense to spend much more to acquire customers, even if this means that the business initially incurs losses to do so. For example, a car dealership may invest in an exceptional facility in order to accommodate customers who are waiting for their vehicles to be serviced, in hopes of selling them more cars in the future.

General Management Measurements

Sales and marketing require very particular skills that may not be readily available on the open market. For example, direct sales can require employees with a flair for hands-on selling transactions, while effective marketing may call for a deep knowledge of the industry. Consequently, employee turnover among the more experienced staff should be an area of great interest.

It is entirely possible that the corporate bottleneck for achieving more sales is the sales staff itself. This is especially likely to be the case when individual sales require significant sales expertise, or selling relationships require a long time to mature, or there are specific technical aspects to certain parts of the selling process flow. The situation is exacerbated if there are few salespeople in the industry who have the required skill set, or if a long period of time is required to educate new salespeople. Under these circumstances, a business may find that its sales could potentially be devastated by the loss of just a few people in the sales department. If so, employee turnover is an especially pernicious problem that must be guarded against proactively.

Also, pay particular attention to the compensation being paid to the sales staff. This group may be highly motivated by compensation, so employee turnover can be closely linked to how well employees are being paid in comparison to the median rate for the industry.

These two measurements are usually monitored by the human resources department, but should also be a key concern of the sales manager and marketing manager. In essence, if turnover among the senior staff increases for any reason, then many of the performance measurements described in this chapter will decline.

Summary

The traditional focus of sales and marketing measurements has been on increasing the gross sales of a business. In this chapter, we have continually advocated the use of throughput as a much more appropriate outcome, since it is tied more directly to the ultimate profitability of an organization. However, in order to use throughput, a company must have a system in place that easily states the throughput for every product or service, without a great deal of cost accounting analysis. The simplest way to do so is to estimate the standard cost associated with each product or service, and publish the resulting standard throughput figures as the de facto throughput numbers that employees will henceforth use to manage the business.

Glossary

A

Accrual basis of accounting. The recognition of revenue when earned and expenses when incurred.

Asset base. The sum total of all assets used by a business to generate revenue.

Asset turnover. The proportion of the sales generated by a group of assets.

Available balance. The balance in a cash account where there is a delay by the controlling bank in crediting funds to the account.

B

Backlog. The amount of firm orders from customers that have not yet been processed.

Balance sheet. A report that summarizes all of an entity's assets, liabilities, and equity as of a given point in time.

Bill of materials. A listing of the parts used in a product.

Book value. Total assets minus total liabilities.

Borrowing base. The total amount of collateral against which a lender will lend funds to a business.

Bottleneck. A chokepoint through which work must flow before goods can be delivered to a customer.

Breakeven point. The sales level at which a company earns exactly no profit.

C

Capital lease. A lease in which the lessor only finances the lease, and all other rights of ownership transfer to the lessee.

Carrying amount. The original cost of an asset, less any accumulated depreciation and impairment.

Cash basis of accounting. The recognition of revenue when cash is received and expenses when cash is paid.

Cash conversion cycle. The time period from when cash is expended for the production of goods, until cash is received from customers in payment of those goods.

Cash flow. The net amount of an entity's incoming cash receipts and outgoing cash payments over a period of time.

Cash sweeping. The practice of automatically transferring cash at the end of each business day from an account into an investment option that earns interest income.

Collateral. An asset pledged as security for the repayment of a loan.

Cost of capital. The cost of funds for a business.

Current asset. An asset expected to be converted into cash within one year.

Current liability. A liability for which payment is due within one year.

Current ratio. The current assets of a business, divided by its current liabilities.

D

Depreciation. The gradual charging to expense of an asset's cost over its useful life.

Direct mail. Sales offers sent to recipients via standard mail or e-mail.

Discretionary cost. A cost that can be avoided in the short term without interfering with the basic operation of a business.

Dividend payout ratio. A comparison of dividends paid to net earnings, used to evaluate the level of dividend payments made by a business.

E

EBITDA. Earnings before interest, taxes, depreciation, and amortization. It is a rough measure of the cash flows of a business.

Economic order quantity. The number of units ordered that minimizes the costs of order placement and holding inventory.

Effective interest rate. The actual interest rate paid, as computed by dividing the actual amount of interest paid by the amount of the principal that the borrower is obligated to repay.

Engineering change order. A scheduled change to the contents of a product.

F

Financial leverage. The proportion of debt to equity used to fund the operations of a business.

Financial statements. A collection of reports that describe the financial results, condition, and cash flows of an entity.

First in, first out. The assignment of costs to sold goods based on the assumption that the first items entering inventory are the first ones sold.

Fixed asset. An asset with a useful life greater than one year, and which exceeds an entity's minimum capitalization limit.

Free cash flow. The net change in cash generated by the operations of a business, minus cash outlays for working capital, capital expenditures, and dividends.

Full-time equivalent. The number of working hours that equates to one full-time employee.

G

Goodwill. That portion of an acquisition price that cannot be assigned to the tangible or intangible assets of the acquiree.

Gross sales. Sales before deductions for sales returns and allowances.

H

Hedging. A risk reduction technique whereby a derivative or similar instrument is used to offset future changes in the fair value or cash flows of an asset or liability.

I

Impairment. A reduction in the value of an asset.

In the money. When the designated exercise price of an option or warrant is below the current market price of a company's common stock.

Income investor. An investor that invests based on the dividends paid by the issuers of stock.

Income statement. A financial report that summarizes an entity's revenue, cost of goods sold, gross margin, other costs, and net income or loss.

Intangible asset. A non-physical asset having a useful life spanning more than one accounting period.

Inventory buffer. A buffer placed in front of a constrained resource, to keep the operation running in the event of a shortfall in incoming deliveries.

L

Last in, first out (LIFO). A cost layering concept under which the cost of the last items added to inventory are assigned to the first items sold from inventory.

Leverage. The use of borrowed funds to increase profits.

Lifetime value. The present value of the profits that will be generated from a customer over the life of the relationship.

Line of credit. A commitment from a lender to pay a company whenever it needs cash, up to a pre-set maximum level.

Lower of cost or market. An accounting requirement mandating that inventory be recorded at the lower of its cost or market value.

M

Margin of safety. The reduction in sales that can occur before the breakeven point of a business is reached.

Mark to market. The practice of recording an asset or liability at its current market value.

N

Net book value. The original cost of an asset, less any accumulated depreciation, accumulated amortization, and accumulated impairment.

O

Opportunity cost. The cost of an alternative course of action that is being foregone.

P

Price elasticity. The degree to which changes in price impact the unit sales of a product or service.

Procurement card. A company-sponsored credit card used to make purchases on behalf of the company.

Purchase order. A formal authorization to buy goods and services under the terms stated in the authorization document.

Q

Quick ratio. The ratio of cash, marketable securities, and accounts receivable to current liabilities. The ratio does not include inventory or prepaid expenses.

S

Sales returns and allowances. Reductions in gross sales caused by merchandise returns and credits granted to customers.

Shareholders' equity. The share capital of a business, plus its retained earnings, less any treasury stock.

Short interest. The number of shares that investors have sold short, and which they have not yet closed out.

Short selling. The sale of borrowed stock, which a short seller expects to buy later on the open market at a lower price, earning a profit on the decline in price.

Soft close. The process of closing the books for a reporting period, using fewer than the normal set of closing activities in order to reduce the work required to close the books.

Statement of cash flows. A part of the financial statements that summarizes an entity's cash inflows and outflows in relation to financing, operating, and investing activities.

Stock-keeping unit. A unique identification code assigned to a product or service.

T

Takt time. The average rate at which units must be produced in order to meet demand.

Tangible assets. Assets that occupy physical space, such as equipment and buildings.

Tangible book value. Book value minus the recorded cost of all intangible assets.

Target balance. The amount of cash that a company plans to hold in an account.

Three-way matching. The process of comparing the authorizing purchase order to a receiving document and supplier invoice, to ensure that a supplier invoice is approved, and that the billed goods were received.

Throughput. Revenue minus all totally variable expenses.

W

Working capital. Cash plus accounts receivable and inventory, minus accounts payable.

Index